T5-CVN-118

ENGLISH CAROLINE SCRIPT
AND MONASTIC HISTORY

Caroline minuscule script was adopted in England in the mid-tenth century in imitation of Continental usage. A badge of ecclesiastical reform, it was practised in Benedictine scriptoria but was also taken up by members of the royal writing office; the chancery occupied an important place in the pioneering of calligraphic fashions. Caroline script developed a number of forms during its approximately two-century history in England, in part reflecting different tendencies within the Reform-cause. The Rule of St Benedict was focal for this movement: at royal instance it was translated into English by Bishop Æthelwold. An important manuscript of that bilingual Rule is here made the centrepiece of a study of how the script was promoted by St Oswald, bishop of Worcester and founder of many Benedictine abbeys in midland England. The major role occupied also by St Dunstan and the church of Canterbury in the cultural developments of this period is considered. In the aftermath of the final Scandinavian conquest of England (A.D. 1016) a Canterbury master-scribe created the form of Caroline writing which was to become a mark of Englishness and outlive the Norman conquest; its inventor's career is discussed and his achievement assessed. This volume offers analysis of manuscript evidence as a basis for the cultural and ecclesiastical history of late Anglo-Saxon England.

The author is a Fellow of Girton College, Cambridge, and Reader in the Early Mediaeval History and Culture of the British Isles in the Department of Anglo-Saxon, Norse & Celtic, University of Cambridge.

STUDIES IN ANGLO-SAXON HISTORY
General Editor: David Dumville

Editorial Advisers

Mark Blackburn   Niels Lund
James Campbell   Roger Ray
Simon Keynes   Anton Scharer

Editorial Manager: Clare Orchard

ISSN 0950-3412

Already published

In preparation

ENGLISH CAROLINE SCRIPT AND MONASTIC HISTORY:

Studies in Benedictinism, A.D. 950–1030

DAVID N. DUMVILLE

THE BOYDELL PRESS

© David N. Dumville 1993

All Rights Reserved. Except as permitted under current legislation
no part of this work may be photocopied, stored in a retrieval system,
published, performed in public, adapted, broadcast,
transmitted, recorded or reproduced in any form or by any means,
without the prior permission of the copyright owner.

First published 1993 by The Boydell Press, Woodbridge

The Boydell Press is an imprint of Boydell & Brewer Ltd
PO Box 9, Woodbridge, Suffolk IP12 3DF, UK
and of Boydell & Brewer Inc.
PO Box 41026, Rochester, NY 14604, USA.

ISBN 0 85115 323 2

British Library Cataloguing-in-Publication Data
Dumville, David
   English Caroline Script and Monastic History: Studies in
   Benedictinism, A.D. 950–1030. – (Studies in Anglo-
   Saxon History Series, ISSN 0950-3412; Vol. 6)
   I. Title II. Series
   271
   ISBN 0-85115-323-2

   Library of Congress Cataloging-in-Publication Data
Dumville, D. N.
   English Caroline script and monastic history : studies in Benedictinism,
A.D. 950–1030 / David N. Dumville.
      p. cm. – Studies in Anglo-Saxon history, ISSN 0950-3412 ; 6)
   Includes bibliographical references and indexes.
   ISBN 0-85115-323-2 (alk. paper)
   1. Great Britain–History–Anglo-Saxon period, 449–1066–Historiography.
2. England–Church history–Anglo-Saxon period, 449–1066. 3. Manuscripts,
Latin (Medieval and modern)–England. 4. England–Charters, grants,
privileges. 5. Benedictines–England–Historiography. 6. Monasteries–
England–Historiography. 7. Manuscripts, English (Old). 8. Paleography,
English. 9. Scriptoria–England. 10. Writing, Minuscule. I. Title. II. Series.
DA152.D84 1993
942.01'7–dc20   92-434238

The paper used in this publication meets the minimum requirements
of American National Standard for Information Sciences –
Permanence of Paper for Printed Library Materials, ANSI Z39.48-1984.

Printed in Great Britain by
St Edmundsbury Press Ltd, Bury St Edmunds, Suffolk

CONTENTS

LIST OF ILLUSTRATIONS
(between pp. 54 and 55)

Grateful acknowledgment is hereby made to the following, who hold copyright in the illustrations reproduced in this book: the Master and Fellows of Corpus Christi College, Cambridge (III, IV, VIII–X, XV, XVI); the Syndics of Cambridge University Library (II); Biblioteca Medicea Laurenziana, Firenze (XII); Kestner-Museum, Hannover (XIII); the British Library Board (I); Bibliothèque nationale, Paris (XI, XIV); Biblioteca Apostolica Vaticana (VI, VII); Bibliothèque municipale, Rouen (V).

GENERAL EDITOR'S FOREWORD

That a study of palaeographical as well as textual evidence can be made the foundation of a book on Anglo-Saxon cultural history is an indication of how far research into that era's manuscripts has progressed in recent decades. Building on previous work, and principally that of T.A.M. Bishop, the chapters of this book seek to offer insights into the Benedictine revolution which convulsed the English Church in the mid- and later tenth century and to make a contribution to our understanding of the development of script as well as the transmission and reception of texts. The author's previous volumes in this series provided some of the background against which ideas in this book developed; and Patrick Conner's *Anglo-Saxon Exeter* offered much inspiration. The General Editor very much hopes that approaches to Anglo-Saxon history based on close study of manuscript evidence can be a continuing feature of contributions to this series.

David N. Dumville
Girton College,
Cambridge

IN ERINNERUNG
AN EINEN GESCHÄTZTEN GELEHRTEN,
GROSSZÜGIGEN LEHRER UND GUTEN FREUND
– BERNHARD BISCHOFF (1906–1991)

PREFACE

The germ of this book belongs in my search for the answers to two questions about the history of handwriting in late Anglo-Saxon England: first, what kinds of script were written (and when) in specific ecclesiastical scriptoria and in the English royal chancery in the 140 years which the kingdom enjoyed from its inception in 927 until the cataclysm which was the Norman conquest; and secondly, how to explain to new students of palaeography the essentials of the development and dissemination of Anglo-Caroline minuscule. I have spent more than fifteen years probing the detailed work on and the outline history of English Caroline script, which my first teacher of palaeography, T.A.M. Bishop, published from 1953 to 1971. In as much as I now seek to organise the evidence into different patterns and to modify some of the conclusions which he reached, it is proper that I should acknowledge at once the inspiration which Mr Bishop provided: without his seminal work, this attempt at a further step would not have been possible. I must refer also to the very remarkable mediaevalist to whose memory this little book is dedicated: thanks to introductions from Mr Bishop and Professor Bruce Dickins, I was able in 1971 to begin study of the wider history of Caroline writing under the guidance of Professor Bernhard Bischoff at the Ludwig-Maximilian Universität in Munich and to acquaint myself with the extraordinary resources of the Bavarian State Library. I owe a great deal to the willingness of both Mr Bishop and Professor Bischoff to continue to advise me during the two decades which have elapsed since I left their formal tutelage: the generosity of these fine scholars and kind friends has provided a continuing stimulus to my studies of the script of the British Isles in the central middle ages. One other debt due in Munich must also be recorded: from Professor Helmut Gneuss's interest in and keen pursuit of the manuscripts and texts of Anglo-Saxon England I have derived much profit, both in personal exchange and through study of his publications; my warmest thanks must be given here.

Study and teaching of the palaeography of these manuscripts has mostly been undertaken while I have been employed in Cambridge. To two fine colleagues and valued friends, Julia Crick and Michael Lapidge, I owe much insight gained while we have worked in harness on the same sources and in the same pedagogic cause. They have read drafts of much of this book and it has profited from their characteristically keen and imaginative scrutiny. Michael Lapidge indeed has blazed some textual

trails ahead of me, particularly towards Ramsey. To Peter Clemoes I owe
the unique opportunity to develop, in tandem with Michael Lapidge,
undergraduate teaching in palaeography within the context of an
interdisciplinary approach to the cultures of the Insular world in the early
and central middle ages. The discipline provided by the necessity to
explain what is all too often left unstated or unorganised in palaeographical scholarship has been of inestimable benefit to me; to have had to do so
too in terms of cultural history has offered a welcome and humane
framework for the enterprise.

Other friends and colleagues, to all of whom my grateful thanks are
here extended, have also contributed much to the making of this book.
Drafts of chapters I and IV here been read critically by Susan Kelly,
Michael Korhammer, Patrick McGurk, and Tessa Webber, and I have
discussed a number of the wider issues with them, to my profit. In a
period when an interest in liturgical manuscripts has necessarily been
kindled in me, I have been fortunate to number among my friends Alicia
Corrêa who with characteristic verve has joined in debate on several
problems and has done more, materially and intellectually, to aid my
suspicious probings of the 'Leofric Missal' than I could ever have hoped
for. Various of the issues here I have discussed with Lesley Abrams,
Bruce Barker-Benfield, James Carley, Thomas Charles-Edwards,
Patrick Conner, Kent Emery, Margaret Gelling, Antonia Gransden,
Scott Gwara, Peter Jackson, Simon Keynes, Brigitte Langefeld, Richard
Marsden, Uaininn O'Meadhra, Andy Orchard, Susan Rankin, Yoko
Wada, Nicholas Webb, Michael Winterbottom, and Neil Wright, many
of whom have also helped on specific points of difficulty.

If I had had to word-process this book, as well as write it, it might
never have seen the light of day. That it does so is due to the efforts and
skill of Ruth Johnson, Anne Rendell, Helen Saunders, and Sarah-Anne
Wood: they have stood between author and abyss.

As so often, I am indebted to Richard Barber for his imaginative
response to my proposal of a book. It seems appropriate that my contract-
date is the thousandth Feast of St Oswald of Worcester, 28 February,
1992.

David N. Dumville

I

INTRODUCTION

From the last generation's work on English script and book-production in the period before the Norman conquest, a number of themes for meditation, issues for debate, and fields requiring further cultivation can be seen to have emerged. One of the themes is the introduction of Caroline minuscule script into England and its development from the mid-tenth century as a major, canonical bookhand employed in both royal service and ecclesiastical scriptoria. One of the crucial issues is how and why that script was first adopted in (southern) England and whether its employment – not to mention its various forms – may be reckoned to have held an ideological significance for, or conferred a party-label upon, its practitioners. Among the requirements for further research, therefore, is enhancement of our understanding of the various and developing styles of Anglo-Caroline minuscule, their chronology, and the centres at which they were practised.

The period before the wholehearted adoption of Caroline writing by Anglo-Saxon scribes, that is to say anterior to *ca* A.D. 960, remains the murkiest phase of its English history. Two decades' work by T.A.M. Bishop, culminating in 1971,[1] gave considerable definition to the history of that script in the first two generations of its full use and pointed the way to an understanding of its eleventh-century development.[2] Bishop identified two broad streams of practice within the canon of Anglo-Caroline script.

One embodied a wholehearted rejection of inherited English script-forms: not for the practitioners of this style the frequent Continental reality of the creation of a regional variety of Caroline writing which represented a fusion of local scribal habits with an imported ideal of canonical Caroline practice.[3] The consequences of this absolute attitude

---

[1] The fundamental study of the subject is his *English Caroline Minuscule*.
[2] 'Notes on Cambridge manuscripts'; 'An early example of Insular-Caroline'; *Aethici Istrici Cosmographia*; 'Lincoln Cathedral MS 182'.
[3] On regional developments of Caroline minuscule on the Continent see Bischoff, *Latin Palaeography*, pp. 112–26. Cf. Hessel, 'Zur Entstehung' and 'Studien zur Ausbreitung'.

were striking: Anglo-Caroline of 'Style I' (for so Bishop named it)[4] was in the first instance (and largely remained) monumental in proportions and rotund of aspect; and it was by definition free of local, non-Caroline features. Its models must have been either early specimens of Caroline from the schools of Corbie and Tours or (and more likely) grand liturgical books of ninth-century date.[5] In so far as the origins of specimens of Style-I Anglo-Caroline have been ascertained, they are to be placed in the royal chancery and in the scriptoria of ecclesiastical houses associated with Æthelwold, bishop of Winchester (963–984).[6]

The other stream of Anglo-Caroline practice was different indeed. An English regional hybrid of Insular and Caroline practices, 'Style II' conformed in that respect to the Continental pattern which manifested itself during the spread of the Caroline minuscule outside the script's heartlands. Style-II Anglo-Caroline, over the course of its relatively brief history, displays a greater variety of forms and occurs in a greater number of specimens than does Style I.[7] It must have been easier for the average English scribe, also having to practise a native version of Insular minuscule, to write a style of Caroline which would happily admit an admixture of Insular forms. In the surviving specimens of Style II, the script tends to be significantly smaller than in most Style-I manuscripts. To some extent it is mistaken to think of Style II as being a script-form parallel to Style I, for it is effectively an umbrella-term for an attitude to the new script, an attitude which in practice produced a number of local, indeed scribal, varieties. The question has been raised, but not yet properly attended to, as to what were the Continental styles of Caroline minuscule which stood as models for the new, English practitioners of Caroline writing;[8] if this matter can be sorted out, the solution will bring us a wide variety of knowledge and insights in its train.

[4] *English Caroline Minuscule*, pp. xxi–xxii.
[5] On Corbie and Tours see Lowe, *Codices Latini Antiquiores*, VI, pp. xxii–xxvi, xxvii–xxix, and Rand, *Studies in the Script of Tours*, I. If such were the direct models, however, their distinctive hierarchy of scripts was not reproduced by their English imitators. For the possibility of influence from rather later Caroline liturgical manuscripts, see Bishop, *English Caroline Minuscule*, p. 12 (no. 14) and plate XII. See also Dumville, *Liturgy*, pp. 146–52.
[6] For the earliest datable specimens of Style I see Sawyer, *Anglo-Saxon Charters*, no. 690, dated 961 (second scribe), a product of the royal chancery; London, British Library, MS. Cotton Vespasian A.viii, fols 3v–33v (Sawyer, *ibid.*, no. 745), dated 966 (but sometimes thought – as by Wormald, 'Late Anglo-Saxon art', pp. 23–6 –, for no very obvious reason, to be a little later), from the New Minster at Winchester; London, British Library, MS. Additional 49598, datable 963 x 984 – edited in facsimile by Warner & Wilson, *The Benedictional of Saint Æthelwold* –, from the Old Minster at Winchester.
[7] Bishop, *English Caroline Minuscule*, pp. xxii–xxiii, has stressed the greater number rather than the greater variety.
[8] Bischoff, *Latin Palaeography*, p. 124. Cf. n. 5 above, and also Bishop, 'Notes', p. 333.

Style II, then, is unlike Style I in a number of ways. It represents a relatively relaxed attitude to the Continental minuscule and whatever message that script was deemed to embody. It was perhaps not therefore the mark of a party, tendency, or spiritual family-group in the tenth-century English Church. However, the contrast with Style I can be pursued a little further in those terms. The first localisable specimens of Style-II Anglo-Caroline are associable with Dunstan, archbishop of Canterbury (959–988).[9] It is noteworthy that the phase of life which linked Dunstan and Æthelwold was when Æthelwold was a monk at Glastonbury during Dunstan's abbacy. Glastonbury as a point of origin in the 940s or earlier 950s for the native cultivation of Caroline minuscule would provide an explanation for both men's presumed support for the script in subsequent years. Æthelwold's pursuit of stricter ideals may have led also to the writing of a purer strain of the Continental script under his auspices. Be that as it may, Glastonbury has indeed been taken, in Bishop's account of the script,[10] to be the *fons et origo* of Anglo-Caroline minuscule: this perception fits a long-standing historical model,[11] but in fact no specimen of early Anglo-Caroline can be securely assigned a Glastonbury origin.[12] A number of distinctive house-variants of Style II probably came into existence at different scriptoria; they are certainly seen at the two Canterbury minsters (Christ Church and St

[9] Oxford, Bodleian Library, MS. Auct. F.4.32 (*S.C.* 2176), a complex codex united only by the work of a single English scribe, has become the type for mid-tenth-century Glastonbury work: it has been edited in facsimile by Hunt, *Saint Dunstan's Classbook*. The same hand is deemed to recur in additions to a number of other manuscripts: Bishop ('An early example of Insular-Caroline', pp. 399–400) has noted four possible specimens of varying credibility; for a fifth, see Parkes, 'A note on MS Vatican, Bibl. Apost., lat. 3363'. But in fact the association is rather with Dunstan than with tenth-century Glastonbury.

[10] Bishop, *English Caroline Minuscule*, pp. 1 (no. 1) and 2 (no. 3); but note his caveat (*ibid.*, p. xxii), 'The evidence that Glastonbury was the first home of Style II is less substantial than could be wished'. The evidence for association of the script with Dunstan himself is more impressive. Bishop (*ibid.*, pp. 1–2, and 'An early example of Insular-Caroline') is perhaps responsible for a more generous view of manuscript output by a Glastonbury scriptorium than the evidence will permit.

[11] See Gasquet & Bishop, *The Bosworth Psalter*, pp. 15–27, 126. But cf. Dumville, *Liturgy*, chapter II.

[12] 'St Dunstan's Classbook' (n. 9, above) was at Glastonbury in the second half of the fifteenth century and the first half of the sixteenth; but we do not know that it was not brought thither from one of the other churches which Dunstan ruled in the course of his long career, whether in his lifetime or soon or long thereafter. More probably associable with Glastonbury is a Square-minuscule manuscript, Oxford, Bodleian Library, MS. Hatton 30 (*S.C.* 4076), which bears on fo 73v the inscription, 'Dunstan abbas hunc libellum scribere iussit'. MS. Hatton 42 (*S.C.* 4117), a Breton manuscript (as is Auct. F.4.32, fos 1–9), augmented at Canterbury and subsequently found at Worcester, has been given a similar history; but there is no credible reason for linking it to Glastonbury (cf. Dumville, 'Wulfric cild').

Augustine's).[13] The differences between Style I and Style II can be considered in various ways: in the history of the tenth-century Church Æthelwold has often been seen as the extremist and ideologue, Dunstan as more moderate and pragmatic in pursuit of essentially similar goals; it would be easy to fit the aforementioned script-history into this pattern.

These two styles may be seen in Anglo-Caroline manuscripts of the second half of the tenth century and the very early years of the eleventh. As the separate approaches of different houses and groups within the English Church of the revolutionary era, they maintained their distinctive qualities to the end of the second generation of clergy who were inspired by the Benedictine upheaval of Edgar's reign. At the end of that second generation, in the 1010s, we begin to see signs of change – of accommodation of the two approaches to one another – leading to the creation in the late 1010s and early 1020s of the model for what has been described as 'a generically English Caroline . . . of the eleventh century'.[14] In the second quarter of the century the results of this new scribal fashion were almost everywhere to be seen.

Before we turn to that national style, another local variant requires brief attention. One of the ways in which the history of Anglo-Caroline writing might have developed was towards pronounced regional or local varieties. That, in the event, such was not the trend may (as we shall see) be a testimony to the influence and strength of the see of Canterbury in the last half-century of the Anglo-Saxon state. Style II had, by its very nature, been prone to local variation. In the later tenth century Style I had seemed – perhaps as a result of the stricter aims of its creators or the closer links between the houses whose scriptoria practised it – secure against such development. Worcester Cathedral in the time of St Oswald, bishop from 961 to 992, had been reformed from Oswald's own foundation at Ramsey but it has often been thought to have enjoyed also significant links with Winchester.[15] We find Anglo-Caroline of Style I

---

13 Bishop, *English Caroline Minuscule*, pp. xxii–xxiii, summarising his accounts in 'Notes', pp. 323–36, 93–5, 412–23, and in *Aethici Istrici Cosmographia*, introduction.

14 Bishop, *English Caroline Minuscule*, p. xxiii. But *ibid.*, p. xviii, Mr Bishop remarked that the manuscripts of the mid-eleventh century 'show intellectual curiosity and Anglo-Latin letters alive but hardly flourishing' – for a controversial but productive assessment of the pre-Conquest century, see Thomson, 'The Norman conquest and English libraries'; cf. Gneuss, 'Anglo-Saxon libraries', for a different perspective.

15 From both textual and manuscript studies liturgical links between Winchester and Worcester in the eleventh century have been asserted. The evidence is provided principally by the New Hymnal (cf. Gneuss, *Hymnar*, pp. 70–1) and by three manuscripts: Cambridge, Corpus Christi College, MSS. 146 and 391, and Worcester, Cathedral Library, MS. F.173 (cf. Hohler, 'Some service-books', pp. 73–4; on the last see Warren, 'An Anglo-Saxon missal at Worcester', and Turner, 'The churches at Winchester'); but little of this will withstand scrutiny. That there were comparable

practised at Worcester in the second half of the tenth century, but alongside the native Square minuscule.[16] By the early eleventh century, however, partly perhaps under the influence of that Anglo-Saxon script, a local style had emerged. It was identified, but not thoroughly described, by T.A.M. Bishop. Unfortunately, his attempts to discuss its origins and history were clouded by consideration of irrelevant matter. He was undoubtedly correct, however, in describing it as 'outside the main categories of English Caroline'.[17] It is characterised above all by deliberately broken or hesitant strokes. Its practice would seem to be attributable to a brief period in the earlier eleventh century. In recognition of its unusual position in the history of Anglo-Caroline writing, I have designated it 'Style III' in continuation of Bishop's definition of the outstanding movements in the history of that script.[18]

The effective life of the three distinctive styles practised during the first two generations of extensive Caroline writing in England cannot be prolonged beyond the first quarter of the eleventh century, however. The route by which the diversity of these generations' practice was converted or assimilated into a single national style may be discovered by following developments at Christ Church, Canterbury.[19]

What was achieved there *ca* 1020 was the creation of a calligraphic style essentially derivative of the Æthelwoldian tradition of Anglo-Caroline but not spurning all aspects of the more hybrid forms of that script. The inspiration for this development, probably ultimately in the previous generation, may have orginated at Christ Church or may instead be seen in the work of royal-chancery scribes; if the latter, however, the transition in that context did not survive King Cnut's first years. Reversing the direction of the preceding years' ecclesiastical traffic, this Style-IV Anglo-Caroline was diffused rapidly to Winchester and probably elsewhere. Royal diplomas do not, however, show its influence in the 1020s or 1030s. In the 1040s it starts to be (re-)adopted for such purposes, and in the 1050s is discoverable in use at Exeter and Worcester. While the script of these centres remains essentially faithful to the original Canterbury type, we see a stiffer, more awkward variety

---

connexions between the two centres in the last third of the tenth century remains to be demonstrated in detail. Dr Alicia Corrêa is investigating this subject anew.

[16] A good example of both scripts written coevally in the same manuscript is provided by London, British Library, MS. Royal 13.A.xv: Bishop, *English Caroline Minuscule*, p. 16 (cf. p. xiv and n. 1).

[17] *Ibid.*, p. 20, referring to Cambridge, Corpus Christi College, MS. 178, part 2. The description is better applied to other Worcester manuscripts of the period, however; see below, pp. 68–75.

[18] For discussion of the context in which Worcester scribes experimented with new styles, see chapter II.

[19] See chapters III and IV.

5

of Style IV written elsewhere in the second half of the eleventh century, datable specimens indicating that this was a pre-Conquest development.[20] What needs to be stressed, however, is that the new Anglo-Caroline form practised at Christ Church, Canterbury, *ca* 1020 had come by 1066 to be employed wherever in England Latin script was being written. In the scribal context it had become a defining mark of Englishness and was in some parts of the country to retain this national characteristic for another seventy-five years.

[20] See, for example, Hinkle, 'The gift', on Reims, Bibliothèque municipale, MS. 9.

II

THE DISSEMINATION OF
ANGLO-CAROLINE MINUSCULE:
THE EVIDENCE OF THE OXFORD MANUSCRIPT OF
THE OLD ENGLISH BENEDICTINE RULE

Of fundamental importance to the Carolingian perception of proper Church-order was the Rule of St Benedict.[1] In as much as monasticism began to be appreciated among the English aristocracy in the first half of the tenth century,[2] it is reasonable to suppose that there was some awareness of the centrality of that Rule to the contemporary Continental experience of monasticism. When revolutionary Benedictine ideologues gained power in the English Church with the accession of King Edgar to the throne of England,[3] the Rule became a document of enormous

---

[1] For an introduction see Wallace-Hadrill, *The Frankish Church*, pp. 229–31, 264–5, 356–8, 381; Ganshof, 'L'église et le pouvoir', pp. 118–19. Cf. John, ' "Saecularium prioratus" '. For commentaries on *Regula sancti Benedicti*, see Schroll, *Benedictine Monasticism*; *Der Basiliuskommentar*, ed. Hafner (cf. Zelzer, 'Untersuchungen zu einer Gesamtedition'); *Smaragdi Abbatis Expositio*, edd. Spannagel & Engelbert. Cf. Semmler, 'Benedictus II', pp. 31–47, on Smaragdus.

[2] Dumville, *Wessex and England*, chapters IV–VI.

[3] The best introduction remains that of John, 'The King and the monks', reprinted in his *Orbis Britanniae*, pp. 154–80. There has been a wide variety of comment on the English monastic movement of the second half of the tenth century. On possible sources of reform see Dauphin, 'Le renouveau monastique'; Hamilton, 'The monastic revival'; Leclercq, 'The tenth century English Benedictine reform'; Rosenwein, *Rhinoceros Bound*, pp. 48–9, 87–90, 108; Bullough, 'The Continental background'; Wormald, 'Æthelwold and his Continental counterparts'; *The Monastic Ritual of Fleury*, ed. Davril. For the palaeographical dimension see Keller, *Angelsächsische Palaeographie*, I.28–9; Hessel, 'Studien zur Ausbreitung'; Boutemy, 'L'enluminure anglaise'; Vezin, 'Manuscrits des dixième et onzième siècles', pp. 283–5. On the course and significance of the revolution (variously called 'reform', 'reformation', and 'revival' by different scholars), see for example (in addition to the work of Eric John, cited *passim*), Turner *et al.*, *The Benedictines in Britain*; Stenton, *Anglo-Saxon England*, pp. 433–69; Darlington, 'Ecclesiastical reform'; Fisher, 'The anti-monastic reaction'; Deanesly, *The Pre-Conquest Church*, pp. 251–352, and *Sidelights*, pp. 37–170; Knowles, *The Monastic Order*, *passim*; Schmitz, *Histoire de l'ordre*, I.192–209 (and vols I, II, VII, in general); Whitelock, *English Historical Documents*, pp. 90–8 (cf. 36–51); Godfrey,

consequence and status in the Anglo-Saxon world. Commentary on the Rule and glossed copies of the Rule are prominent among English manuscript survivals from the century or so before the Norman conquest.[4]

The Church in Anglo-Saxon England, pp. 294–410; Barlow, *The English Church, 1000–1066*; *Tenth-century Studies*, ed. Parsons; *Councils*, edd. Whitelock *et al.*, I; Vollrath, *Die Synoden*, pp. 210–413, 424–70 (and 'König Edgar'); Gransden, 'Traditionalism'. For a thoughtful and important study of the unreformed and the secular clergy, see Caraman, 'The character'.

[4] The most useful introduction to the Benedictine Rule is *The Rule*, ed. Fry. Pre-Conquest English manuscripts of *Regula sancti Benedicti* are, apart from the five copies of Æthelwold's bilingual edition, seven in number; we probably also have the remains of another copy, now containing only related texts. These seven are: Cambridge, Corpus Christi College, MS. 57, *saec.* x/xi (Gneuss, 'A preliminary list', no. 41; cf. *The Rule*, ed. Chamberlin); CCCC 368, attributed to *saec.* x/xi (Gneuss no. 101); Cambridge, Trinity College, MS. O.2.30 (1134), fos 129–172, *saec.* x *med.* (Gneuss no. 189); Cambridge, University Library, MS. Ll.1.14 (2143), fos 70–108, *saec.* xi^2 (Gneuss no. 29); for a copy glossed in Old English, see below; London, British Library, MS. Harley 5431, *saec.* x^2 (Gneuss no. 440); the seventh is a survival from before the First Viking-Age, Oxford, Bodleian Library, MS. Hatton 48 (*S.C.* 4118), *saec.* viii (Gneuss no. 631). Three of these (Gneuss nos 29, 41, 440) have associated with them two Carolingian texts, *Memoriale qualiter* and *Collectio capitularis*, which bear directly on the Rule: the same texts are found also in London, British Library, MS. Cotton Titus A.iv, *saec.* xi *med.* (Gneuss no. 379), one of the manuscripts of Æthelwold's bilingual; in Rouen, Bibliothèque municipale, MS. U.107 (1385), fos 20–26 (but with the unique copy of the *Acta praeliminaria* of the Synod of Aachen, A.D. 816, instead of *Collectio capitularis*), which lacks the Rule but is presumed to be a fragment of a manuscript which once contained it (Gneuss no. 926); and in London, British Library, MS. Cotton Tiberius A.iii, fos 2–173, *saec.* xi *med.* (Gneuss no. 363), which contains – in addition to a copy of the Rule (glossed in Old English: ed. Logeman, *The Rule*; cf. *The Old English Version*, ed. Napier, pp. 119–28, for another glossed Benedictine text from the same manuscript) – the English *Regularis concordia*. Furthermore, copies of the commentaries by Smaragdus, abbot of Saint-Mihiel, are also known from Anglo-Saxon England (cf. Witters, 'Smaragde au moyen âge'; Rädle, *Studien*). His *Expositio in Regulam* is found in Cambridge, University Library, MS. Ee.2.4 (922), *saec.* x *med.* (Gneuss no. 3), and Paris, Bibliothèque nationale, MS. latin 4210 (Gneuss no. 883). There are post-Conquest copies in London, British Library, MS. Royal 10.A.xiii, *saec.* xii^2 (from Christ Church, Canterbury – Kauffmann, *Romanesque Manuscripts, 1066–1190*, pp. 115–16, no. 92); Oxford, Bodleian Library, MS. Bodley 543 (*S.C.* 2588), *saec.* xii *ex.* (from Worcester or Ramsey); *ibid.*, MS. Hatton 40 (*S.C.* 4104), *saec.* xii (from Worcester); Paris, Bibliothèque nationale, MS. latin 12638, *saec.* xii/xiii (from Reading). Smaragdus's *Diadema monachorum* is in Cambridge, University Library, MS. Ff.4.43 (1286), *saec.* x *ex.* (Gneuss no. 8); CCCC 57 (as above). There are post-Conquest copies in Cambridge, Clare College, MS. 17, *saec.* xi/xii; Oxford, Bodleian Library, MS. Bodley 451 (*S.C.* 2401), *saec.* xi/xii (from the Nunnaminster, Winchester); and Wisbech, Town Library, MS. 9, *saec.* xii^1. His *Expositio libri comitis* (cf. Souter, 'Prolegomena', pp. 570–1, 'Contributions', and 'Further contributions') is in Oxford, Bodleian Library, MS. Barlow 4 (*S.C.* 6416), *saec.* ix (Continental, at Worcester *saec.* xi *in.*) (Gneuss no. 539), and Worcester, Cathedral Library, MS. F.91, *saec.* x^2

The Old English Benedictine Rule

An aspect of Anglo-Saxon ecclesiastical culture – and particularly, since the reign of Alfred of Wessex, in southumbrian England – was the relatively extensive use of the vernacular tongue in written contexts.[5] To render a Latin text into English gave it easier circulation among native ecclesiastics as well as making it available to many members of the secular aristocracy.[6] In as much as one of the aims of English ecclesiastical policy since the days of King Alfred seems to have been to revive monasticism by encouraging reform-ideals among the laity,[7] it might have seemed that a vernacular version of the Rule of St Benedict would have received official blessing, particularly in Edgar's reign. That it did, indeed that the very act of translation flowed directly from a royal commission, is stated bluntly in an early twelfth-century text, *Libellus quorundam insignium operum beati Æthelwoldi* in §49:[8]

Æadgarus rex et Alftreð dederunt sancto Æðelwoldo manerium, quod dicitur Suðburn, et cyrographum quod pertinebat, quod comes qui dicebatur Scule dudum possederat, eo pacto ut ille regulam sancti Benedicti in anglicum idioma de Latino transferret. Qui sic fecit. Deinde uero beatus Æðelwoldus dedit eandem terram sancte Æðeldreðe cum cyrographo eiusdem terre.

The *Libellus* had itself been translated – into Latin from English – at the order of Hervey, bishop of Ely from 1109 to 1131.[9] It was known in twelfth-century Ely as 'liber de terris sancti Æðelwoldi' and 'liber terrarum quem librum sancti Æðelwoldi nominant'.[10] It survives in two manuscripts, of which one was written in 1139 or 1140,[11] and it was used in *extenso* in the writing of *Liber Eliensis*, a cartulary-chronicle of Ely, in

---

(Gneuss no. 762). Finally, one is tempted to wonder in this context about the significance of the apparent popularity of other monastic literature in late Anglo-Saxon manuscripts – for example, works of Cassian and Sulpicius's *Vita sancti Martini* (cf. Gneuss nos 201, 264, 296, 782, 915). Still useful, though inevitably heavily dated, surveys of the reception of monastic rules in England are the century-old articles by Tupper, 'History and texts', and Bateson, 'Rules for monks'.

[5] See, for example, Dumville, *Wessex and England*, chapter VI; Keynes, 'Royal government and the written word'.

[6] Kelly, 'Anglo-Saxon lay society'.

[7] Dumville, *Wessex and England*, chapters IV and VI.

[8] The following text is quoted from Book II, chapter 37, of *Liber Eliensis*, ed. Blake, p. 111, with minor editorial alterations. On *Libellus Æthelwoldi* see D. Whitelock, *apud* Blake, pp. ix–xviii.

[9] Blake, *ibid.*, p. xxxiv.

[10] *Ibid.* and n. 9. One may compare this title with the *Liber terrarum* of Glastonbury Abbey and perhaps of similar date.

[11] *Ibid.* It has been edited from this manuscript and translated by Keynes & Kennedy, *Anglo-Saxon Ely*.

the period 1131 x 1174.[12] The *Libellus* has been held to be a source of the highest value for the history of Ely in the last Anglo-Saxon century, for its author clearly drew extensively on the archives of the house.[13] What is not so clear is the date of the underlying English text. The author's statement about the history of Sudbourne (Suffolk), and therefore about the origins of the Old English Rule of St Benedict, has been widely accepted.[14] In other words Bishop Æthelwold made a vernacular translation of the Rule in return for a royal grant of an estate which he subsequently gave to the church of Ely. Christopher Hohler has delightfully characterised this royal act of literary and religious patronage as also educational: 'King Edgar, by telling St Aethelwold to produce him a translation of the Rule of St Benedict, no doubt had a most stimulating effect on higher education'.[15] Helmut Gneuss's studies of the developing vocabulary characteristic of Æthelwold's school certainly display the results of stimuli provided by the necessity of translation and interpretation.[16]

Indeed, the important work of the current generation of Anglo-Saxon scholarship on the Old English Rule of St Benedict, and on the circulation of the Latin text in England, has been that of Helmut Gneuss and Mechthild Gretsch.[17] We now have detailed studies of the author's methods of translation, of the vocabulary used, and of the development of the Old English text after publication. What is clear is that the Latin *Regula sancti Benedicti* had some circulation in England before the tenth century, that new copies of the text were imported in the tenth century (and later), what were the textual sources of Æthelwold's English translation, that the translator probably drew also on the commentary on

---

[12] *Liber Eliensis*, ed. Blake, pp. xlviii–xlix, but neither terminus seems very securely established. For difficulties in insisting on 1131 see Brett, 'John of Worcester and his contemporaries'.

[13] Whitelock, in *Liber Eliensis*, ed. Blake, pp. ix–xviii; Keynes & Kennedy, *Anglo-Saxon Ely*.

[14] This has been documented by Whitelock, 'The authorship', and Gretsch, *Die Regula*, pp. 9–11.

[15] 'Some service-books', p. 74, illustrating an assertion that 'The principal force upholding competence at Latin seems to have been relentless pressure from kings'. Hohler's contention quoted in the text goes beyond the Latin of *Libellus Æthelwoldi* ('dederunt . . . eo pacto ut ille regulam . . . transferret') but hardly beyond natural interpretation of the context of the transaction.

[16] See particularly Gneuss, *Hymnar* and 'The origin of Standard Old English'; cf. Hofstetter, *Winchester* and 'Winchester and the standardization'.

[17] Gneuss as in n. 29, below; Gretsch, *Die Regula* and 'Æthelwold's translation', and as in n. 19, below (on the Wintney version). For further comment see Oetgen, 'The Old English *Rule*'. Among older scholarship see Keim, 'Aeþelwold'.

the Rule by Smaragdus of Saint-Mihiel, that the Latin text continued to circulate in England independently of the translation, that most of the surviving manuscripts of the translation contain also the Latin text, that two major revisions of the Old English translation had been undertaken by the middle of the twelfth century, and that the continuous Old English gloss to one copy of the Latin text is independent of Æthelwold's prose translation.

What is perhaps less apparent is the originally intended shape of the whole. I do not wish to take up here the unresolved question of whether the original translation was intended (with appropriate indications of gender) for monks or for nuns or whether two gender-differentiated versions existed from the first.[18] But of some interest is another problematic question. Eight manuscripts attest to Æthelwold's translation (as does – at a further remove – the Early Middle English version from the Cistercian nunnery of Wintney, Hampshire, preserved in London, British Library, MS. Cotton Claudius D.iii, fos 55–140[19]). In format these copies fall into three groups: those which interleave Latin and Old English text, the latter following the former chapter by chapter through the work;[20] the one in which the entire Latin text precedes the continuous Old English translation;[21] and those in which the Old English alone appears.[22] What does this evidence tell us about the original layout of the text after Æthelwold's act of translation?

Mechthild Gretsch has summarised the evidence from study of the textual history.[23]

It seems remarkable that . . . among the manuscripts closest to the translator's conjectural exemplar . . . [are] . . . the four manuscripts which contain the

---

[18] For a summary of this question, see Gretsch, 'Æthelwold's translation', pp. 137–9. Cf. Sgarbi, 'Sulla tradizione manoscritta'. The matter is being tackled afresh by Richard Marsden in a forthcoming paper.

[19] Ker, *Catalogue*, p. xix. Cf. M. Gretsch in *Die Winteney-Version*, ed. Schröer, pp. 179–93, and Gretsch, 'Die Winteney-Version'.

[20] Ker, *Catalogue*, nos 41.B, 186 (an excerpt), 200, 353, 395 (two substantial fragments, now Wells, Cathedral Library, MS. 7), and the Wintney manuscript.

[21] Ibid., no. 109.

[22] *Ibid.*, nos 117 (an excerpt) and 154.B. It would seem very likely that the monolingual excerpt of §4 (albeit a fragment, and therefore perhaps once containing later excerpts) in no. 117 is a derivative of the same, but bilingual, excerpt in no. 186 (see n. 20).

[23] 'Æthelwold's translation', p. 135. The 'four manuscripts' to which she refers are Ker, *Catalogue*, nos 41.B, 109, 200, 353. In a footnote ('Æthelwold's translation', p. 135, n. 2) Gretsch has associated the fragments in Ker's no. 395 with this group. The bilingual excerpt (§4) in no. 186 was not discussed in this context; neither was the Wintney bilingual text (n. 19 above).

Latin text side by side with the Old English Rule. This indicates that the two texts were combined from the very beginning, when Æthelwold's translation was first copied to be sent to the reformed monasteries. Moreover we can conclude that the Latin text which accompanied the Old English version in Æthelwold's 'master copy' was largely, if not wholly, identical with the text he had used for his translation.

This evidence would indeed suggest that the bilingual format was, if not the translator's first layout, at least archetypal for the circulated text. And in particular it would suggest that the format of alternating chapters of Latin and Old English, attested in the five earliest of the eight witnesses to the Old English text (and in the Wintney version), was original. This is not the only known layout for Old English translations, but it is familiar from the Rule of Chrodegang, *Capitula Theodulfi*, and Marvels of the East.[24] However, two problems present themselves, in the form of the two latest Old English witnesses to the complete text. In Durham, Cathedral Library, MS. B.iv.24, the entire Latin text precedes the entire Old English translation. And in London, British Library, MS. Cotton Faustina A.x, only the Old English appears, but with two further and interesting items.[25]

In theory one might suppose that these two late manuscripts show the progressive abandonment of the original layout: first the two languages were separated and two continuous monolingual texts created; then the Latin was lost or discarded. But the unique matter in MS. Faustina A.x must give pause. The presence in this manuscript of a unique, if textually acephalous and physically fragmentary, copy of Æthelwold's supplementary history of monasticism endows the immediately preceding copy of the Old English Rule with an interest, if not necessarily an authority, which deserves respect. In the Faustina manuscript this supplement is not physically separable.[26] At the same period, however, William of

---

[24] For manuscripts of these texts, see Ker, *Catalogue*, nos 46, 97, 128 (Chrodegang); 318 (Theodulf, but in no. 50 another translation has a different format – see *Theodulfi Capitula*, ed. Sauer); 193 (Marvels). (In spite of Ker's appreciation of the importance of manuscripts in this format, none has yet been facsimiled: this is a significant desideratum.) The same layout occurs in the F-text of the Anglo-Saxon Chronicle (Ker no. 148), but here English – as the primary language of the text – precedes its Latin version in most instances. The parallel-text arrangement (Latin in the left-hand column, English in the right) of the Paris Psalter (Ker no. 367) might be held to be a variant of the alternating-language format, as might the natural layout of Latin-Old English glossary-manuscripts. For Ælfric's Grammar as a species of alternating bilingual text, see Ker, *Catalogue*, p. xxvi.

[25] Ker, *Catalogue*, nos 109 (second half of the eleventh century) and 154.B (first half of the twelfth century). One unique item in the latter is a table of contents: cf. Ker, *ibid.*, pp. 194–5 for the details of this.

[26] On this history see Whitelock, 'The authorship'; cf. *English Historical Documents*, transl. Whitelock, pp. 920–3 (no. 238); Robinson, *The Times*, pp. 159–68; Wormald,

Malmesbury saw a manuscript of the Old English Rule with a *prefixed* copy of the historical supplement; in his *Uita sancti Dunstani* he wrote that 'in cuiusdam prologo legi, qui regulam Benedicti Anglico enucleabat fuso, . . .'.[27] We must suppose that this supplement, whether prologue or postscript, originally stood on a quire separable from the Rule, as for example did King Alfred's preface to his translation of St Gregory's *Regula pastoralis*.[28] That the latest manuscript of Æthelwold's translation should uniquely if fragmentarily preserve his own historical supplement to it is a warning to us that our understanding of the whole work's circulation remains poor, in spite of all the important and fruitful research of recent years. A new edition of Æthelwold's 'preface' and bilingual Rule, from all the available witnesses, remains an urgent desideratum and would do much to improve our knowledge of the work's textual history.[29]

Æthelwold's translation was commissioned by King Edgar and Queen Ælfthryth, according to the author of *Libellus Æthelwoldi*. It is therefore possible to give some chronological termini to the creation of Æthelwold's version. The eleventh-century D-text of the Anglo-Saxon Chronicle places their marriage in 965,[30] but charter-evidence has rather suggested that it took place no later than 964 (and certainly not earlier than 962, when Ælfthryth's first husband was still alive).[31]

---

[27] 'Æthelwold and his Continental counterparts', pp. 40–1. On the physical condition of the manuscript, see Ker, *Catalogue*, pp. 194–6: he made it clear that the acephalous text begins in mid-page (fo 148r) after the end of the Rule, and that there is a lacuna of uncertain length between fos 148 and 149; the text ends, apparently complete, on fo 151v.

[27] *Memorials of Saint Dunstan*, ed. Stubbs, p. 290.

[28] On this see Sisam, *Studies*, pp. 140–7; *The Pastoral Care*, facs. ed. Ker; Ker, *Catalogue*, pp. 384–6 (no. 324). This is by no means a unique case. Similar evidence is available for the Old English Bede (Cambridge, University Library, MS. Kk.3.18 [2004]) and the *Historia Dunelmensis ecclesie* attributed to Symeon of Durham (*ibid.*, MS. Ff.1.27 [1160]). For a very clear case (closely comparable to that posited here for Æthelwold's work, in the textual history of another twelfth-century Latin narrative) see Dumville, 'An early text', pp. 16–17.

[29] The existing edition, *Die angelsächsischen Prosabearbeitungen der Benedikti-nerregel*, ed. Schröer, is inadequate, in spite of the excellent supplement by Helmut Gneuss (pp. 263–84) and the availability, as a control, of Mechthild Gretsch's work. It is to Gretsch that we owe the very demonstration of the faults of Schröer's work, first published in 1885–8. In a new edition, one would hope that the Latin text could be presented from Gretsch's MSS. w, s, i*, j, x, u (Ker, *Catalogue*, nos 41.B, 109, 186, 200, 353, 395) and the Wintney book.

[30] 'Her on þissum geare Eadgar cyning genam Ælf⟨ðr⟩yðe him to cwene; heo wæs Ordgares dohtor ealdormannes.' Cf. *An Anglo-Saxon Chronicle*, edd. Classen & Harmer, p. 49. The entry occurs also in the F-text, but as a marginale (on possible relationships between D and F, cf. Dumville, 'Some aspects of annalistic writing').

[31] By a royal diploma dated 964 – Sawyer, *Anglo-Saxon Charters*, no. 725 – King Edgar granted an estate in Berkshire to Ælfthryth, 'lateranee mee mihique dilecte': on this

Since Edgar died in 975, the limits of date for the translation must be (962–)964 x 975.[32] Helmut Gneuss has given it as his opinion, on vocabulary-evidence, that it 'was doubtless carried out at an early stage of his career as a teacher in Winchester',[33] in other words early in the period 964–984.[34]

Once executed, the translation of the Benedictine Rule would have had a guaranteed clientele. Its patrons – presumably proud of what they had commissioned – would have ensured its celebrity at Court. The king and queen, in their roles as guardians of those in monastic communities,

---

terminology, see *Asser's Life of King Alfred*, ed. Stevenson, pp. 200–2. While this charter was once regarded with suspicion, modern commentators have given it the benefit of the doubt: John, *Orbis Britanniae*, p. 98; Keynes, *The Diplomas of King Æthelred*, pp. 19–20. Ælfthryth is listed as a witness in the controversial charter Sawyer 731, also dated 964. Stenton, *Anglo-Saxon England*, p. 372, gave the date of the marriage as 964, without comment. Ælfthryth was the widow of Æthelwold II, ealdorman of East Anglia, who is supposed to have died in 962: on him, and his place in Edgar's family-connexions, see C. Hart, 'Athelstan', pp. 127–31 (which includes a discussion of Edgar's marriages). The date 962 for Æthelwold II's death (stated but not justified by Hart, *ibid.*, p. 130) is deduced from his last attestation of an acceptable charter, which falls in that year (Sawyer, *Anglo-Saxon Charters*, no. 703, surviving as an apparent original).

32 This may be contrasted with the datings 965 x 975, or '*c*. 970', usually given.

33 'The origin of Standard Old English', p. 78. He has appeared to spoil this conclusion by the following remarks (*ibid.*, p. 79): 'The Old English Benedictine Rule thus clearly represents an intermediate, but rather advanced, stage between an older, partly unsettled usage and that of the Winchester group. There is another [witness] which seems to hold a similar position in the development of vocabulary usage; this is [BL] Royal 2.B.v, a Latin psalter with Old English interlinear gloss, written about the middle of the tenth century, perhaps at the New Minster, Winchester, or at the Nunnaminster.' The reader begins to suspect that this 'Regius Psalter' – on which see most recently Davey, 'The commentary of the Regius Psalter' – is being attributed to Æthelwold's Winchester. But this impression is rapidly corrected: 'Wildhagen thought that the Regius gloss was the first fruit of the Benedictine reform, but this [hypothesis] seems to be obscured . . .'. There is no evidence other than that of vocabulary to associate the manuscript with Winchester in the period in question. The manuscript itself is written in Phase-III Square minuscule which was practised in the period 939–959; by the time of Æthelwold's succession to Winchester a very different style (Phase IV) of that script was being written there. A scribal relative of the 'Regius Psalter', BL Royal 4.A.xiv, has a Worcester provenance. If we are to associate the developing vocabulary seen in 'Regius Psalter' and Benedictine Rule with Æthelwold himself (and it would seem that the thrust of recent studies, inspired by Gneuss himself, is in this direction rather than towards attributing it to pre-Reform Winchester and/or seeing it as a source of inspiration for Æthelwold), then we should do better to suppose that Royal 2.B.v and 4.A.xiv were written at Glastonbury or Abingdon before 960, which would suit the palaeographical evidence without any strain whatsoever.

34 I give 964, rather than 963 (the beginning of Æthelwold's episcopate), as the date of inception of Æthelwold's school: in view of the nature of the reform in 964, one can scarcely imagine that any teaching which Æthelwold might have offered in pre-Reform Winchester would have been productive. The date 964 also coincides conveniently with the earlier terminus for the translation of the Rule.

would also have been keen to see the work circulated to the reformed (and perhaps even unreformed) religious houses, and no doubt to all the bishops, and we may be sure that Bishop Æthelwold needed no urging. The availability of this work in the vernacular may have encouraged lay aristocrats and secular clergy to read it, if they could gain access to a copy. Buf if the original published form was bilingual, this may by itself have caused transmission to be limited to circles (the reform-houses in particular) where a latinate audience was also present.[35]

In any event, the presumptions that the Old English Rule was sent to each reform-house in existence at the time of the translation's publication and that it was subsequently provided for each newly reformed house or newly established monastery have given a sense of the minimum size of the circulation of this work.[36] If we admit the figure of forty-six Benedictine monasteries in England before 1066,[37] we have a number with which to compare the six surviving copies of complete texts. If we suppose, as well we might, that any given house might own more than one manuscript of the work, we lose track of possible numbers of mediaeval copies. And when we note that certainly one, and possibly two, of the extant manuscripts of the Old English Rule can be recognised as of post-Conquest date, we realise – as the Wintney version also indicates – that Æthelwold's work had a continuing relevance and usefulness long after 1066, thus increasing still further the size of mediaeval circulation.[38] We are not automatically authorised to suppose, however, that the process of dissemination of the text was so complex that widespread contamination of vertical textual relationships prevents us from assessing the place of the surviving witnesses within the transmission of the work:[39] it will be the task of the next editor to bring light into what has remained obscure hitherto. In particular, as will appear, we need to know how high up the tree of textual relationships the two earliest witnesses stand.[40]

---

[35] Some questions need to be asked about the reason(s) for the development of the alternating-language format of the tenth-century translations mentioned earlier (cf. n. 24). Was it to ensure that the original Latin remained as a control on the English, to prevent excessive corruption of the vernacular text in the course of successive copyings? Was it a teaching aid, to help more readers of English to be brought to a knowledge of Latin?

[36] Gretsch, *Die Regula*, pp. 200–34, and 'Æthelwold's translation', pp. 140–3.

[37] Gneuss, 'Englands Bibliotheken', p. 120.

[38] Ker, *Catalogue*, no. 154.B belongs to the first half of the twelfth century, and no. 109 to the second half of the eleventh – both datings are palaeographical.

[39] Cf. Gretsch, *Die Regula*, pp. 200–34, especially 233–4; 'Æthelwold's translation', pp. 142–3.

[40] Ker, *Catalogue*, no. 353 (cf. plate II and p. xxvi), assigned by him to the second half of the tenth century, and no. 41.B to the first half of the eleventh; cf. Bishop, *English Caroline Minuscule*, pp. xxii and 20 (with plate XX).

Caroline minuscule script in England

One aspect of the revival of Frankish ecclesiastical and cultural life in the later eighth and earlier ninth centuries was the development of the Caroline minuscule script as a testimony to and vehicle for the results of that revival.[41] The extent to which use of that script received royal and consequent official encouragement has been a matter of uncertainty, but a presumption has nonetheless been created that there was such support. Whether that aspect of the early history of Caroline writing could have been known in late ninth- and in tenth-century England is even more uncertain. Books written in that script would have become familiar to English ecclesiastics and in England before the eighth century was out, but we have no certain evidence for any scribal performance in Caroline minuscule in England before the reign of Æthelstan (924–939); even then, the earliest known specimens are the work of foreigners, and the first available examples by English scribes are datable 948 x 958. Anglo-Saxon knowledge of Carolingian books seems to have provoked reactions other than attempts to learn and imitate their script.[42]

The wide external contacts of Æthelstan's England may indeed provide the context in which Caroline minuscule achieved favour – first, no doubt, at Court – just as it is in that period that the first English manifestations of reformed monasticism become apparent.[43] It is presumably an accident of survival which brings to us the first two dated specimens of Anglo-Caroline minuscule (in two very different styles) as royal diplomas from the archive of Æthelwold's reformed foundation at Abingdon:[44] but this serves to remind us that it seems to have been only on the eve of the Benedictine *coup* of 964 that Caroline writing began to make a significant direct public impact in England.

For the English Benedictine reformers a central fact was clear. While we are not aware of the name by which they would have known Caroline minuscule, they would have recognised that the books which they

---

[41] Bischoff, *Latin Palaeography*, pp. 112–20 (cf. 202–11), for an introduction. Cf. Hessel, 'Zur Entstehung'.

[42] Cf. Dumville, 'English Square minuscule script: the background and earliest phases', pp. 154–5. See also below, pp. 151–2.

[43] See Dumville, *Wessex and England*, chapter IV, for the context. For a specimen of Caroline minuscule written by a foreigner in England in A.D. 929 x 939, see Keynes, 'King Athelstan's books', pp. 147–51 (and plate IV), on London, British Library, MS. Cotton Tiberius A.ii, fo 15r; cf. Lapidge, 'Some Latin poems', pp. 93–7. This scribe may have been working either in the royal court or at Christ Church, Canterbury. For Caroline products associated with Frithegod at Canterbury in A.D. 948 x 958, see Lapidge, 'A Frankish scholar'. On these points, cf. pp. 92–4, below.

[44] Sawyer, *Anglo-Saxon Charters*, no. 594 (A.D. 956: BL Cotton Augustus ii.41: *Facsimiles*, ed. Bond, III.18), and no. 690 (A.D. 961: BL Cotton Augustus ii.39: *Facsimiles*, ed. Bond, III.23). Cf. Bishop, *English Caroline Minuscule*, pp. xix and 9.

imported from abroad – particularly those containing texts of ideological importance for their cause and those emanating from reformed Continental houses – were usually written in that script. They may have suspected that the development of the script was coeval with the Carolingian ecclesiastical (and educational) reforms in which they were finding inspiration. In contrast, by *ca* 930 the universal script-form in Southumbrian England was the newly developed Anglo-Saxon Square minuscule.[45] In as much as the reformers wished increasingly to distance themselves from their English ecclesiastical predecessors,[46] they – or the more radical among them – might seek to differentiate visually their approved texts from those of inherited books and in this respect, as no doubt in many others, to wear with pride a badge of internationalism. The beginnings of Caroline writing in England remain poorly understood. It has been argued that one phase of that development may be placed at Glastonbury Abbey during the rule of Dunstan (940x956), where Æthelwold was also for a time a monk;[47] if Dunstan encouraged such scriptorial innovation in his first period of command, he is likely to have done so during his subsequent careers as bishop of Worcester (?958–961?), bishop of London (959–961?), and archbishop of Canterbury (959–988).[48] By the year in

---

[45] Dumville, 'English Square minuscule script: the background and earliest phases', pp. 148–9, 173–8.

[46] This ideology is most apparent in Æthelwold's historical supplement to his translation of the Rule and in the Lives of tenth-century English reformers. For comment, see the references cited in n. 26, above, on Æthelwold's text, and cf. John, *Orbis Britanniae*, pp. 154–264, 271–91, and 'The church of Winchester'.

[47] On this phase, which supposedly produced the hybrid (Insular/Caroline) 'Style II' of Anglo-Caroline minuscule, see Bishop, 'An early example of Insular-Caroline', and *English Caroline Minuscule*, p. 1 (no. 1). Note also Bishop's comment, *ibid.*, p. xxii: 'The evidence that Glastonbury was the first home of Style II is less substantial than could be wished'. See also *Saint Dunstan's Classbook*, facs. ed. Hunt.

[48] On this point we have no evidence which can certainly be dated to Dunstan's tenure of Worcester and London. For Canterbury, see Bishop, *English Caroline Minuscule*, pp. xxii–xxiii, xxv–xxvi, 4–7 (nos 6–9), and Brooks, *The Early History*, pp. 243–78. The principal discussions of Dunstan himself have been by Stubbs, *Memorials of Saint Dunstan*; Robinson, *The Times*; Pontifex, 'St Dunstan in his first biography'; and in numerous papers by Symons ('The monastic reforms'; 'The English monastic reform'; 'Some notes on English monastic origins'; 'The Regularis Concordia and the Council of Winchester'; 'Notes on the life'; 'St Dunstan in the "Oswald" tradition'); cf. also *Regularis Concordia*, ed. & transl. Symons, introduction. (And see now Semmler, 'Das Erbe', pp. 44–50.) In apparent reaction, the last generation has seen considerable stress laid by scholars on the prominent role of Æthelwold, bishop of Winchester, in the English Benedictine revolution. However, this has led to some rather unsubtle contrasts being pointlessly drawn to the disadvantage of Dunstan. There are at last a few signs in the scholarly literature of a more balanced assessment of the evidence for the interaction of the protagonists of ecclesiastical change in tenth-century England.

which Dunstan was driven from the abbacy of Glastonbury and indeed from England, practice of the script had reached the royal chancery.[49] But it is not clear that the route thither was from Dunstan's Glastonbury.

Such evidence as we possess from Abingdon suggests the use there of Square minuscule in the second half of the tenth century;[50] but from the time of Æthelwold's revolution at Winchester in 964 we have ample evidence for the development of a remarkable style of Caroline writing – pure and monumental – known first to us from a royal diploma dated 961.[51] What has come to be called 'Style-I' Anglo-Caroline minuscule is associated particularly with Winchester in the late tenth century; but scholars generally allow that it was practised at the other houses founded or reformed under Bishop Æthelwold's influence.[52] Among the various uncertainties which remain in the history of Caroline writing in pre-Conquest England, however, are the extent and the speed of dissemination of Style I. It has become clear that, at the latest by the beginning of the eleventh century, Style I was being practised alongside the predominant Style II at Christ Church, Canterbury,[53] and that there, *ca* 1020, a fusion of the two styles was achieved (Style IV) which was highly influential for the next half-century.[54] But the monumental quality which had been imitated from Continental liturgical books,[55] and refined in England in the same context,[56] was to remain influential through the central decades of the eleventh century.[57]

One further question which requires discussion here concerns the differentiation of scripts by linguistic function. This begins to become

---

[49] Sawyer, *Anglo-Saxon Charters*, no. 594 (as above, n. 44). On the chancery in this period, see Keynes, *The Diplomas of King Æthelred*, pp. 14–83 (on S.594, see pp. 11, 26–7, 50–4, 62–3, 68).

[50] I have discussed this fully in 'The scriptorium and library of Abingdon Abbey, A.D. 954–1066' (forthcoming). For whatever reason, there is no evidence for the practice of Caroline script at Abingdon before the mid-eleventh century. T.A.M. Bishop's idea that Style-I Anglo-Caroline was pioneered there (*English Caroline Minuscule*, pp. xxi–xxii and p. 9, no. 11) rested on mistaken deductions from charter-evidence: I have discussed these in 'English libraries before 1066'.

[51] Sawyer, *Anglo-Saxon Charters*, no. 690 (as above, n. 44); see Keynes, *The Diplomas of King Æthelred*, pp. 11–12, 36, 70–9. Cf. pp. 52–3, below.

[52] Now following Bishop, *English Caroline Minuscule*, pp. xxi–xxii.

[53] Bishop, *ibid.*, pp. 6 (no. 8) and 8 (no. 10) illustrate the point (cf. p. xxv also): the two styles appear side by side in no. 8, Cambridge, University Library, MS. Ff.4.43 (1286). I have discussed this matter further in chapters III–IV, below.

[54] Bishop, *English Caroline Minuscule*, pp. xxiii, 22–24 (nos 24–5, 27–8). Cf. chapter IV, below.

[55] *Ibid.*, pp. xxi–xxii, 12 (no. 14).

[56] *Ibid.*, pp. 10 (no. 12) and 14 (no. 16).

[57] *Ibid.*, p. xxiv, n. 2, lists (*inter alios*) many specimens of this type; cf. p. xxiii.

apparent in the second half of the tenth century.[58] In the Anglo-Saxon eleventh century the use of Insular minuscule for English but of Caroline minuscule for Latin provided a system which was adhered to with some rigidity,[59] with scribes prepared to change script word by word in some contexts. In the later tenth century, the rigidity is not yet present but the intention to differentiate comes clearly into view in both books and documents. The impulse which gave birth to this system of alphabetic apartheid remains undefined: the distinction may reflect a spirit of compromise on the part of the proponents of Caroline writing, permitting the native Square-minuscule script to be retained for one of its functions; or we may interpret their attitude as more haughty, allowing that the word of God was transmitted in Latin and that it should therefore be written in the script which in their eyes had great status, while Englishmen's earthly vernacular grunts might be rendered in an uncouth alphabet. Whatever the motivation, the division of functions proved effective, presumably popular, and enduring.[60] For the first reform-generation, however, this was an experiment, whatever its motives, and the results match these circumstances.

Oxford, Corpus Christi College, MS. 197

One of the bilingual manuscripts of that first generation of scribal differentiation by script-type contains the earliest surviving copy of Æthelwold's version of the Benedictine Rule. Oxford, Corpus Christi College, MS. 197 was described by Neil Ker as 'the most interesting of these manuscripts' containing bilingual prose texts.[61] The principal, and sole original, content of the manuscript – the bilingual Rule – occupies fos 1r–105r4. Some additions, Latin and Old English, of the eleventh and twelfth centuries occupy fo 105r6–13 and an added quire,

---

[58] *Ibid.*, pp. xi, xx–xxi (N.B. his observation that 'The Caroline minuscule is not to be considered apart from a script [viz, Insular minuscule] antecedently and concurrently written, equally esteemed and intimately associated'), 9 (discussion of no. 11). For the more consistent differentiation in the earlier eleventh century, see *ibid.*, pp. 15 (no. 17) and 20 (no. 22). Cf. Ker, *Catalogue*, pp. xxv–xxvi, xxvii, and plates II, IV–V.

[59] For some exceptions to this rule, see *ibid.*, p. xxvii, for his nos 1, 32, 43, 56, 158, and 288, to which nos 157 and 239 should be added (cf. his pp. 201, 312).

[60] Cf. *ibid.*, pp. xxvi–xxvii for usage in the period 1066–*ca* 1200, and cf. his plate VII (of no. 325). A great deal more could be written about usage of the period 1150–1300 in this respect than has in fact been done. Wright, *English Vernacular Hands*, produced a rather muddled book whose title advertised linguistically based distinctions of script but which failed to point precisely to the differences of usage.

[61] Ker, *Catalogue*, p. xxvi.

fos 106–109;[62] fo 105v, the last page of the original book, has remained blank. That original manuscript is constructed in thirteen quires: I¹⁰ (2, 7 canc.) (fos 1–8); II⁸–V⁸; VI¹⁰ (3, 9 canc.) (fos 41–48); VII⁸–XII⁸; XIII¹⁰ (lacks 10) (fos 97–105).[63] The added fourteenth quire, XIV⁴ (fos 106–109), will be discussed later. In the original quires the old Insular practice of arranging the leaves HFHF was adhered to; but pricking is found in the outer margins only; leaves were ruled in batches of four.[64]

To all appearances, a single scribe wrote the whole text. For the most part the Latin is written in Caroline and the English in Insular minuscule. In principle this should cause difficulties of scribal identification. In fact the aspect of the whole is so uniform that there can be little doubt that we have to do with a holograph. And where features of one script intrude into the other, the identity of form with those features where they occur in their proper linguistic and scribal context assures the student of this volume that one scribe was initially responsible for the whole book. Neil Ker wrote as follows about the manuscript.[65]

The bilingual copies of the Rules of St. Benedict, of Chrodegang, and of Theodulf, and the manuscripts of Ælfric's Grammar, where Latin and OE occur together on every page, provide ample material to demonstrate that the scribes were trained to observe the conventional distinctions of letter-form with the utmost care . . .. The most interesting of these manuscripts is the bilingual copy of the Rule of St. Benedict now at Corpus Christi College, Oxford . . ., since it is the only one of them which was written at a time when Anglo-Saxon minuscule was still a living script. We find in it not only two sets of letter-forms, but two distinct scripts. The scribe wrote the OE chapters in Anglo-Saxon minuscule and the Latin chapters in caroline minuscule of a heavy and not markedly English type. The script, both in Latin and in OE, has a certain resemblance to that of a Latin charter of 984 from Worcester, with OE boundaries . . ..

---

[62] These additions are discussed below, pp. 30–4.

[63] This collation differs from Ker's (*ibid.*, p. 431) in two respects: I have described differently the half-sheets of quire I; and Ker missed the same kind of complexity in quire VI. The missing last leaf of quire XIII was presumably blank and accordingly removed as otherwise usable parchment. The manuscript bears no quire-signatures.

[64] Ker, *ibid.*; cf. pp. xxiii–xxv.

[65] *Ibid.*, p. xxvi. In reading this passage one should bear in mind Ker's view of the history of native script in England, that it ended with the abandonment of Square minuscule, being replaced not by what many would call 'Anglo-Saxon minuscule of the eleventh century' (which for Ker would have been a contradiction in terms) but by a species of Caroline minuscule in which some special letter-forms were employed (*ibid.*, pp. xxv–xxvi and xxxii–xxxiii, for example). Cf. comment by Dumville, 'Beowulf come lately', p. 58. The charter mentioned at the end of the quotation is Sawyer, *Anglo-Saxon Charters*, no. 1347.

In the general context of script-history, Ker stressed the distinctions to be drawn between the scribe's performances in English and Latin. Incidentally Ker drew attention to two other matters which will be of central concern in this chapter: the nature of the Caroline script, and the place of origin of the manuscript. However, when describing the manuscript in detail,[66] Ker's emphasis shifted somewhat. He began, as one would expect from his introductory comments quoted above, by stressing and reporting in detail the differences between the scribal usage in English and Latin.[67]

OE is distinguished from Latin not only by the forms of **a**, **d**, **e**, **f**, **g**, **h**, **r**, and **s**, but in other ways also. For example, in OE only, **c** and **o** begin, like **e**, with a slight projection or horn to the left, the bow of **p** is open, and the end of the bow of **t** is often curled up. Another less conspicuous difference is in the form of the shaft of **t**, which is more curved in OE than it is in Latin. **e** differs from **e** in Latin, not only, as usual, in the way it is begun, but also in the way it is completed, with a slight downward twist to the end of the tongue. The mark of abbreviation is a horizontal stroke with a slight hook at each end, not, as in Latin, a wavy stroke. Punctuation within the sentence is by means of a point only: in Latin both the point and the inverted semicolon are used . . .. The different appearance of the Latin and OE passages is due partly to the differences of letter-form, especially the much more common use in OE of heavy left-to-right downward diagonals (**c**, **e**, **o**); partly also, it seems, to a deliberate varying of the duct of the hand, so that the OE looks like square Anglo-Saxon minuscule and the Latin like caroline minuscule of a rather heavy and not typically English type, such as we find in the Benedictional of St. Athelwold.

However, he continued by drawing attention to facts which point to another aspect of the scribe's training – one which has some implications of consequence for the history of script.[68]

The scribe seems to have been more at home in the insular than in the caroline script. He occasionally used letter-forms proper to OE when writing Latin (e.g. **o**, **p**, **r**, **t** on ff. 89, 102, 103) and he wrote the whole of chs. 56 and 59 of the Latin, as well as the [end] of ch. 50 and the [beginning] of ch. 58, in full insular script. He used insular script also whenever Latin words occur in an OE context: . . .

---

[66] Ker, *Catalogue*, pp. 430–2.

[67] *Ibid.*, p. 431. The ambiguity of the last clause of the passage quoted here is troubling. Did Ker think the Benedictional's script to be of a typically English type? Or did he take it to be 'of a rather heavy and not typically English type'? Bishop (*English Caroline Minuscule*, p. 10) has more recently characterised the script of BL MS. Additional 49598 as 'medium-large, slightly sloping, broad, round, clear, characteristic of an early type of English Caroline'.

[68] Ker, *Catalogue*, p. 431. In the penultimate sentence of the quotation I have corrected a pair of related errors.

These are observations and conclusions from which one might be tempted to draw further, chronological, inferences. Caution is required, however. Ker dated the manuscript very conservatively, to the second half of the tenth century. But he drew attention, as we have seen, to a scribal performance in both scripts which offers 'a certain resemblance' to that seen in CCCO 197.[69] In the scholarly literature this comparison with a Worcester episcopal charter of A.D. 984 has perhaps proved productive more in respect of place than of date. It is with dating that we must first be concerned, however. Helmut Gneuss has written that CCCO 197 'was made about one or two decades after the completion of the original version' of the bilingual Rule.[70] We have seen that the chronological parameters for the commissioning of the text are 964 x 975. The earliest possible date for the text itself, and therefore for any manuscript of it, is accordingly likely to have been 965. Gneuss's one or two decades will consequently take us to ten years after 965 and twenty after 975, to give a maximum approximate date-range of 975 x 995. The centre of gravity is effectively provided by the charter of A.D. 984 – two decades after 964 and about one after 975 – which was no doubt an influence on Gneuss's dating. By considering the date of the text, we can shrink Ker's dating from the second half to the last third of the century. If we adopt Ker's palaeographical comparison more wholeheartedly than he did, we can restrict dating still further, to the last quarter of the tenth century.

If CCCO 197 is to be dated so late in the century, some questions arise about the centre(s) in which its scribe was trained and employed. The general impression conveyed by the manuscript is that the scribe was reasonably competent, but no more than that. Given that the original manuscript is a holograph and that no other performances by the same scribe have been identified with assurance,[71] it is not possible to speak with confidence of anything more than a one-person scriptorium. (However, our scribe's performance does offer some evidence for the traditions of the house in which he or she was trained.) The scribe's treatment of rubrics creates an immediate impression of muddle, and perhaps more so in the last couple of quires than elsewhere. The rubrics were usually written in mixed majuscules, but several are found in minuscule (for example, fos 29v2, 38r12, 47r24, 52r10) and at least one is only partly in minuscule (51r17);[72] there is an incomplete rubric in green at 69v6. A Latin *capitula*-list occupies 6r17–7v15: like two other

---

[69] *Ibid.*, p. xxvi; and quoted above, p. 20.
[70] 'The origin of Standard Old English', p. 74.
[71] I return to this question below, pp. 27–8.
[72] The scribe seems to have begun this practice for unnumbered rubrics (for example, those in Old English).

copies, this embodies an error by which *capitula* 63–65 (of 70) have been omitted.[73] In the body of the text, the distributed rubrics have by no means all been numbered. At the beginning (§§ 2–7) an effort was made to give Old English rubrics for the vernacular version of each chapter. In the rest of the manuscript a line has often been left blank between the Latin text of a chapter and its following translation, but the practice is far from invariable. The scribe clearly did not always anticipate the need to leave space for rubrication, either at all or to the extent required by the length of the rubric: the result is that, where rubrics are found, they are cramped, or are badly placed, or even hang vertically down the right-hand margin. There is obviously no doubt that textual rubrication was carried out subsequent to the writing of the body of the text, not concurrently with it.[74]

These indications of scriptorial muddle and incompetence may serve as background to our examination of the script and the execution of copying. The evidence of scribal correction suggests that the initial transcription was not done with great accuracy.[75] On the other hand great attention seems to have been given to correction. Errors were eliminated by simple erasure (for example, 12r5, *bið*), by writing a correction on an erasure (for example, 12v15, 15r13), by erasure and superscript (for example, `under ´þeod*, 73r11), or by the addition of letters or a word above the line with an insertion-mark placed below the line. Six larger supplied passages, all needing repatriation as a result of omission by scribal *saut du même au même* (four in Old English and two in Latin), have been placed in lower margins, marked by + in both margin and text (15r, 37r, 40v–41r, 63r, 63v, 71v).[76] Correction appears, therefore, to have been efficient.

In his description and discussion of the scripts of our book, Neil Ker concluded that the scribe was more competent in Insular than in Caroline

---

[73] This feature was identified by Ker, *Catalogue*, p. 63 (*s.n.* 41.B). The manuscripts other than CCCO 197 are Cambridge, Corpus Christi College, MS. 178 and London, British Library, MS. Cotton Titus A.iv.

[74] There is an important discrepancy between the Latin *capitula*-list on 6r–7v and the rubrics distributed through the text, but its significance has not yet been discovered. In the list, masculine forms are used. However, in the rubrics, a feminising process may be seen at work. In the heading to §59 we read 'De *filiabus* nobilium aut pauperum que offeruntur' (86v18); for §58 (83r17) we find the rather bizarre 'De disciplina suscipiendarum *fratrum*'!

[75] I leave aside the question of existing textual error, in as much as examples of this are often likely to have been inherited.

[76] The last two are the Latin examples. It would be possible to argue from all but one (63r) of these instances that the scribe's exemplar had a line-length of 20–22 characters, or from all but two (37r, 63r) that its line-length was 40–44 characters. But the scribal *saut* may of course occur in a number of different environments.

minuscule.[77] I turn first to a consideration of this Caroline performance. The script is rather large and very heavy in appearance.[78] This pair of features develops over a couple of quires at the beginning of the book: in the first quire, strokes and therefore letters are narrower; they appear thicker in quire II; and from quire III the full thickness of strokes, found in the rest of the volume, has been achieved. Throughout the book, the Caroline script is forward-leaning, but this feature is more pronounced in the first quire. It is a striking characteristic of the script that round letters seem very round indeed. Among other Caroline features may be recorded the sparing use of abbreviations, an **a** of strikingly Uncial sort, a **g** with an open (and very generously proportioned) lower member, and the occasional employment of continuation-lettering (**on**, **ri**, for example). Suspension-marks are generally very restrained. Among impure features one may mention that Caroline **r** and **s** both drop slightly below the line, the ampersand is found within (as well as at the end of) words, the **st** ligature occurs throughout, and some use is made of accents. The Capital NT monogram is found at word-end and line-end. For Classical *ae*, **e**-caudata is found, but not obtrusively, as also are **æ** and **ae** itself. That the scribe had an Insular background might be held to be suggested by the wedging of the ascender in **b** and **d**, and sporadically in **l**; by the occasional use of accents; by a rare example of tall **i**-longa (*iudicio*, 19r21); and by hints (though no more) at a knowledge of tall-**e** ligatures (97r). If the Old English in Insular minuscule were not present in the book, there would still – I think – be no doubt that this is Anglo-Caroline script.[79]

Indeed, a striking feature of the scribe's Caroline performance is that, notwithstanding the features just mentioned as possibly indicating an Insular background, the Caroline minuscule found in this manuscript cannot be characterised as hybrid. There is no sustained importation of Insular letter-forms, ligatures, or abbreviations into the Caroline context, and generally no writing of letter-forms of one script in a duct characteristic of the other. This is Style-I Anglo-Caroline minuscule.

---

[77] *Ibid.*, p. 431; quoted above, p. 21.

[78] Only two published facsimiles of parts of this manuscript are known to me: Ker, *Catalogue*, plate II (part of fo 89v); Watson, *Catalogue of Dated and Datable Manuscripts c. 435–1600 in Oxford Libraries*, II, plate 15 (part of fo 51r).

[79] Ker, *Catalogue*, p. xxxii, drew attention to a bilingual document dated A.D. 997 in which the scribe successfully avoided wedges in Caroline minuscule but employed them in the Old English part of the diploma: London, British Library, Stowe Charter 34 (Sawyer, *Anglo-Saxon Charters*, no. 890; *Facsimiles*, ed. Sanders, III.35). Ker's descriptions of the Caroline script of CCCO 197 as 'of a heavy and not markedly English type' and as looking 'like caroline minuscule of a rather heavy and not typically English type' (*Catalogue*, pp. xxvi, 431) suggest that he was thinking of Bishop's 'Style II' (formally defined thus only in 1971 in *English Caroline Minuscule*, pp. xx–xxiii) as being the Anglo-Caroline standard.

However, Ker was undoubtedly correct to observe that the scribe was more at home in Insular script. The evidence is provided by random lapses into Square-minuscule forms. These occur most dramatically in quires X and XI where, as Ker noted, in the Latin text the end of §50 (74v17, *abba*, –23), the whole of §56 (82r10–14), the beginning of §58 (83r17–v1), and the whole of §59 (86v18–87r15), are all written in Square minuscule when they should have been in Caroline script. These lapses of concentration are paralleled at more local, particular levels. Within these Square-minuscule passages we find lapses back into Caroline forms – for example, *suae* 83r24, *inuoluant* 86v22, *faciant* 87r5, or *nihil habent* 87r13. Ker remarked the large amount of Latin which remained in the 'translation' and commented that the scribe 'used insular script . . . whenever Latin words occur in an OE context'; this is not the whole story, however. While such is the case in 37r21 (*cantemus*), at 36v15 the scribe wrote 'D*eus* misereatur no*stri*' with the emboldened letters in non-Insular forms; the **st** is ligatured, while **ri** give an example of continuation-lettering. Likewise, in Caroline contexts one meets occasional lapses into Insular forms: in *hon*e*statem*, 103v23, for example, we see an Insular **e** + **s** ligature and an example of an Insular **a**.

What must be stressed is that these examples are visibly random lapses.[80] They indicate neither intention to create a hybrid script nor inability to shrug off in Caroline minuscule the duct of Insular script. They show that the scribe did not always concentrate sufficiently and that, as Ker diagnosed, Square minuscule was the scribe's primary medium. The scribe must have been trained originally to write only Square minuscule. If we bear in mind the practically certain fact that the bilingual text is not older than 965 (and that the manuscript can hardly therefore be any older than the last third of the tenth century), we shall be clear that this is not an early Anglo-Caroline performance. Neither does it stand very close in its aspect to the script of the royal diploma of A.D. 961 in which the first dated specimen of Style I is found,[81] or to the Benedictional of St Æthelwold or other Winchester products of the last third of the century. It is nonetheless undoubtedly a specimen of Style-I Anglo-Caroline.

It is customary – and, on the available localised evidence, probably correct – to associate Style-I Anglo-Caroline with houses connected with Æthelwold. That the first recorded specimen issues from the royal chancery is not a difficulty, for royal scribes are likely to have been

---

[80] A very curious linguistic lapse may be noted. 83r21 reads (in §58) 'æt inlatas sibi iniurias æt dificultatis in-' where 'et . . . et . . .' is intended. The error is orthographic, but, with Old English everywhere in the manuscript, one wonders what was in the scribe's mind.

[81] Sawyer, *Anglo-Saxon Charters*, no. 690, as above, p. 18.

drawn from ecclesiastical houses and Æthelwold's influence at Edgar's court is well known.[82] The alternative to accepting the equation is to allow that our book was not written in an Æthelwoldian house.[83]

The question must first be put, therefore, whether a scribe taught first to write Square minuscule might have been trained thus in a house of the Æthelwoldian connexion. There are two aspects to this matter. First, was Square minuscule written at all at such churches? The answer must be affirmative: all such manuscript evidence as survives from tenth-century Abingdon indicates the practice of Square minuscule there;[84] and writing in Old English continued to be in Insular script at all Æthelwoldian houses from which evidence survives. Secondly, in such a church, what would the relationship be between learning to write Square minuscule and learning to write Caroline script? Caroline minuscule has been described as 'the most difficult of scripts'.[85] In an English scriptorium in which Caroline and Insular minuscules were both in current use, trainee scribes might be introduced first to Square minuscule: it was an easier script to produce to a reasonable standard; and as the script increasingly employed (as the tenth century drew towards its close) for the writing of the native language, it would provide work in an easier linguistic context for one still seeking full competence as a scribe.

These arguments might suggest that it would be natural enough for scriptoria where Style-I Anglo-Caroline was practised to train their new

[82] On the provenance of royal scribes, see Dumville, 'English libraries before 1066'. As noted above, if we were to associate characteristically Æthelwoldian endeavours with a period before he gained full control of Winchester's minsters in 964, we must attribute them to Abingdon or even to Glastonbury. While textual and linguistic matters might be carried back to Glastonbury and the early 950s (or earlier), it is perhaps unlikely that he would have had the scope to encourage a new style of Caroline minuscule there, given that that is where we are supposed to see 'Style II' developing. If we associate the *origins* (rather than the subsequent patronage) of Style I with Æthelwold, the Caroline scribe of Sawyer, *Anglo-Saxon Charters*, no. 690 is likely to have been trained at Abingdon Abbey. Such an association must be balanced against the point made above about tenth-century Abingdon (p. 18) and discussed further immediately below (cf. n. 84). Likewise, the role of Bishop Oswald in this diploma's creation must be considered: see below, pp. 52–3.

[83] As we shall see later in this chapter (pp. 48–68), such evidence as is available may be found to demonstrate the practice of Style I in another major group of churches.

[84] Dumville, 'The scriptorium and library of Abingdon Abbey, A.D. 954–1066' (forthcoming). But we have nothing in Latin which can be shown to be associated with Abingdon before the mid-eleventh century. It could perhaps be argued that the period from 985 when Abingdon was ruled by an intruded, simoniacal abbot, Eadwine, was a watershed in the history of the Abingdon library, just as it was for the landed endowment. Only one Abingdon book written before that date is known to survive – London, British Library, MS. Cotton Tiberius A.vi, fos 1–34 + Tiberius A.iii, fo 178, containing the B-text of the Anglo-Saxon Chronicle, written in 977/8 – and it may have had a complex history from soon after it was written.

[85] Bishop, *English Caroline Minuscule*, p. xxiii.

scribes first in the inherited native script. Two difficulties attend this approach, however. Unless we may judge from what Ælfric said, a generation later, it is still very unclear what attitude the Benedictine reformers took towards pre-Reform English literature, even the works which King Alfred inspired or undertook.[86] It is not clear that, until the new surge of approved vernacular works had begun to appear, there would be enough for a monoglot Reform-scribe to do. Neither do we know what was the attitude of Reformers to Insular script, although their championing of Caroline minuscule invites an obvious – but perhaps much too simplistic – deduction.[87] And the danger posed by teaching Insular minuscule first would be that scribes might be unable to make a clean – uncontaminated – transition to writing Caroline minuscule. In some measure the scribal performance in CCCO 197 illustrates that point.[88]

It is perhaps necessary to pursue a little further the nature of the partial inadequacy of our scribe's performance. That performance was in more than one respect undisciplined. Lack of adequate planning for rubrication, copying of uneven accuracy (but rather good correction), and sporadic inattention to conventions of script-differentiation are the principal charges. On the other side of the scales, however, is the relatively pure quality of the scribe's Caroline minuscule. We do not see an inability to learn that script, but rather a lack of scriptorial discipline. One is perhaps brought back, therefore, to a question raised earlier:[89] one wonders whether this scribe might not have been working in isolation or in a context where adequate supervision and assistance were unavailable.

Three possibilities seem to be open to us. We may allow that Anglo-Caroline Style I was not the only medium for Latin writing in Æthelwoldian houses: this is not, perhaps, an unthinkable proposition, but to document it does not seem possible. If, therefore, we turn aside from that option, we must suppose that the scribe was trained outside the Æthelwoldian family. Since we know that Square minuscule was still being practised as a Latin script at Glastonbury in Dunstan's time, the scribe, if a man, could have been trained there (given that the chronology were appropriate) but would have had to have escaped before being contaminated by any knowledge of the Style-II Anglo-Caroline supposedly developed there under Dunstan's auspices.[90] Otherwise, and probably more likely, we should think in terms of an ecclesiastic from an unreformed minster being attracted to one of Æthelwold's houses where

---

[86] Cf. Clemoes, 'Ælfric'; Dumville, *Wessex and England*, chapters IV and VI.

[87] Cf. discussion above, pp. 1–4, 16–17, 18–19.

[88] As witness the evidence discussed above, pp. 23–5.

[89] See above, p. 22.

[90] On the tenth-century scripts of Glastonbury see my remarks, pp. 3, 17–18, 50–1, 89–90, 142–3, 153.

it was then necessary for Anglo-Caroline Style I to be added to the scribe's repertoire. The third possibility allows that the scribe was originally trained outside the Æthelwoldian family but that the minster in which he or she was trained was brought into that family by being reformed. In view of what we learn about the nature of the reform of the Winchester houses, it is highly unlikely that our scribe learned the craft there before 964.[91] But a variety of other houses was reformed in the succeeding years and there should be no shortage of possible candidates.[92]

All these options lead to a consideration of the problem of dating our scribe's activity. We may start by asking how we would date this scribe's Caroline minuscule if it occurred alone, not in conjunction with comparable amounts of Insular script. This is not easy to answer, for the surviving quantity of scribal performances in Style-I Anglo-Caroline is not great and criteria for recognising development within that style have not been clearly worked out. We may say with modest confidence that our manuscript belongs, on the evidence of the Caroline script, to the period from *ca* 960 to *ca* 1010,[93] but that at a minor house a later date would not be unimaginable. Dating more precisely within that period would at present depend on argument from historical considerations rather than from palaeographical criteria. Such criteria sometimes appear to be involved in a context of this sort whereas in fact the reasoning tends to be essentially historical: to point to the retention of Insular features in Caroline writing is commonly taken as a sign of a date relatively early in the history of Anglo-Caroline. A caution issued by T.A.M. Bishop should be remembered, however: 'native practices might be naturally acceptable to a possibly long succession of scriptoria and scribes taking up the Continental script for the first time'.[94]

So it is with our manuscript, and we must turn instead to the scribe's Square minuscule in the hope of gaining more precision. The history of

---

[91] On that reform see Anglo-Saxon Chronicle, *s.a.* 964A, and Wulfstan *cantor*, *Vita S. Æthelwoldi*, §§16–22 (edd. & transl. Lapidge & Winterbottom, *Wulfstan of Winchester*, pp. 28–39).

[92] On the houses of the Æthelwoldian connexion, see *ibid.*, pp. xliv–li.

[93] The *termini* are those of the documented scribal performances in Style I. In the succeeding decade, 'Eadwig Basan' at Christ Church, Canterbury, began Style IV by merging characteristics of Styles I and II with several other ingredients to create a new (and in due course very influential) variety of Anglo-Caroline minuscule. Until Style IV was generally adopted at Winchester, perhaps in the second third of the eleventh century, Style I might have continued to be used – but further study of the Winchester scriptoria is required. On Style IV (my terminology, not that of Bishop who did not continue his numbering beyond Style II), see chapter IV, below, and Bishop, *English Caroline Minuscule*, pp. xxiii and 22–24.

[94] *Ibid.*, p. xxii. In the eleventh century one may mention as an example the scribe Ælfric of Bath: Dumville, 'Beowulf come lately', p. 61, n. 60.

English Square minuscule is such that, within the confines of the tenth century, rather rapidly changing fashions often allow surprisingly narrow dating bands for specimens of that script.[95] This example does not disappoint. We see here an Insular script which is still within the Square-minuscule tradition, but only just: our scribe wrote a heavy, late type of that script. Among the salient features, one may mention first that the characteristic Square-minuscule **a** is not found here, having been abandoned in favour of the round Insular form of the letter,[96] a known feature of some late styles of this script. **c** shows movement towards a broken-backed form; **d** has a heavy appearance, round and low-backed. **e** has in some examples the form with a hooked back. We find tall **e** in ligature with following **m, n, o, r, s, t** – but not consistently; in this context **e** is usually, but by no means invariably, closed at the top; it seems perhaps notably large and tall in ligature with **n** and **o**; and wasp-waisted tall **e** may be seen (for example, at 86v21). In **æ** the e-element is found in tall and two-line forms; in **æt** we find **e** tall and open (for example, 63r, lower margin; *hpæt*, 81r24). **g** is flat-topped and open bowled. Where **i**-longa occurs, it has a foot. **o** is angular. **r** is long-stemmed; it often occurs in a laterally compressed form with a narrow aperture. **s** occurs in the taller and lower forms; majuscule, round **s** is also found (for example, at 86v18). **t** is heavy in appearance and has a curled-up toe. **y** occurs in all three forms.[97]

The history of Square-minuscule script ends, as far as can be seen at present, in the first decade of the eleventh century, a decade of transition between Insular script-forms in England.[98] Our manuscript should not be dated later than *ca* 1010, therefore. It is somewhat more difficult at present to place an earlier limit. Ker and Bishop drew attention, as a comparandum, to a private charter of A.D. 984;[99] although this does not provide especially close parallels to the scripts of CCCO 197, we may accept it as a rough indication of what the date-range should include. Manuscripts from the 960s display more than one style of Square minuscule,[100] but none resembles that of CCCO 197. The 970s remain for the moment something of a grey area in the history of this script.[101]

---

[95] I have discussed this point *ibid.* and in 'English Square minuscule script: the background and earliest phases', pp. 149–50.

[96] On this letter, see *ibid.*, p. 153.

[97] For comparison of these forms with other specimens comprising the canon, cf. Ker, *Catalogue*, pp. xxv–xxxiii (which also contain scattered observations on this manuscript, his no. 353). For his comments on ligatured e in this manuscript, see p. xxiii (cf. xxviii), and for his specific remarks on CCCO 197 see pp. 431–2, mostly quoted above, p. 21.

[98] Dumville, 'Beowulf come lately'.

[99] See above, p. 20 (cf. 22).

[100] Dumville, 'English Square minuscule script: the mid-century phases'.

[101] The only single-sheet documents dated in or attributed to the 970s are Sawyer, *Anglo-*

The broadest date-range for our manuscript is therefore at present from the 970s to the 1000s, 970 x 1010 stating the very outermost limits.

Our manuscript continued to be used in the eleventh and twelfth centuries. Old English rubrics to some chapters were added in the eleventh century; §7 was divided into thirteen parts and the numbering of subsequent chapters had to be revised. Further correction of the text occurred in the same period. In the twelfth century some Old English glosses were added at 80r17–18 and 80v2–3. A drypoint *neq*; may be found in the lower margin of 83r, and a (presumably twelfth-century) pedant went obsessively through the Latin text correcting enclitic *-que*, when fully written out, to the abbreviated *-q;* form! But the most substantial evidence for the use of the manuscript comes from larger additions. In the middle of the eleventh century a small quire was added to the book: XIV⁴ (fos 106–109).

Almost all of the texts on the added quire are documentary.[102] They show that by the mid-eleventh century this book was in the possession of the Suffolk abbey of Bury St Edmunds.[103] The first addition occupies 106v1–108r6. It is datable broadly by script but more specifically by its contents, a series of notes recording possessions and rents of St Edmund during the abbacy of Leofstan (1044–1065).[104] These are followed (108r7–23) by two series of notes of grants and dues from the time of Abbot Baldwin (1065–1097/8).[105] A fourth set of notes (108v1–11) is datable after the death of King William I (1087) but with a *terminus ante quem* provided only by a palaeographical date of *saec.* xi/xii.[106]

Saxon Charters, nos 779 (970: non-contemporary), 786 (972: disputed), 792 (973: fifteenth-century), 794 (974: non-contemporary), 795 (974), 801 (975: disputed), 804 (975: fifteenth-century), ?808 (963 x 971: fourteenth-century), 830 (976), 832 (977: non-contemporary), 1451 (972 x 978), 1487 (975 x 1016: probably eleventh-century), 1494 (962 x 991: probably eleventh-century), 1497 (undated, but *saec.* x²), 1501 (961 x 994: non-contemporary), 1539 (undated but tenth-century). Given this unpromising situation, and the absence of books clearly datable to the 970s, caution is necessary in describing the Insular script-fashion(s) of that decade.

102 They were summarily described and dated by Ker, *Catalogue*, pp. 430–2. The additional texts have been partially published and translated by Douglas, 'Fragments of an Anglo-Saxon survey'; Hervey, *Corpus Christi College, Oxford, MS. 197*; Robertson, *Anglo-Saxon Charters*, pp. 192–201, 440–7.

103 By a slip, Watson, *Catalogue of Dated and Datable Manuscripts c. 435–1600 in Oxford Libraries*, I.129 (no. 776), has dated this matter a century too late: 'Added documents on fols. 106ᵛ–9 show that it had reached the abbey of Bury St Edmunds by *c.* 1150'.

104 For these records, see Robertson, *Anglo-Saxon Charters*, pp. 192 (line 14)–196 (line 19), with facing-page translation (pp. 193–7).

105 For these see *ibid.*, p. 196 (lines 20–35) and facing translation. On this abbot see Gransden, 'Baldwin, abbot of Bury St Edmunds'.

106 For these notes, see Robertson, *Anglo-Saxon Charters*, p. 198 (lines 1–13) and facing translation.

This fourth series seems at first sight to mark a point of transition in record-keeping at Bury, for whereas all the preceding notes were in Old English these are in Latin. The impression is reinforced by what follows. On 108v12–22, in another hand of the same date as what immediately precedes, we find, as a fifth text, a Latin version of the two series of records from Baldwin's abbacy.[107] What is more, in a hand contemporaneous with this activity, the Old English notes of Leofstan's abbacy have been partially glossed in Latin.[108] On this evidence we might be forgiven for thinking that English was on the wane as a language of record at Bury, or at least that those more comfortable with Latin than English had to be catered for. Such a development might suit the years after the death of Abbot Baldwin (1097 or 1098), the last abbot of Bury elected before the Norman conquest. Such a conclusion might seem premature, however, when it is remarked that the last of the documentary texts in this manuscript (occupying 109r1–12) is again in Old English, written in a hand dated by Neil Ker to the first half of the twelfth century;[109] one might wonder whether such a circumstance could be due to the eventual accession of an English abbot – Ording, in 1138 and 1148–1156. The last addition to our manuscript is non-documentary and seems to indicate that this book's function as a register of grants and dues was at an end. On 109v a twelfth-century scribe wrote an 'Ymnus de sancta Maria Magdalene', beginning 'Electa Christi famula'.[110]

This account of the texts on the supplementary quire overlooks one other significant addition to the book. On 105r6–13 in a hand palaeographically datable to the years on either side of 1100 (*saec.* xi/ xii),[111] a scribe has added two historical notes in annalistic format, each occupying four lines. These annals would by themselves have been sufficient to tell us that our manuscript had arrived at Bury St Edmunds. The scribe left one line blank after the conclusion of the bilingual Rule of St Benedict before writing the following text.[112]

---

[107] For these see *ibid.*, p. 198 (lines 14–29) and facing translation.

[108] Albeit by a scribe who also used Old English: Ker, *Catalogue*, pp. 430–1 (item 3). For the glosses see Robertson, *Anglo-Saxon Charters*, p. 196 (lines 10, 12, 14, 16, 18).

[109] For these notes of rents in kind due to St Edmund, see *ibid.*, pp. 198 (line 30)–200 (line 10) with facing-page translation. For the date of the script see Ker, *Catalogue*, p. 431 (item 8); on p. 432 he noted that this scribe no longer used the Insular form of a – one might recall that at Peterborough (on the evidence of Oxford, Bodleian Library, MS. Laud misc. 636 [*S.C.* 1003]) this transition took place between 1131 (when Insular a was used by scribe 1 of Anglo-Saxon Chronicle E) and 1154 (when scribe 2 did not employ it).

[110] Ker, *Catalogue*, p. 431 (item 9).

[111] *Ibid.*, p. 430 (item 2).

[112] Previously printed by Coxe, *Catalogus*, II, pt 3, p. 79, and (with translation) by Hervey, *Corpus Christi College, Oxford, MS. 197*, pp. 2–3.

M'.xx.   Hic denique presul Ælfuuinus sub comite Thurkillo constituit regulam monachorum sancti EADMVNDI in monasterio et sub uoluntate licentiaque Cnutoni regis permanet usque in presens.

M'.xxxii. Hic sub Cnutono rege constructam basilicam beate memorie archipresul Ægelnothus consecrauit in honore Christi et sanctę Marię sanctique Eadmundi.

The wording of each annal marks them down as non-contemporary notices of the events in question. In the item dated 1020 we are told that something (the syntax is uncertain and the meaning consequently ambiguous) continues to the present – plainly some time after 1020. And in the item dated 1032, Archbishop Æthelnoth (who ruled at Canterbury from 1020 to 1038) is referred to as 'of blessed memory'. Further, the stress on the office-holders of the time in each item gives an air of distance from the event. How much later these annals were composed is a nice question.

Below those annals, in an early modern hand, we read 'Sic et Florentius Wigorniensis ad hunc annum'. Certainly in the Chronicle of John of Worcester (first published in 1131),[113] the annal for 1032 is devoted to a brief notice of the dedication of St Edmund's Abbey. More to the immediate point, however, is the fact that a mid-twelfth-century manuscript – Oxford, Bodleian Library, MS. Bodley 297 (*S.C.* 2468) – preserves a copy of John's Chronicle, transcribed at Bury where the text was extensively interpolated with local matter. In that version these notes recur as follows.[114]

p. 350b9–25 *ad an.* 1020 (in text):
Eodem etiam anno, indictione .iiiᵃ., Canutus rex Anglorum aliarumque gentium plurimarum, cum consilio et decreto archiepiscoporum episcoporum et optimatum suorum, maxime uero Ælfgyuę `.i. Emme´ reginę suę et Alfuuini presulis Orientalium Anglorum[115] et Turkilli comitis, constituit monachos in monasterio quod Badriceswrde uocatur, in quo sanctissimus rex et martyr Eadmundus incorrupto corpore diem expectat beatę resurrectionis; pręfecitque eis patrem et abbatem nomine Vuium, uirum scilicet humilem modestum mansuetum et pium, presbyteros uero qui inibi inordinate uiuebant aut in eodem loco ad religionis culmen erexit aut datis aliis rebus de quibus habundantius solito uictum et uestitum haberent, in alia loca mutauit.

---

113 On John's Chronicle and its early (including informal pre-publication) circulation, see Brett, 'John of Worcester and his contemporaries'.

114 Previously published in *Memorials of St. Edmund's Abbey*, ed. Arnold, I.341–2. On the manuscript and Bury historiography, see Brett, 'John of Worcester and his contemporaries'; cf. Dumville in *The Anglo-Saxon Chronicle*, gen. edd. Dumville & Keynes, XVII.lx–lxi.

115 An erasure of about five letters follows here.

p. 353b2–7, *ad an.* 1032 (in text):
Constructam basilicam apud Będrichesuurtham beatę memorię Dor-
obernensis archipresul Ægelnothus consecrauit in honore Christi et sanctę
Marie sanctique EADMVNDI regis et martyris, die .xv. kal. Nouembris.

It is possible that the notes in CCCO 197 were the source of these, for
their script is a generation older than that of Bodley 297. However, as
Ker noted, there is another possible source. In an English psalter written
in the second quarter of the eleventh century (the evidence for the date is
palaeographical and art-historical) for or at Bury St Edmunds Abbey, we
find the same annals recurring. Roma, Biblioteca Apostolica Vaticana,
MS. Reginensis lat. 12 is known as 'the Bury Psalter':[116] it may have
been written at Bury, or it may have been a product of the scriptorium at
Christ Church, Canterbury;[117] if the latter, perhaps it was commissioned

---

[116] Temple, *Anglo-Saxon Manuscripts*, pp. 100–2 (no. 84); Wilmart, *Codices*, I.30–5.
For various aspects of the manuscript, see *English Kalendars before A.D. 1100*, ed.
Wormald, pp. 239–51; Wilmart, 'The prayers'; Heimann, 'Three illustrations'. For
its later history see Wilmart, *Analecta Reginensia*, pp. 9–17.

[117] There is a controlling negative argument concerning the origin of this manuscript –
and of London, British Library, MS. Harley 76, 'the Bury Gospels', of Bury St
Edmunds provenance *saec.* xi *ex.* (Temple, *Anglo-Saxon Manuscripts*, p. 93, no. 75)
– which may be quoted in Temple's words: 'It is unlikely, however, to have been
produced there since Bury Abbey, founded in 1020 and consecrated in 1032, could
hardly have had a workshop organized for the production of luxury manuscripts *c.*
1030' (*ibid.*); 'The manuscript could hardly, however, have been made at Bury since
the new foundation was probably not organized in the second quarter of the 11th
century for the production of richly decorated books' (*ibid.*, p. 101). For a more
sensible, positive assessment, see Clemoes, *Manuscripts from Anglo-Saxon England*,
p. 15 (no. 26). Temple (*Anglo-Saxon Manuscripts*, p. 93) has supposed MS. Harley
76 to be of approximately the same date (she has placed it in the 1020s) and to have
the same Canterbury origin as Vat. Reg. lat. 12. However, the script of the two books
is quite different: Vat. Reg. lat. 12 is written in a full-blooded Style-IV Anglo-
Caroline (for the type, cf. chapter IV, below); Harley 76, on the other hand, displays
sporadically some features which come to be characteristic of that style (tall **a**; small
majuscule **H**; the characteristic mixed majuscules, including tall **S**) but is essentially a
specimen of Style I. Written by more than one scribe in a single style, it is clearly a
scriptorium-product. That scriptorium had been in touch with Fleury, for Harley 76 is
among the English manuscripts in which one finds that house's characteristic
abbreviation for *est*: Bishop, *English Caroline Minuscule*, p. xii(–xiii), n. 2; cf.
Pellegrin, *Bibliothèques retrouvées*, p. 169. On the evidence of its appearance in
gloss-script in Paris, Bibliothèque nationale, MS. latin 14380 (attributed to Christ
Church, Canterbury, by Bishop, *English Caroline Minuscule*, p. xxvi), we can
suppose that such usage was not wholly foreign to the cathedral scriptorium. In as
much as Harley 76 has the distinctive abbreviation preponderantly, the usual one
sporadically, and some correction of the former to the latter, we may regard it as
originating in a period of transitional usage in this respect. The same is suggested by
my preceding remarks on the script. However, if it was written at Christ Church, its
distinctive scribal practices must find a place in that already potentially crowded
decade, the 1010s: cf. chapters III and IV, below. Among the few English

for Æthelnoth to present on the day of the consecration in 1032. But, if the manuscript's cataloguer presented the palaeographical evidence correctly, the book must be rather later. Easter-tables for A.D. 1000–1095 occupy 16v–19r: in them the principal scribe has added historical notes.[118] Alongside the years 1020–1024 and 1032–1035 (both on 17v) we find two familiar annals.[119]

[1020(–4)] Hinc[120] denique presul Aelfwinus[121] sub comite Thurkyllo[122] constituit regulam monachorum sancti Eadmundi monasterio;[123] et sub uoluntate licentiaque Cnutoni regis permanet usque in presens.

[1032(–5)] Hic sub Cnutono rege constructam basilicam beate memorie archipresul Aegelnoðus[124] consecrauit eam[125] in honore Christi et sancte Marie sanctique Eadmundi.

Plainly this view of Bury's history in Cnut's reign was established already in the mid-eleventh century. The annals must still be regarded, on the evidence of their wording, as non-contemporary, but the margin of time must be fairly narrow. If the surviving three witnesses to this historical tradition represent Bury's total output on the subject from the mid-eleventh century to the mid-twelfth – itself a very doubtful, positivistic assumption –, we should have to suppose that the text of these annals in CCCO 197 derived from the Bury Psalter.

The Corpus manuscript probably remained at Bury St Edmunds for the rest of the middle ages. It still bears the fourteenth-century Bury librarian's *ex-libris* and press-mark at the head of 1r: 'Liber Sancti

---

manuscripts in which the 'Fleury' abbreviation has been noted in use in text rather than gloss is Lincoln, Cathedral Library, MS. 182: cf. n. 259, below. A highly distinctive feature of the hands of MS. Harley 76 is a tall, crossed z, which I do not recall encountering elsewhere, except as an occasional (and perhaps in part secondary) usage in Cambridge, Pembroke College, MS. 301. Given that most of the pre-Conquest books in the Pembroke collection have a Bury provenance, I wonder whether MS. 301 should be assigned thither and Bury be deemed to be the origin of both it and Harley 76. Cf. also Heslop, 'The production', p. 175.

[118] Wilmart, *Codices*, I.31, identified the scribe. It is accordingly not the case that Hermann's *De miraculis S. Edmundi* 'is the earliest authority for the universally held belief that St Edmund's abbey was founded in 1020 by King Canute': Gransden, 'The legends', pp. 9–10; cf. 11, 11–12. The same, rather odd, range of years is likewise (and apparently uniquely) represented in paschal tables in the earlier liturgical book, Rouen, B.M., MS. Y.6 (274): see *The Missal of Robert of Jumièges*, ed. Wilson, pp. 28–32.

[119] These may be seen in facsimile in *The New Palaeographical Society Facsimiles*, edd. Thompson *et al.*, 2nd series, plates 166–8.

[120] *Hic* in CCCO 197.

[121] *Ælfuuinus* in CCCO 197.

[122] *Thurkillo* in CCCO 197.

[123] *in monasterio* in CCCO 197.

[124] *Ægelnothus* in CCCO 197.

[125] Not in CCCO 197.

Eadmundi Regis et Martyris. .R.70.'.[126] It was given to its present owners in the seventeenth century by William Fulman (1632–1688), Fellow of the College.[127]

The early history of Bury St Edmunds Abbey

Edmund, king of East Anglia, was killed in November 869 by a Danish army which had invaded his kingdom. The minster which came to bear his name, and which served as the cult-centre for this royal martyr, was previously called Bedricesworth.[128] According to the first narrative account of St Edmund's martyrdom – that of Abbo of Fleury, written in 985 x 987 – this was a royal vill to which the holy body had been translated from its first place of burial near where the king had been killed.[129] This translation took place not later than the time when Theodred was bishop of London (926–951).[130] Two further pieces of evidence support the conclusion that a minster had been established not later than the middle of the tenth century: in their wills, both datable within the period 942 x *ca* 951, Ealdorman Ælfgar[131] and Bishop Theodred[132] made bequests to the church of St Edmund at Bedricesworth. It may indeed be possible to put a date on its origin, for we have a

---

[126] On the Bury library and that librarian see Thomson, 'The library of Bury St Edmunds Abbey', and Rouse, 'Bostonus Buriensis' (cf. Gransden, *Historical Writing*, II.401–3).

[127] At the foot of 1r we read 'liber C.C.C. Oxon.' and 'Ex dono Gulielmi Fulman A.M. hujus Collegii quondam Socii' (Fulman ceased to be a Fellow in 1669). College reference-numbers are found at the head of the page: 'No. 1664.197. E.2.11'.

[128] Abbo Floriacensis, *Passio S. Eadmundi*, §13, gives a place-name form rather at variance with that which I have used in the text (and which is the normal early name for Bury St Edmunds). Abbo's text as transmitted reads, 'in uilla regia quae lingua Anglorum Bedricesgueord dicitur, latina uero Bedricicurtis uocatur'. This has provoked the comment (*Three Lives*, ed. Winterbottom, p. 82, n. *ad* 13/24) that '-*gueord* = OE *geard* "yard, enclosure" '. Either Abbo had received a false etymology (but, given his local information, this seems unlikely) or his foreigner's spelling of an English name has given rise to misunderstanding: his -*gu*- stands, as commonly in Franco-Latin usage, for /w/ and his -*d* for /θ/.

[129] Abbo Floriacensis, *Passio S. Eadmundi*, §13: *uilla regia*. Cf. Sawyer, 'The royal *tun*', p. 291.

[130] Abbo Floriacensis, *Passio S. Eadmundi*, §15 (ed. Winterbottom, *Three Lives*, pp. 83–5), for Theodred. The dates given are minimal: cf. p. 38 and n. 149, below.

[131] Sawyer, *Anglo-Saxon Charters*, no. 1483, datable 946 x *ca* 951. For Ælfgar, *uir religiosus*, cf. Abbo Floriacensis, *Passio S. Eadmundi*, §16 (ed. Winterbottom, *Three Lives*, pp. 85–6). See further Hart, 'The Mersea charter'.

[132] Sawyer, *Anglo-Saxon Charters*, no. 1526, datable 942 x *ca* 951. *Ibid.*, no. 1213 is a private grant to St Edmund's Abbey, *Beodrichesworth*, dated 962 (for the land, cf. no. 1527, datable *ca* 1000 x 1038): cf. Hart, *The Early Charters of Northern England*, p. 379, on the donor.

diploma in the name of King Edmund I and dated 945 which presents itself as the foundation-charter of this minster:[133] the diploma, surviving only in twelfth-century and later copies (it appears first as an addition to John of Worcester's Chronicle in MS. Bodley 297), has often been denounced as a forgery, but Dr Cyril Hart has made a persuasive case for a new and less severe look at it.[134]

Bury St Edmunds, founded on a royal estate and perhaps by King Edmund I (939–946), was to grow into a wealthy abbey. But the circumstances of the minster's origins remain a subject for conjecture. A great deal of the legendary matter obscuring its early history has been cleared away in recent years, notably by Dr Antonia Gransden.[135] That exercise has thrown into sharp relief three phases of the minster's history which require more attention than they have received: the immediate background to the original foundation; the transition, between 969 and 1016, to observance of the Benedictine Rule (a phase not even recognised until lately); and developments in the reign of Cnut.

It is necessary first to be clear about what is certain, and that is not much. The minster existed by the mid-point of the tenth century. A generation later, the monks of the Benedictine abbey of Ramsey commissioned a distinguished visitor – Abbo of Fleury – to write an account of St Edmund's passion and miracles.[136] That they did so implies most insistently an important connexion between Ramsey and Bury St Edmunds.[137] In the last quarter of the tenth century, Æthelflæd of Damerham, widow of King Edmund I, bequeathed property to Bury,[138] as did Ælfflæd, her sister, wife of Ealdorman Byrhtnoth, ca A.D. 1000;[139] their father was the Ealdorman Ælfgar whose bequest to Bury in the mid-tenth century I have already noted. It is clear, then, that in that century St Edmund's minster had important patrons in the upper reaches of the aristocracy. By the mid-eleventh century Bury was in the king's hands, to judge by his appointment of Abbot Baldwin: indeed, Edward the Confessor seems to have regarded St Edmund as a kinsman and to have

---

133 Sawyer, *Anglo-Saxon Charters*, no. 507. As Hart, 'The East Anglian chronicle', p. 277, has pointed out, the donor and the saintly donee shared their name; one is bound to wonder whether King Edmund I had some fellow-feeling for his namesake on that account.

134 Hart, *The Early Charters of Eastern England*, pp. 54–8 (no. 74). In 1975, however, he retracted that opinion: *The Early Charters of Northern England*, p. 385. In 1981 ('The East Anglian chronicle', p. 277) he was edging back towards a more benign view of this document.

135 Gransden, 'The legends', with references given there.

136 Abbo Floriacensis, *Passio S. Eadmundi*, preface (*Three Lives*, ed. Winterbottom, pp. 67–8).

137 Hart, 'The East Anglian chronicle', p. 277; Gransden, 'The legends', p. 3.

138 Sawyer, *Anglo-Saxon Charters*, no. 1494.

139 *Ibid.*, no. 1486.

taken a special interest in his abbey.[140] Whether this direct royal control stretches back to the reign of Cnut (and of Queen Emma, Edward's mother)[141] is a nice question. The annalistic notices quoted above from Vat. Reg. lat. 12 and CCCO 197 are ambiguous as to that king's involvement in the history of Bury.[142] At all events, by the mid-eleventh century the view disseminated from Bury and Canterbury was that Bury had been brought under the Benedictine Rule in 1020 and that in 1032 a new church had been consecrated by Archbishop Æthelnoth.[143]

The context of the first foundation of the minster at Bury St Edmunds must almost certainly remain largely in the realms of speculation. Nevertheless, it is worth pursuing for a moment the idea advanced by Cyril Hart that Ealdorman Æthelstan Half-king[144]

was responsible for settling at Bury the clerics guarding the remains of the martyred East Anglian King Edmund. The settlement occurred while the Half-King was at the height of his power, and was an important event in the consolidation of Christianity in East Anglia after its reconquest from the Danes.[145] The charter of privileges granted to the clerics in 945 by the martyred king's namesake King Edmund set out the *banleuca* of Bury St Edmunds. The surviving text has been tampered with, but there is no need to doubt the historicity of the transaction it records, nor can one doubt that the young King Edmund issued the privilege under the Half-King's influence.[146]

There can, and probably should, be a great deal of doubt about the two points most vigorously asserted without evidence. The contextual observations are accurate, however, and – if moderately stated – the suggestions about the roles of Ealdorman Æthelstan and King Edmund may be regarded as reasonable speculations. If, as Abbo stated, Bedricesworth was indeed a *uilla regalis*, the settlement there of St Edmund's remains is perhaps unlikely to have taken place without the involvement of the ealdorman and, by implication, the king; unfortunately, questions remain as to the accuracy of Abbo's information and the

---

[140] *Anglo-Saxon Writs*, ed. & transl. Harmer, nos 18 (pp. 160–1) and 24 (pp. 164–5): Sawyer, *Anglo-Saxon Charters*, nos 1078 and 1084. (The Bury diplomas in Edward's name appear to be spurious: *ibid.*, nos 1045, 1046.)

[141] *Ibid.*, no. 980 (*Facsimiles*, ed. Keynes, no. 33), Cnut to Bury, datable 1021 x 1023. In it, Cnut is made to confirm his queen's transfer to Bury of the four thousand eels due to her annually from Lakenheath.

[142] Cf. pp. 31–4, above.

[143] Cf. pp. 31–4, above, and pp. 38–41, below. On 1032, cf. also Gransden, 'The question', pp. 59–60, where for 'Eadnoth' read 'Æthelnoth'.

[144] 'The East Anglian chronicle', p. 277.

[145] Here Hart referred to Whitelock, 'The conversion', pp. 172–3.

[146] Here he referred to Hart, *The Early Charters of Eastern England*, pp. 54–8, unfortunately not very helpfully on the point at issue.

fidelity of the transmitted text of the *Passio* to Abbo's own words.[147] As for the charter attributed to King Edmund and A.D. 945, that does indeed deserve favourable reconsideration.[148] For the present, it is sufficient to note that Æthelstan was ealdorman of East Anglia from 932 to 956 and Theodred was bishop of London (apparently with responsibility also for East Anglia) from 909 x 926 to 951 x 953.[149] Their interest in the development of the cult and the minster is likely to have been decisive.

The next major royal intervention in the history of Bury St Edmunds has been attributed to King Cnut (1016–1035). The annals which we have already noted attribute significant events to the years 1020 and 1032, though with some measure of ambiguity as to the king's role:[150] the view which they represent took shape between 1038 and a palaeographically-determined mid-century date. The refoundation-charter attributed to Cnut has usually been rejected as spurious by commentators,[151] as have the further grants of privileges attributed to his son King Harthacnut[152] and to Edward the Confessor.[153] With these points in mind, we can return to the year 1020. According to the Bury annal in question,[154] Ælfwine, bishop of East Anglia 1012 x 1019–1023 x 1038, in the time of Thorkel (the Tall),[155] earl of East Anglia 1017 x 1021, established *regulam monachorum* (presumably the Rule of St Benedict) at Bury St Edmunds, perhaps by the authority of King Cnut.[156] No other pre-Conquest source has any information on this alleged event. We can proceed only by an argument from the context.

The Anglo-Saxon Chronicle for the year 1020 (MSS. CDEF) has a notice of the consecration of a minster at *Assandun* where on 18 October,

---

[147] On the former point see Gransden, 'The legends', pp. 3–8; for the latter, Gransden, 'Baldwin, abbot of Bury St Edmunds', p. 72.

[148] Cf. n. 134, above. My colleagues Susan Kelly and Simon Keynes tell me that they see no diplomatic evidence which would lead them to question the authenticity of Edmund's diploma.

[149] Hart, *The Early Charters of Northern England*, pp. 299 (cf. Hart, 'Athelstan') and 360; on Theodred see further Whitelock, *Some Anglo-Saxon Bishops of London*, pp. 17–21.

[150] Cf. above, pp. 31–4.

[151] See above, n. 141; cf. n. 165, below.

[152] Sawyer, *Anglo-Saxon Charters*, no. 995, datable to 1038/9.

[153] *Ibid.*, nos 1045 and 1046, both undated.

[154] See above, p. 34.

[155] '*sub* comite Thurkillo', where *sub* seems to carry the sense of 'in the period of office of'.

[156] The clause 'et sub uoluntate licentiaque Cnutoni regis permanet usque in presens', which gives an unlikely meaning (that King Cnut allowed it to continue to the present), should perhaps be broken up so as to read 'sub uoluntate licentiaque Cnutoni regis *et* permanet usque in presens'. Thus reorganised, the sentence would express Cnut's will that the Rule be adopted.

1016, had been fought the decisive battle in Cnut's campaign to seize the kingdom of England.[157] In what follows, text in roman represents the agreement of MSS. CD (qualified by bracketed matter); text in bold shows the consensus of MSS. CDEF.

And on ðisum geare se cyng for (᛫ Þurkyl eorl, *MS. D*) **to Assandune** ᛫ Wulfstan arce*bisceop* (᛫ Þurkil eorl, *MS. C*) ᛫ {manega (C)/oðre (D)} bisceopas (᛫ eac abbodas ᛫ manege munecas, *MS. D*) (mid heom, *MS. C*) ᛫ gehalgodan þæt mynster æt Assandune. (*MS. F, after 'to Assandune'*: ᛫ let timbrian ðar an mynster of stane ᛫ lime far ðare manna sawle ðe ðar ofslagene wæran ᛫ gief hit his anum preoste þas nama was Stigand.) (And Liuing arce*biscop* forðferde, *MSS. EF*.) (᛫ Æðelnoð munuc {᛫ (EF)/se þe wæs (D)} decanus æt Cristes cyrcan wearð on þam ilcan geare [on Idus Nouembris, *MS. D*] to biscop [arce*biscop*, *MS. F*] [into Cristes cyrcan, *MS. D*] [from Wulstane arce*biscop*, *MS. F*], MSS. DEF.)

And in this year the King (and Earl Thorkel, *MS. D*) went to *Assandun*, and Archbishop Wulfstan (and Earl Thorkel, *MS. C*), and (with them, *MS. C*) {many (C)/other (D)} bishops (and also abbots and many monks, *MS. D*), and they consecrated the minster at *Assandun* (*instead of the last clause, MS. F has*: and had a minster built there of stone and mortar, for the souls of the men who had been slain there, and gave it to a priest of his who was called Stigand). (And Archbishop Lyfing died, *MSS. EF*.) (And the monk Æthelnoth who was dean at Christ Church was consecrated bishop [archbishop, *MS. F*] [for Christ Church on 13 November, *MS. D*] in that same year [*MSS. DEF*] by Archbishop Wulfstan [*MS. F*].)

The base-annal told that King Cnut, Earl Thorkel, Archbishop Wulfstan, and other bishops went to *Assandun* (probably Ashdon, Essex, on the Suffolk border) where they consecrated the (Hadstock) minster.[158] To this, three levels of Canterbury accretion may be seen.[159] The archbishop of Canterbury seems not to have been present at what must have been an important event within his own province: Lyfing died 12 June; his successor was consecrated 13 November.[160]

---

[157] *The Anglo-Saxon Chronicle*, ed. & transl. Thorpe, I.286–7, for parallel texts, on which I draw. The translation depends on that of Whitelock, *English Historical Documents*, p. 252, but I have modified her version (which is incomplete in detail) in the light of the textual comparison made here.

[158] Cf. Hart, 'The site', on the location. *Ibid.*, p. 8, n. 33, and p. 9, Hart has asserted that Thorkel 'built the church at *Assandun*'; but this is not what the Chronicle says. John of Worcester's account is that King Cnut and Earl Thorkel *construxerant* the church and that, *illis praesentibus*, Archbishop Wulfstan dedicated it.

[159] The first level (if indeed it was not itself two) was the notices of Lyfing and Æthelnoth. The second was the record (found only in MS. D) of the date of Æthelnoth's consecration. The third was the expansion of information about the church of *Assandun*, mentioning Stigand, and found only in MS. F.

[160] Cf. Hart, 'The site', p. 9, n. 47.

With reference to the event attributed to 1020 at Bury St Edmunds, two opposed arguments may be made. The transition at Bury – involving king, earl, and bishop – never occurred, and the notice of it (and perhaps that about 1032) was modelled on knowledge of what happened at *Assandun*.[161] The alternative is to argue, with Cyril Hart, that this year saw Cnut taking in hand the ecclesiastical affairs of eastern England,[162] bringing Bury St Edmunds under his patronage as a part of this process. The previous patrons of religious activity in this area had been the family of Æthelstan 'Half-king';[163] the demise of that kindred as a result of the battle of *Assandun* left a political vacuum within ecclesiastical life, and it was a nice question as to how the filling of that vacuum would affect institutions whose patrons and rulers had opposed Swegen and then Cnut until late 1016. In Hart's view, in 1020 'King Cnut celebrated his victory by setting up Bury St Edmunds as an autonomous abbey'.[164]

To interpret matters thus requires one to take seriously the evidence of the refoundation-documentation associated with Cnut and Emma. All of this can, however, be accounted for – if one is so minded – by reference to later documents of unimpeachable authority from which the information offered in the refoundation-charter could have been constructed after the Norman conquest and perhaps indeed in the first half of the twelfth century.[165] If one discounts the diplomatic material,

---

[161] This view must nevertheless allow that such a history had been created for Bury within a generation (if the palaeographical information reported at p. 34 and n. 118, above, is accurate).

[162] On Cnut and Ramsey, cf. Hart, 'Eadnoth', pp. 66–7; on Ely, see Hart, 'The site', p. 11. On Cnut's alleged relationship with the abbey of St Benedict at Holme (Norfolk), see Hart, *The Early Charters of Eastern England*, pp. 64–5, 81; cf. Gransden, 'The legends', pp. 15–18, on this point, and p. 10 (and n. 4) more generally on Cnut's dealings with the Fenland houses. Cf. also Heslop, 'The production', p. 158 and n. 17. The alleged relationship between Holme and Bury has been demolished by Gransden.

[163] Hart, 'Athelstan'.

[164] 'The East Anglian chronicle', p. 279. Cf. Hart & Syme, 'The earliest Suffolk charter', p. 171.

[165] Sawyer, *Anglo-Saxon Charters*, no. 980, surviving first in a twelfth-century single sheet (*Facsimiles*, ed. Keynes, no. 33), in a twelfth-century copy in the 'Bury Gospels' (London, British Library, MS. Harley 76, fos 138r–139r), in the Bury copy of John of Worcester's Chronicle (pp. 353–354: see above, n. 114), and in a late twelfth- or early thirteenth-century Bury cartulary (Cambridge, University Library, MS. Mm.4.19 [2367]: Davis, *Medieval Cartularies*, p. 16, no. 118; Thomson, *The Archives*, pp. 119–21, no. 1277). The fullest study of the documents of Bury St Edmunds, A.D. 1016–1066, may be found in *Anglo-Saxon Writs*, ed. & transl. Harmer, pp. 138–66, where some trenchant comments are made about the authenticity of the Bury diplomas of Cnut, Harthacnut, and Edward. For older studies see MacKinlay, *Saint Edmund*, pp. 352–411; *Corolla*, ed. & transl. Hervey; Davis, 'The liberties'; Douglas, 'Fragments of an Anglo-Saxon survey'; Hervey, *Corpus*

which would in any case refer to 1021 x 1023,[166] there is nothing to sustain the Bury annal for 1020 concerning which doubts have already been expressed and which seems very unlikely to have been a contemporary record.

What does seem likely to have happened at Bury St Edmunds in Cnut's reign is that a new church (*basilica*) dedicated to St Mary and St Edmund was consecrated. According to the annal in the 'Bury Psalter' this occurred in 1032. According to the kalendar in the same manuscript, 'Dedicatio basilice sancte Mariȩ et sancti Eadmundi' (in gold majuscules) took place on 18 October.[167] That was the anniversary of the battle of *Assandun*: the coincidence of dates is striking;[168] but what conclusion is to be drawn from it? Was a connexion seen between 869 and 1016, as well it might have been? Had the church or the cult of St Edmund been affected by the battle? Or was the day also a memorial of another event? The coincidence is the more striking in that 18 October, 1032, was not a Sunday, the day on which (one might expect) such an event would most naturally have taken place.

If the parallel, drawn above, between the event at *Assandun* in 1020 and that alleged to have taken place at Bury in the same year, is apposite,[169] then one must wonder further about a connexion with the consecration at Bury in 1032. The natural date for the consecration of the minster at *Assandun* would have been the anniversary of the battle, and this is certainly a possible choice.[170] But there seems to be no source which specifies the day of that dedication.

Other events commemorated in the kalendar of the 'Bury Psalter' have been associated with Cnut's reign[171] – the translation of St Hiurmin (24

Christi College, Oxford, MS. 197; Goodwin, *The Abbey*, pp. 3–22, 83–4; *Feudal Documents*, ed. Douglas; Lobel, *The Borough*, pp. 1–15. For an example of a popular essay on the subject, see Houghton, *Saint Edmund*.

[166] Sawyer, *Anglo-Saxon Charters*, no. 980.

[167] *English Kalendars before A.D. 1100*, ed. Wormald, p. 249. The date recurs in the annal in MS. Bodley 297: see above, p. 33. *Historia regum Anglorum* (Part 2), attributed to Symeon of Durham, *s.a.* 1032 (ed. Arnold, *Symeonis Monachi Opera*, II.157), goes one stage further than John of Worcester's account: it has the church dedicated 'in qua rex Canutus monachos posuit, eiectis presbyteris', making a typical Reform-story out of the event. Cf. Gransden, 'The legends', pp. 13–15, who has said that this view appeared at Bury only in the reign of Henry II (it is not in §17 of Hermann's *De miraculis sancti Eadmundi*: ed. Arnold, *Memorials of St. Edmund's Abbey*, I.47).

[168] Hart, 'The site', p. 9, n. 46.

[169] Cf. *ibid.*

[170] However, Hart (*ibid.*, p. 9, n. 47) has wondered whether the day might have been 17 June, 1020, the festival of St Botulf who was the patron-saint of this (viz Hadstock) church.

[171] Temple, *Anglo-Saxon Manuscripts*, p. 101.

January)[172] and of St Botulf (15 February),[173] both of which are recorded in gold majuscules as feasts of the highest status. Botulf is unhistorically described as bishop of the East Angles.[174] In the mid-twelfth century it was thought that these translations had been effected by Abbot Leofstan (1044–1065).[175]

Similarly recorded in the same source are two translations of St Edmund himself – on 30 and 31 March. The former reads simply 'Translatio sancti Eadmundi', but the latter is more elaborate: 'Hic translatus est sanctus rex Eadmundus ab Ælfrico episcopo'.[176] Unfortunately there were three bishops Ælfric of East Anglia: in 966 x 970–970 x 974; in 1023 x 1038;[177] and (immediately following Ælfric II) in 1039–1042/3. The last of these, if correctly identified, is known in post-Conquest Bury benefactor-lists as Ælfric the Good (*cognomento bonus*).[178] It is possible, then, that the translation in question could have happened in Cnut's reign – but, if so, not in 1020 (when there was a bishop of another name) and probably not in 1032 (for the great event of that year was on 18 October). 31 March was a Sunday in 1023, 1028, and 1034 (but also, in the time of Ælfric I, in 967 when it was Easter Day and in 972).

What the translation of 30 March was is not known – it is just possibly that of the initial translation to Bedricesworth not later than *ca* 950. In 1095 SS. Edmund, Botulf, and Hiurmin were all translated together to a new position of honour in the east of the abbey-church. This translation, on 29 April, was the one subsequently remembered at Bury.[179]

---

[172] There is an account of Iurminus in *Nova legenda Anglie*, edited from a fourteenth-century Bury manuscript, now Oxford, Bodleian Library, MS. Bodley 240 (*S.C.* 2469), p. 764, by Horstman, II.542–3, where the translation is attributed to the reign of Cnut.

[173] This commemoration is unique in the Anglo-Saxon kalendarial tradition. From its disposition on the page in the 'Bury Psalter', there is room for suspicion that it is an addition.

[174] For Botulf's role in early East Anglian history, see Whitelock, 'The pre-Viking Age Church', pp. 10–12.

[175] *Memorials of St. Edmund's Abbey*, ed. Arnold, I.352: information from MS. Bodley 297, p. 397, *s.a.* 1095.

[176] *English Kalendars before A.D. 1100*, ed. Wormald, p. 242. However, the possibility should be kept in mind that both statements refer to the same translation.

[177] For the will of this second Ælfric (Sawyer, *Anglo-Saxon Charters*, no. 1489 where it is attributed to Ælfric III), see *Anglo-Saxon Wills*, ed. & transl. Whitelock, pp. 70–3, 181–4 (no. 26). Cf. Hart, *The Early Charters of Eastern England*, pp. 65 and 82 (no. 88).

[178] *Ibid.*, p. 248 (no. 362).

[179] For details see the account in MS. Bodley 297, p. 397, *s.a.* (ed. Arnold, *Memorials of St. Edmund's Abbey*, I.351–2). Cf. Gransden, 'The question', pp. 60–2. It is the only translation recorded in kalendars later than the eleventh century: see *English Benedictine Kalendars after A.D. 1100*, ed. Wormald. On the physical aspects, see James, *On the Abbey*, pp. 117–18.

That it is not recorded in the kalendar of the 'Bury Psalter' is a guarantee that the book was made before that date.

We are left with some gain but much confusion. That a new church was consecrated at Bury on 18 October, 1032, seems quite likely; that a notable event of some sort occurred there in 1020 seems altogether doubtful. Two translations of St Edmund, and one each of St Botulf and St Hiurmin, had taken place before the Norman conquest and it is not impossible that one or more of these events might be attributed to the tenth century.

In the 1070s Ælfwine, abbot of Ramsey since 1043, testified that already in King Cnut's time Bury had enjoyed the privileges which it was currently asserting.[180] However, there is no good evidence that Cnut was the founder of a Benedictine community there. Neither the annal in the 'Bury Psalter' nor the refoundation-charter can sustain that interpretation. However, Antonia Gransden was certainly mistaken in her assertion that 'the Bury monks adopted Canute as their putative founder in the late eleventh century'[181] and that Hermann, the author *ca* 1100 of *De miraculis sancti Eadmundi*, is the earliest authority for this;[182] already at some date in the middle years of the century the 'Bury Psalter' attests to a belief in the introduction of the Rule in 1020.[183] Nevertheless, the more elaborate stories about Bury in Cnut's reign are first attested in Hermann's work and are to be viewed with the greatest suspicion.[184] From that period onwards we see the rapid and complex development of elaborate and conflicting stories about Bury's history, as Gransden has shown.[185] In particular, the roles attributed to Ely and (above all) the abbey of St Benet of Hulme, in the colonisation of Bury with Benedictine monks, have been discredited in the process.[186]

It is clear that we must take another look at the question of the Benedictinising of Bury St Edmunds, and in a longer historical perspective. In the reign of Edward the Confessor the abbey came to hold a special status. Whether it had enjoyed the favour which Cnut is supposed to have shown to the Fenland abbeys is uncertain indeed. But it is necessary to ask whether reform touched Bury in the period of the Benedictine revolution in the late tenth century.

---

[180] Gransden, 'The legends', p. 11, drawing on Hermann, *De miraculis sancti Eadmundi*.

[181] *Ibid.*, pp. 11–12. It should also be remarked in passing that it is not clear that Cnut did *endow* Bury.

[182] *Ibid.*, pp. 9–10.

[183] This source was apparently unknown to Gransden when she wrote 'The legends'.

[184] *Ibid.*, pp. 9–14.

[185] *Ibid.*, pp. 13–17.

[186] *Ibid.*, pp. 17–18.

Bury St Edmunds, Ramsey, and Worcester

However difficult it may be to see clearly what happened at Bury St Edmunds in the mid-tenth century or in the reign of Cnut, the years between those two periods remain the most obscure of all. The central – indeed, almost the only – fact is the Ramsey monks' commissioning of Abbo to write his *Passio sancti Eadmundi*. Their interest – and presumably that of their founder, Archbishop Oswald[187] – in St Edmund suggests that in 985 x 987 an institutional relationship existed between Ramsey Abbey and the church of St Edmund at Bedricesworth. On this single piece of firm ground we may attempt to build a modest tower of deduction and contextual speculation.

The lay patron of Ramsey Abbey, as of so many other aspects of the religious life in eastern England, was Æthelwine, *amicus Dei*, ealdorman of East Anglia 962–992. The ecclesiastical founder, Oswald, bishop of Worcester (961–992) and archbishop of York (971–992), had established his Fenland abbey at Ramsey in 968/9. It was one of the remarkable series of Fenland monasteries established in the second half of the tenth century.[188] Our principal source of information about the circumstances of foundation is provided by the *Uita sancti Oswaldi* written by Byrhtferth of Ramsey in 997 x 1005.[189] From the late thirteenth-century house-history of Ramsey, based in part on the monastery's archival records, we learn that Ealdorman Æthelwine had his hall and kept his court at Upwood (Huntingdonshire), near Ramsey.[190] In 968, it would seem, 'Æthelwine had erected at Ramsey a tiny wooden chapel and installed three monks there'.[191] Meanwhile, Bishop Oswald seems to have

[187] Gransden, *ibid.*, pp. 3–4. For new discussion of the date of Abbo's visit to England and his writing of the *Passio sancti Eadmundi*, see Mostert, 'Le séjour', and *The Political Theology*, pp. 40–5. Cf. Bullough, 'The educational tradition', pp. 482–5.

[188] On these see *Wulfstan of Winchester*, edd. & transl. Lapidge & Winterbottom, pp. xlviii–l, 38–45.

[189] Ed. Raine, *The Historians*, I.399–475. For the date see Lapidge, 'The hermeneutic style', p. 91; for a slightly broader dating, 995 x 1005, see his 'Byrhtferth and the *Vita S. Ecgwini*', p. 333. For earlier assessments of the text, see Crawford, 'Byrhtferth of Ramsey', and Robinson, 'Byrhtferth'. On the place of Oswald in the ecclesiastical upheavals of his generation, see John, 'St Oswald and the tenth-century Reformation'.

[190] *Chronicon Abbatiæ Rameseiensis*, ed. Macray, pp. 52–5. Cf. Hart, *The Early Charters of Eastern England*, pp. 231–2 (no. 311).

[191] Hart, 'Athelstan', p. 137; cf. *ibid.*, pp. 136–7, for all the matters discussed in the rest of this paragraph. Hart has there said that the funeral was at Glastonbury Abbey, and that Oswald sent twelve monks from Westbury to Ramsey. I can find reference neither to the location of the funeral nor to that precise number of monks in Byrhtferth's Life of St Oswald.

been searching for a suitable site on which to found or refound a monastery in eastern England – he inspected, but was dissatisfied with, Benfleet (Essex), Ely (Cambridgeshire), and St Albans (Hertfordshire). Meeting at a funeral, Æthelwine and Oswald brought their plans together. Oswald visited Ramsey, approved it as a suitable choice, and despatched thither monks from an earlier foundation of his at Westbury-on-Trym (Gloucestershire) which had been established in 963/4. Other foundations or refoundations by Oswald seem to have been the abbeys at Evesham (Worcestershire), Pershore (Worcestershire), and Winchcombe (Gloucestershire).[192]

Æthelwine, his family, his friends and dependants, all poured very considerable resources into the endowment of Ramsey Abbey. Cyril Hart has shown[193] how this process differed from that of the foundation of Bishop Æthelwold's Fenland monasteries at Ely, Peterborough, and Thorney in the years 964 x 971,[194] where Æthelwine provided support for the bishop's efforts but was not personally heavily involved in the endowment. By Æthelwine's death on 24 April, 992, two months after Oswald's (29 February), Ramsey was already formidably well endowed. Although the family by no means lost interest in the abbey, the momentum of development slowed considerably – not least, no doubt, because Æthelwine's family lost control of the East Anglian ealdordom. In 1016, Abbot Wulfsige and Bishop Eadnoth (of Dorchester-on-Thames; Wulfsige's predecessor as abbot of Ramsey) were killed on King Edmund's side at the battle of *Assandun*, as was Æthelweard, one of Æthelwine's sons;[195] the uncertainties which must have begun to afflict the abbey with the worsening security-situation after the battle of Maldon in 991 became grave with the eventual seizure of the country by the Danes in 1016.

Æthelwine's father, and predecessor-but-one in the East Anglian ealdordom (932–956), Æthelstan 'Half-king', had been a supporter of ecclesiastical revival and reform since the reign of King Æthelstan.[196] It was in his household, if the thirteenth-century Ramsey chronicle is to be credited, that the future King Edgar was fostered from 944;[197] at least part of Edgar's education was placed in the hands of Æthelwold, abbot of

---

[192] Byrhtferth, *Vita S. Oswaldi*, §4, wrote that Oswald built seven monasteries in *Wiccia* (the diocese of Worcester, the ancient kingdom of the Hwicce). Even counting Worcester Cathedral itself, this list reaches only five.

[193] 'Eadnoth', pp. 61–2, 65–6; 'Athelstan', pp. 136–7, 122. On Ælfwold, Æthelwine's brother, see *ibid.*, pp. 131–2, 136; see also below, pp. 68–75.

[194] Cf. *Wulfstan of Winchester*, edd. & transl. Lapidge & Winterbottom, p. xlviii.

[195] Anglo-Saxon Chronicle, *s.a.* 1016 CDEF.

[196] Hart, 'Athelstan', pp. 120–8.

[197] *Ibid.*, pp. 123–4.

Abingdon.[198] In the reign of King Edmund I, as the military strength of the kingdom increased and as the evidence for ecclesiastical revival becomes more compelling (notably in the series of royal land-grants to religious women aristocrats),[199] Ealdorman Æthelstan and his family were dominant in the king's counsels, and Dunstan was made abbot of Glastonbury; in the reign of that very devout chronic invalid, Eadred, Ealdorman Æthelstan was regent, Dunstan was a significant force to be reckoned with, Æthelwold was given the abbey of Abingdon, and the king's will is a remarkable testament to piety.[200] When the Benedictine revolution got under way in the 960s, it is no surprise, therefore, to see Æthelwine playing a significant role.

If the foundation of a church of St Edmund at Bedricesworth is to be associated with the aftermath of the region's seizure from Danish control in 917 or (perhaps more likely) its recovery by King Edmund I in 942,[201] it occurred at a time when Bishop Theodred and Ealdorman Æthelstan not only were concentrating on the revival of ecclesiastical life in East Anglia but also were powerful in the counsels of the realm as a whole.[202] There is a significant likelihood that, under such circumstances, the ealdorman would have been seen as the protector, and even the patron, of St Edmund's church, and that such a relationship would have continued with the relatives who were his successors in office until 992. One is therefore led to wonder about how that relationship would have developed in the period of the family's support for the full-blown Benedictinism of the period from 959.

Cyril Hart has argued that the acquisition (during Ramsey's first twenty years) of estates in the neighbourhood of Bury St Edmunds is an indication of or led to the close interest of Ramsey Abbey and its patrons in the affairs of the church of St Edmund.[203] However, this is a suggestion

---

[198] The evidence for this is provided by Æthelwold's historical preface to his version of the *Regula sancti Benedicti*: for discussion, cf. Whitelock, 'The authorship', pp. 126–7, and *English Historical Documents*, p. 921; Robinson, *The Times*, pp. 162–4; John, *Orbis Britanniae*, pp. 158–60, 191; Lapidge, 'Æthelwold as scholar', p. 98.

[199] Cf. Dumville, *Wessex and England*, pp. 213–14.

[200] Sawyer, *Anglo-Saxon Charters*, no. 1515. I have made a special study of this text – 'The will of King Eadred and the early history of the Winchester Nunnaminster'.

[201] On A.D. 917 and its aftermath, see Hart, 'The church of St Mary', pp. 109–11, and 'The hidation of Huntingdonshire', pp. 55–7. Cf. Dumville, *Wessex and England*, pp. 181–4. I have not seen a discussion of the fate of East Anglia during the crisis of A.D. 940–942 nor, therefore, of how those years' events affected its future government.

[202] Whitelock, *Some Anglo-Saxon Bishops of London*, pp. 17–21, and 'The conversion'; Hart, 'Athelstan', p. 122.

[203] 'The East Anglian chronicle', p. 277. Cf. Hart & Syme, 'The earliest Suffolk charter', p. 171.

of uncertain import, taken by itself. It is possible that the relationship did not progress beyond that point – that the minster at Bedricesworth and the Benedictine abbey at Ramsey had the same patron and held neighbouring estates. Equally, however, we might suppose that the religious climate of the generation after Edgar's accession to power in that region in 957 (and one might think that Ealdorman Æthelstan's family was likely to have been in that year the prime mover in the secession of England north of the Thames from King Eadwig's rule) would have provided the circumstances in which St Edmund's minster could be reformed into a Benedictine community. It seems to me that the interests of the Ramsey community as expressed to Abbo in the 980s are best explained by the recent or impending reform of Bury St Edmunds.

Antonia Gransden has advanced the view that late thirteenth-century and later statements that Bury St Edmunds was colonised by monks from the abbey of St Benedict of Holme, a story which she has shown to have no reasonable basis in fact,[204] may ultimately derive from lost information that Bury was Benedictinised by transplant from another abbey of St Benedict, that of Ramsey.[205] This argument lacks cogency, however. It requires that such knowledge was lost or suppressed by the mid-eleventh century when the annal for 1020 was written in the 'Bury Psalter'. It requires information to resurface far away from Bury and be associated with the minor Norfolk abbey of Holme,[206] but yet only after some further lapse to be adopted at Bury itself. We must, it seems to me, regard the double dose of St Benedict as coincidental.[207]

The case for a familial association of Ramsey and Bury St Edmunds in the years on either side of 1000 must therefore rest on Abbo's evidence. Any further deductions about the nature of that association are speculative arguments from context. Nevertheless, taken together with the doubts about the general and specific evidential value of the annal for 1020 in the 'Bury Psalter' (and any other evidence which may be deemed to bear directly on an alleged refoundation and Benedictinisation of the abbey by King Cnut), these deductions seem sufficient to open up the possibility that the minster at Bury St Edmunds was reformed in the 970s

---

[204] Gransden, 'The legends', pp. 15–18.

[205] *Ibid.*, pp. 18–21.

[206] The first indication of a role for Holme in the history of Bury occurs with a statement in a controversialist episcopal tract from Norwich (datable 1103 x 1119) that a monk of Holme, one Uuius, was appointed prior of Bury by Bishop Ælfric (ed. Galbraith, 'The East Anglian see', p. 226; cf. Gransden. 'The legends', p. 16).

[207] It is a nice question as to how much further that argument could be carried, in a *reductio ad absurdum*. How many other houses – particularly of the Oswald connexion – were dedicated to St Benedict? Could the house at Holme have been colonised from Ramsey or from another house dedicated thus?

or 980s, that one of the translations of St Edmund took place then,[208] and that reformed Bury belonged to the group of houses associated with St Oswald. It follows that books, and particularly books containing Reform-literature, might have been owned and written there up to half a century earlier than has previously been allowed.[209] Such books might be expected to partake of the characteristics displayed by those known from the principal centres of Oswald's activity, Ramsey and Worcester – and perhaps York.[210]

The introduction of Caroline minuscule to houses of the Oswald connexion

In the course of the tenth century (if not before) Continental manuscripts written in Caroline minuscule script were probably reaching Worcester. A census of such ninth- and tenth-century books of later Worcester provenance produces the following modest list.

1. Cambridge, Corpus Christi College, 279 (*saec.* ix², Tours or region)[211]
2. London, British Library, Royal 5.E.xiii (*saec.* ix *med.*, Brittany)[212]
3. London, British Library, Royal 15.A.xxxiii (*saec.* x *in.*, Reims)[213]

---

[208] And just possibly also one or both of the translations of St Iurmin and St Botulf.

[209] Arguments made on the basis that book-production at Bury would not have been possible before A.D. 1020 (or even a generation thereafter) must accordingly be disallowed: as I have noticed elsewhere in this volume (cf. pp. 33–4, 78–9), they are very prominent in the accounts given by Temple, *Anglo-Saxon Manuscripts*, pp. 71, 93, 101.

[210] We may note the survival of Ramsey hagiography uniquely in a manuscript written at Worcester (in the second half of the eleventh century): London, British Library, MS. Cotton Nero E.i + Cambridge, Corpus Christi College, MS. 9. Cf. Lapidge, 'Byrhtferth and the *Vita S. Ecgwini*', pp. 332–3. For the problem of books associated with Abbot Germanus (of Winchcombe, Ramsey, and Cholsey), see the appendix to this chapter (below, pp. 79–85). Furthermore, there is evidence for mutual archival penetration: on Ælfwold and his charters, see below, pp. 68–75; Sawyer, *Anglo-Saxon Charters*, no. 1371 (Archbishop Oswald receives a lease of land in Worcestershire from the Ramsey community and re-leases it to his kinsman, Osulf) is a document from the Ramsey archive yet clearly having much to do with Worcester; *ibid.*, no. 67 (a spurious document dated 624 by which Wulfhere, king of Mercians, grants Dillington) survives as a single sheet of the Worcester archive (London, British Library, Add. Ch. 19788: *Facsimiles*, ed. Bond, IV.1) but concerns land in Huntingdonshire which belonged to Ramsey Abbey in 1066 and 1086 (Domesday Book, vol. 1, fo 204vb) – I propose to devote a full study to this document.

[211] Gneuss, 'A preliminary list', no. 81; *The Bishops' Synod*, ed. Faris; Sharpe, 'Gildas as a Father'; De Brún & Herbert, *Catalogue*, p. 109 (no. 52). For some speculation, cf. Bullough, 'The educational tradition', p. 475.

[212] Gneuss, 'A preliminary list', no. 459; Dumville, 'Biblical apocrypha', p. 331.

[213] Gneuss, 'A preliminary list', no. 490; *Catalogus*, edd. Atkins & Ker, p. 18 and n. 2.

4. Oxford, Bodleian Library, Barlow 4 (*S.C.* 6416) (*saec.* ix)[214]
5. Oxford, Bodleian Library, Hatton 42 (*S.C.* 4117) (*saec.* ix², Brittany)[215]

Worcester, Cathedral Library, MSS. Q.21, Q.28, and Q.78B could be added.[216] It is of course easier to demonstrate that these manuscripts arrived in England in or by the tenth century than that they reached Worcester then. In the absence of a very close study of the Worcester scribes of that period, this is not a surprising state of affairs. Indeed, in one of these instances, such studies have demonstrated that a particular manuscript is likely to have arrived at Worcester early in the eleventh century: the first quire of MS. Hatton 42 is supply-text added at Christ Church, Canterbury, *ca* 1000; immediately thereafter, the book is found in use by Wulfstan, bishop of Worcester and archbishop of York 1002–1023, whose hand is visible in various annotations.[217] However, the study of textual history has suggested instances where a Continental manuscript is likely to have been available for copying at Worcester, even where that manuscript is no longer extant or else has not been identified because it bears no obvious physical signs of its sojourn at Worcester. A likely case in point, where the manuscripts are still identifiable, concerns the *Expositio libri comitis* written by the Carolingian Benedictine author, Smaragdus of Saint-Mihiel, Verdun: it would be quite surprising if Worcester, Cathedral Library, MS. F.91, written there in the second half of the tenth century, were not a copy of MS. Barlow 4 (no. 4 on the list above).[218]

Three successive tenth-century bishops of Worcester had Continental experience which might have caused Caroline books to be imported to

[214] Gneuss, 'A preliminary list', no. 539; cf., for the dating, Pächt *et al.*, *Illuminated Manuscripts*, III.6 (no. 40).
[215] Gneuss, 'A preliminary list', no. 629; Pächt *et al.*, *Illuminated Manuscripts*, I.32–3 (nos 417, 419, 420) and III.4 (no. 29); Lucas, 'MS. Hatton 42'; Dumville, 'Wulfric cild'.
[216] Gneuss, 'A preliminary list', nos 767–9. MS. Q.21, a ninth-century Continental book, was at Worcester in the early twelfth century, but an earlier English provenance has not (as yet, at least) been demonstrated: Ker, *English Manuscripts*, p. 53.
[217] On Canterbury see Bishop, 'Notes', pp. 415, 421, 423; *English Caroline Minuscule*, p. xxvi. On its arguably Canterbury binding, see Pollard, 'Some Anglo-Saxon bookbindings', pp. 143–4 (no. 3). At Worcester in the twelfth century it was believed to have been one of Dunstan's books. (Galloway, 'On the medieval and post-medieval collation', p. 109, has mistakenly reported Pollard as identifying a number of Canterbury books as associated by their bindings with Worcester.) On Wulfstan see Ker, *Books, Collectors*, pp. 22–4.
[218] Bishop, *English Caroline Minuscule*, p. 16 (no. 18), on Worcester MS. F.91. These are the only two copies of this text known from pre-Conquest England. The evidence from Archbishop Wulfstan's manuscripts and copies of them (cf. Sauer, 'Zur Überlieferung', and Clemoes, 'The Old English Benedictine Office') is, when fully evaluated, likely to point to further instances of texts once available at Worcester but not yet identified in books with a demonstrable Worcester history.

their cathedral. Cenwald (928/9–957 x 959) always described himself as a monk:[219] it has been thought that this might have been as a result of a profession made at a Continental house and that a confraternity-bond could consequently have existed. At any rate Cenwald participated in an extensive diplomatic expedition to the Continent on King Æthelstan's behalf in 929.[220] His successor as bishop, Dunstan (957 x 961, perhaps latterly in plurality with London, and possibly then also Canterbury), was recalled from exile on the Continent to Mercia when Edgar became king there in late 957 in secession from King Eadwig's rule; a great deal of evidence attests to Dunstan's subsequent maintenance and development of links with Continental churchmen.[221] Finally, Oswald (961–992) had studied the monastic life at Fleury (Saint-Benoît-sur-Loire) – as, apparently, had his uncle, Archbishop Oda, before him; Oswald returned to England in 958.[222]

The two latter bishops of Worcester, Dunstan and Oswald, are quite directly associable with the origins of Anglo-Caroline minuscule. It is in specimens of Dunstan's own hand that we find the first datable examples of Style II:[223] but the limits of dating remain broad, *ca* 940 x 988. In spite of what has often been asserted, the connexion of Oxford, Bodleian Library, MS. Auct. F.4.32 (*S.C.* 2176), 'St Dunstan's Classbook', with Glastonbury is established only by the evidence of provenance in the second half of the fifteenth century and the first half of the sixteenth:[224] there were many opportunities both in Dunstan's lifetime and subsequently for manuscripts to have travelled from Canterbury (or elsewhere) to Glastonbury.[225] We should be particularly cautious in view

---

[219] In the thirteenth-century text, *De antiquitate Glastonie ecclesie*, §67 (ed. & transl. Scott, *The Early History*, p. 138), Cenwald ('Keneualdus episcopus') is described as having been a monk of Glastonbury, and his death-date is given (see below, p. 51). On all this see Barker, 'Two lost documents', p. 139.

[220] Keynes, 'King Athelstan's books', pp. 148, 158–9, 192, 198–201. On Cenwald and the so-called 'alliterative group' of Anglo-Saxon charters, one at least of which seems to have been written in Caroline minuscule, see below, pp. 141–2.

[221] *Memorials of Saint Dunstan*, ed. Stubbs, *passim*.

[222] Byrhtferth, *Vita Sancti Oswaldi*, §§2–3 (ed. Raine, *The Historians*, I.413–19). Of Fleury (and Oda) he wrote, 'ex quo idem pontifex suscepit monastice religionis habitum'.

[223] Bishop, 'An early example of Insular-Caroline'; Parkes, 'A note on MS Vatican, Bibl. Apost., lat. 3363'. See further chapter III, below.

[224] *Saint Dunstan's Classbook*, facs. ed. Hunt, p. xv. I discount, as being too vague, the evidence drawn by Hunt from the Glastonbury library-catalogue compiled in A.D. 1248. The best case for a Glastonbury origin for the Anglo-Caroline additions would be made by establishing that the component parts of the present codex were separate until towards the end of the middle ages.

[225] For three tenth-century Canterbury manuscripts thought to have done so, see below, p. 93, n. 45. According to §67 of the thirteenth-century *De antiquitate Glastonie ecclesie* (ed. & transl. Scott, *The Early History*, pp. 136–9), four Reform-monks of

of the fact that the one book which can with conviction be attributed to Dunstan's years at Glastonbury (940 x 956) – Oxford, Bodleian Library, MS. Hatton 30 (*S. C.* 4076) – is written in Square minuscule.[226] It could be argued that a more natural context for Dunstan's Style-II Anglo-Caroline would be after his return from Continental exile: in other words, that his brief careers in 957–959 as a Mercian bishop, first without see and then at Worcester and London, or else (or additionally) his long stint at Canterbury from late 959, are the times to which we might better assign his work as recognised in MS. Auct. F.4.32 and in Roma, Biblioteca Apostolica Vaticana, MS. lat. 3363, and perhaps elsewhere.

It is not impossible, then, that Dunstan had started writing a hybrid Caroline minuscule in the period 956 x 958 (encompassing his Continental exile and first establishment in Mercia) and therefore that he had practised it at Worcester. But it might also be argued that his stay there – not beyond Oswald's appointment as bishop in 961 – was too brief for his innovatory scribal practice (as opposed to his continuing acceptance of Square minuscule) to have made much impact on a long-established scriptorium. In this connexion it is curious that a late mediaeval Glastonbury source describes Dunstan's predecessor, Cenwald, as a former member (presumably therefore before 929 – unless after 957 x 959) of that house and preserves his obit, 28 June.[227] For it may have been in Cenwald's time that a copy of the Pseudo-Theodore Penitential, almost certainly of pre-Conquest Worcester provenance, was written in a number of remarkable scripts: apparently incomplete, it now contains fifty-three folios distributed in six quires; the first four quires, displaying a variety of often rather odd Insular scripts, show both archaic and innovative features, while the last two quires are written in a hybrid Insular-Caroline minuscule seemingly unparalleled in the corpus of late

---

Glastonbury became archbishops of Canterbury (Æthelgar, Sigeric, Ælfheah, Æthelnoth): two made gifts to Glastonbury Abbey. Of these, the most interesting is that of Archbishop Æthelnoth (1020–1038) who, apart from a prayerbook illuminated in gold, donated a copy of Hrabanus's *De laudibus crucis Christi* (cf. Keynes, *Anglo-Saxon Manuscripts*, pp. 11–14, no. 4). Curiously, in the will of Ælfwold III, bishop of Crediton (A.D. 986 x 1015), we find a bequest of a copy of 'Hrabanus' to a layman (Sawyer, *Anglo-Saxon Charters*, no. 1492, datable 1008 x 1012): *The Crawford Collection*, edd. Napier & Stevenson, pp. 23–4, 125–33 (no. 10).

[226] Of Phase III. At the end it bears an inscription recording that it was written by *Abbot* Dunstan's command.

[227] Cf. n. 219, above. Scott, *The Early History*, p. 139 and pp. 206–7 (n. 135) has misidentified 'Keneualdus' (Cenwald) with the doubly different name, Cyneward, and taken him to be the bishop of Wells (A.D. 973 x 975). Among attempts to penetrate the gloom of Glastonbury's history before Dunstan's abbacy, special mention must be made of those by Robinson, *The Saxon Bishops of Wells*, and *Somerset*, pp. 1–53.

Anglo-Saxon manuscripts. This remarkable book will receive a much fuller discussion elsewhere:[228] the place of its writing remains uncertain, although Worcester must certainly be a candidate. What it attests to is another attempt – different from that of the Caroline-minuscule royal diploma of A.D. 956,[229] different from the script of Dunstan and its Style-II derivatives –, by scribes trained in the Insular tradition, to get to grips with foreign scriptorial influences including Caroline minuscule. Inelegantly achieved, this is a practical book whose quires show signs of vertical folding.[230]

It is in 961, the year of Oswald's election to the see of Worcester (Oda's and Oscytel's nephew having gained the favour of Dunstan, according to Byrhtferth),[231] that the first still-surviving specimen of Style-I Anglo-Caroline was written. King Edgar's diploma in favour of Abingdon Abbey (and therefore Abbot Æthelwold) for land at Ringwood (Hampshire) was written by two scribes.[232] The first was a practitioner of Square minuscule in Phase IV: this Caroline-influenced form was used in royal charters of the 960s and was written also, it seems, at pre-Reform Winchester.[233] The second scribe wrote Style-I Anglo-Caroline, albeit with an occasional lapse (and, as a few Old English words show, he could manage the native script too). Michael Lapidge has written of the second scribe's text 'that it was indeed Oswald who drafted the eight attestations which are appended to this charter, though it is most unlikely that it was

---

[228] Bruxelles, Bibliothèque royale, MS. 8558–8563 (2498): cf. Ker, *Catalogue*, pp. 8–10 (no. 10). I have a thorough study in preparation. The section in question (Ker's B) is fos 80–131; the only other known copy of the Pseudo-Theodore Penitential is in Cambridge, Corpus Christi College, MS. 190, part 1 (Ker, *ibid.*, pp. 70–3, no. 45.A), written in Style-I Anglo-Caroline, almost certainly at Worcester (its scribe employed non-Insular, non-Caroline **a** – cf. n. 240, below – and a form of **g** like that in London, British Library, MS. Royal 6.A.vii). Fos 132–153 of Bruxelles MS. 8558–8563 (2498) contain two penitential collections: the first (fos 132–139) is found otherwise in Cambridge, Corpus Christi College, MS. 265, pp. 72–82, written at Worcester in the mid-eleventh century (cf. Bateson, 'A Worcester cathedral book'); the second (fos 140v–153v) occurs otherwise in Oxford, Bodleian Library, MS. Laud misc. 482 (*S.C.* 1054), a mid-eleventh-century book of thirteenth-century Worcester provenance.

[229] London, British Library, MS. Cotton Augustus ii.41: Sawyer, *Anglo-Saxon Charters*, no. 594; cf. Bishop, 'Notes', p. 333.

[230] On folded manuscripts (of which part B of 'St Dunstan's Classbook' – cf. facs. ed. Hunt, p. vii – is an example) see Bischoff, *Mittelalterliche Studien*, I.93–100.

[231] *Vita Sancti Oswaldi*, §3 (ed. Raine, *The Historians*, I.420). Cf. Symons, 'St Dunstan in the "Oswald" tradition'.

[232] London, British Library, MS. Cotton Augustus ii.39: Sawyer, *Anglo-Saxon Charters*, no. 690; *Facsimiles*, ed. Bond, III.23; cf. Bishop, *English Caroline Minuscule*, p. 9 (no. 11) and plate IX.

[233] On the scribe known as 'Edgar A', see Keynes, *The Diplomas of King Æthelred*, pp. 70–9; on the evidence of Cambridge, Corpus Christi College, MS. 173, see Dumville, *Wessex and England*, p. 61.

he who copied them into the surviving single-sheet copy'.[234] I see no need for such shyness. If it was this portion only – the *eulogium* or 'testament' – which Oswald composed, is it not rather a coincidence to find it written in a hand other than that of the main body of the diploma? Whether or not we admit that Oswald was the scribe of the Anglo-Caroline portion of this document, it must be allowed as striking that the first surviving witness to Anglo-Caroline Style I occurs in the year of Oswald's elevation and in a document which he partially composed. In as much as the form of Caroline practised at Worcester for the rest of the tenth century seems to have been Style I, the early association is noteworthy. The Caroline scribe was either a Worcester scribe (and possibly Oswald himself) trying out the new style, or else this script-form was being developed in the royal chancery.[235] The first examples from the other principal centre at which Style I came to be written, Winchester, are dated 966 (the New Minster Foundation-charter)[236] and 963 x 984 (the Benedictional of St Æthelwold, and its alleged precursor, Paris, Bibliothèque nationale, MS. latin 987).[237] The possibility therefore arises, however uncertainly, that – rather than Glastonbury and Winchester providing the scriptoria in which the two styles of Anglo-Caroline minuscule were developed – both styles were first written at Worcester.

The observable history – such as it is – of Anglo-Caroline writing at Worcester in the last four decades of the tenth century can leave one in no doubt that it was Style I, and not Style II, which was practised there. It is clear, however, that as at Canterbury (but unlike Winchester) Square-minuscule script continued to be used for Latin writing alongside Caroline until the end of the century. The attributable manuscript, London, British Library, MS. Royal 13.A.xv,[238] written partly in Square

---

234 'Æthelwold as scholar', pp. 92–3 (quotation from p. 93).

235 The role of the royal chancery as a creator of fashion and arbiter of taste in script-development in this period is not to be underrated.

236 London, British Library, MS. Cotton Vespasian A.viii, fos 3–33 (Sawyer, *Anglo-Saxon Charters*, no. 745): on its date, I agree with the remarks of John, *Orbis Britanniae*, pp. 271–5, as against those of Wormald, 'Late Anglo-Saxon art', pp. 23–6.

237 Prescott, 'The structure', pp. 120–1, has explained the textual situation, but it remains to be demonstrated that the Paris *manuscript* is earlier than London, British Library, MS. Additional 49598. This dating limit, as applied to the Paris manuscript, rests on the assumption that Æthelwold was the moving force behind the creation of the text. The Paris manuscript was once, for no very good reason, known as the 'Ramsey Benedictional' (for an early study of the book, see Homburger, *Die Anfänge*, pp. 57–65): but this serves to remind us that an original link of text or manuscript or both with Oswald needs to be considered before it is ruled out (for a brief, but ingenious, reassessment see Vezin, 'Manuscrits des dizième et onzième siècles', pp. 287–90).

238 For reproductions from this manuscript see Warner & Gilson, *British Museum Catalogue*, IV, plate 77: (*b*) shows part of fo 24r, in the Caroline section of the

minuscule and partly in Anglo-Caroline, is linked by a shared Caroline scribe to two wholly Caroline books, MS. Royal 8.B.xi, and Worcester, Cathedral Library, F.91 which contains Smaragdus's *Expositio libri comitis*. An isolated item, perhaps written at Worcester, is Oxford, Bodleian Library, MS. Lat. theol. c.4 (*S.C.* 1926*), in both scripts.[239] A second group of manuscripts with a shared scribe, perhaps written at the very end of the century, attaches to Worcester by the slenderest of threads, the late mediaeval provenance of one of its members:[240]

---

book. Cf. Bishop, *English Caroline Minuscule*, p. 16; also p. xiv and n. 1. The Worcester characteristics described by Bishop as occurring in the Caroline hand common to the three manuscripts named here are 'Ink dark brown or . . . black of the dead mineral quality'; 'The prevalent form of x is confined between the median lines'. Bishop also noted the presence in Worcester MS. F.91 of marginalia in a hybrid minuscule. On BL MS. Royal 13.A.xv see further *Felix's Life of Saint Guthlac*, ed. & transl. Colgrave, pp. 28–30. For a facsimile from BL Royal 8.B.xi, see Warner & Gilson, *British Museum Catalogue*, IV, plate 57(*a*): Bishop has noted that here 'a heavy antenna corrects blind e'.

[239] Bishop, *English Caroline Minuscule*, p. 19 (no. 21) and plate XIX. He has noted that 'of the two forms of x the more prevalent is confined within the median lines'. The marginalia are 'in mixed Caroline-Insular script', described also as 'hybrid script'. The hand of one of the interlinear glossators, *saec.* x/xi, 'resembles a gloss hand in' Cambridge, University Library, MS. Ff.4.42 (1285): cf. Bishop, 'The Corpus Martianus Capella', p. 258 and plate XX; see also n. 242, below.

[240] The other possible scribal connexions are with Fleury and with St Augustine's Abbey, Canterbury, but these do not seem compelling – however, the possibility of interchange between Fleury and the Oswald group of houses is clearly not to be overlooked. The Fleury connexion of this group depends on Mr Bishop's observation that a gloss-scribe in Worcester MS. Q.8 'resembles a hand' in London, British Library, MS. Harley 2506, attributed to Saint-Benoît-sur-Loire and containing hands allegedly both French and English. The St Augustine's connexion depends on identification of the principal scribe of Worcester Q.8 in some glosses in Cambridge, Corpus Christi College, MS. 285, part 2 (Bishop, *English Caroline Minuscule*, pp. xxv, 4, 18). I find neither identification determinative. For El Escorial, Real Biblioteca, MS. E.II.1 (a specimen of 'rough-energy' Style I), given to Horton (perhaps by an abbess of Barking), see *Charters of Sherborne*, ed. O'Donovan, p. lxi; cf. Ker, *Catalogue*, pp. 152–3 (no. 115). The most consistently unusual feature of the script of this group is the employment of non-Insular, non-Caroline a. The textual history of Statius's *Thebaid* has been investigated to the extent that the Worcester fragments (flyleaves from Worcester, Cathedral Library, MSS. F.64 and Q.8, both apparently at Worcester at the end of the middle ages: cf. Ker, *Medieval Libraries*, pp. 211, 213) may be placed in relation to some other witnesses (Williams, 'The Worcester fragments' and 'Two manuscripts'). The resulting stemma is

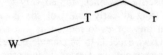

where W is the Worcester fragments, T is a tenth-century Continental manuscript (Paris, Bibliothèque nationale, MS. nouv. acq. lat. 1627) of Tours provenance (presumably therefore lent into England for copying) and r is London, British

dñi panare uias eius dum · Ad clandam
scientiam salutis plebi eius Inremissi
onem peccatorum eorum:- Peruiscer
misereicordie di nri Inquibus uisitauit
nos oriens exalto:- Illuminare his
qui Intenebris & Inumbra mortis sedent
addirigendos pedes nrós Inuia pacis:-

Benedictus es dñe ds patrum
Nostrorum & laudabilis & super
exaltatus Inscla:- & benedictum no
men gloriae tuae scm & lauda
bile & super exaltatum Inomnibus
saeculis· benedictus es Intemplo sco
gloriae tuae & laudabilis & glorio
sus Insaecula· benedictus es Inthrono
Regni tui & laudabilis & super exal
tatus Inscla

I London, British Library, MS. Royal 2.A.xx, fo 14v, detail (see pp. 76–7)

signo a priore omf parite
exp. surgunt; [Stcemof aut
apud antiquof monachorñ
canoñ ut audito unuscuiusq;
horæ figno. celerif omnep
adorationem conuenirent....
orationi simul incumbereñt...
simul orarent: E aborato
ne facto figno a priore
omf parite surge ent; modo
ueo iam apud nof alr ea aeq;
alr habeatur; quãto enim
suouni apprimatur cãto
longiuf utq; meñto. Aban
aquif oftendamuf patonb;; Ut
eñ euñte fpm feruientef dño
feruientef; nof aut teprer

exfaucab; et diaboli uuelocton
rapiat; qñ nobif femp pro
infeftauf; tunc quã maxime
adofiftere infeftauf; cñ nof conte
fe offerre pcer dño uidet...
peftinanf mcē nram abitem
aone orationif; aut cogita
tionib; aut excratuf humo
rib; reuocare; proptea q
breuef quide orationef; fed
frequenter fieri pat es er ñi
tuffñ; breuef ideo. ut infi
diaf diaboli infiftentaf tunc
feapus cum orarñ inipfa bre
uitate urcatre poffiñ; ceperipfam

feruiutii
qñterel auf ideo; iterpipfam
uidedep frequentia orationifetillud
ctuo luffa

... atq; saxonis p̃diuersis criminib; peniten
tiae b̃s utitur modus·

De diuersis poenitentiaru·

De diuersis homicidiis·

tem de poenitentia·

De penitentib; ut apresbiteris ñreconciliento
nisi presbiteris epo exconcilio affricano·

tem exconcilio cartaginensi deeadẽ re·

Item decapitalib; criminibus;

usq̃ capitula **DE PENITENTIAM**·

De inani gloria·

III Cambridge, Corpus Christi College, MS. 190, p. iii, detail (see pp. 52, 55)

me paterno inatrio

^{pfiat} (gloss: pfiat) t obsoletum uasculum caducis

christus ^{ι coniungit} aptat usibus·

^{permittat} init que parte ^{f·me} inanguli ma ^{ι·esse}

nere munus ecce ficule ^{tuas meu delicet tamquam uile} ; ^{& contem nibilem}

^{ingredimur ι·regulem domun} nimus intrix regiam saluas

attamen uel infimam ^{ι·minimam}

eo obsequellam prestuasse pd÷ ^{f·nob} ;

quicquid illud accidit ^{quicquid eueniat}

^{f·me} uuabit ore personasse christum ^{ι·laudasse} ^{ineo}

quo regente uiuimus ^{f·omnia} ;

E A D A M E E V A

V A C O L V M B A F V I T T V H C ^{simplex & innocens}

candida · nigra deinde · ^{ante quä peccare·} ^{ι·postquä peccauit}

f acta· per anguinum male ^{f·est·serpentü}

suada fraude uenenum ; ^{f·diaboli}

inxit & innocuum maculis ^{ι·maculauit f·eua ι·innocenté}

sordentibus adam · ^{foedis turpibus·}

at nudis ficulna draco mox ^{adae & eue ficulas pera folia habet· & significat pruritü libidinis}

tegmina uictor · CAIN ET ABEL

IV Cambridge, Corpus Christi College, MS. 448, fo 91r (see pp. 55–6)

...nibuſ epiſ & can onum ſtatutaſ. excom

...cam' & aliminibuſ ſce di æccte ſegre

...u xpianorum efficimuſ. & niſi cito

...te & nmce mediocritato quam leſerum

...enit : &na maledictione eoſ confundi

...p&uo anathemate condempnamuſ.

...pne iudiciſ incurrant abhereditate

...torum eiuſ alien exiſtant & neq: inp

...mpore communionē cum xpianiſ habeant

...que infuturo do & ſciſ eiuſ partem obtine

...tcum diabulo & miniſtriſ eiuſ ſocient &

...triciſ flamme cum ſempiterno luctu po

...lum æternum exoſi habeant & gehen

...pplicio crucientur inſcto. Maledicta

...domo. maledicti inagro. Maledicta

V Rouen, Bibliothèque municipale, MS. A.27 (368), fo 183v, detail (see pp. 60–1)

VII Roma, Biblioteca Apostolica Vaticana, MS. Reg. lat. 1671, fo 216v, detail showing hand iv (see pp. 69–75)

Nil asperum laurentius:

Refert ad ista aut turbidum.

Sedut paratus obsequi:

Obæmperanter annuit;

Est diues inquit nonnego:

Habæque uitæ ecclesia:

Opnmque ærum plurimum.

Necquisquam inorbe ditior;

Sipse tantum nonhabæ:

Argenteorum enig miratum:

Augustus artæm possidens:

Cui nummius omnis scribiatur;

Sednæc reculo prodere:

Locu pletus artam nummus.

Uulgabo cuncta & proferam:

Preтiosa que xps tenæj

Unum sæ orans flagтo:

Induciarum paululum.

Quo fungar efficacius:

Promissionis munere:

Dum tota digestim mihi:

Xpi sub pellex scribiatur;

Nam calculanda primitus.

Tum sub notanda est summula;

Letus timescit gaudio:

Prefectus, ac spem deuorat:

Aurum uelut iam conditum:

VIII (left)
Cambridge, Corpus Christi College, MS. 23, fo 64r, detail showing hands 1 and 3 (see pp. 105–6)

IX (right)
Cambridge, Corpus Christi College, MS. 23, fo 56v, detail showing hand 2 (see pp. 105–6)

C um predicatur ipse uerborum dictor

Q uis fecit ut uis uocis expressa intimo

P ul mo ne . & oristorta sub testudine

N unc ex palato & repercusos sonos

N unc temperatur dentium depecane

S itque his agendis lingua plectrum mobile

S mandæ idem . faucium sic fistulas

S pirare . flatu concinentes consono

U t uerba in ipsis explicent meatibus

U el extaioris cimbalis profarier

H unc pressa parte labra . nunc hiantia

D ubitas neuera posse naturæ flatum

C ui facta formæ . qualis esse primtaus

h anc nempe factor uertere ut libet potest

P ositas que leges texere ac retexere

L inguam loquela neministram postulet

V issare nostri numinis potentiam

F lucais liquenas aequoris praessic pede

N atura fluxa accenius in solidum eo te

Q uam dispar illis legibus quis condita est

S olæ natatus ferre ; fert uestigia

H abe usitatum munus hoc diuinitas

Q ue uera nobis colitur in xpo & patre

co uas loquelam . perctaum claudis gradu

S ur dis fruendam reddere audientiam

D onare cecis lucis insuetam diem

h aec siquis amens fabulosa existimat

Pones eos ut clibanum ignis in tempore uultus tui ·
dns in ira sua conturbabit eos & deuorabit eos ignis ·
Fructum eorum de terra perdes · & semen eorum
a filiis hominum ·
Quo declinauerunt in te mala · cogitauerunt
consilia · que non potuerunt stabilire ·
Inpones eos dorsum · in reliquus tuis prepa
rabis uultum eorum ·
Exaltare dne in uirtute tua · cantabimus
& psallemus uirtutes tuas · INT PROASSVP
TIONE MATVTINA PSALMVS DAVID ·
DS DS MEVS RESPICE ME · QVARE ME DERELI
quisti · longe a salute mea uerba delictorum meorum ·
Ds meus clamabo p diem & non exaudies ·
& nocte & non ad insipientiam mihi ·
Tu autem in sco habitas · laus istrahel · In te spera
uerunt patres nri speraueri & liberasti eos ·
Ad te clamauerunt & salui facti sunt · in te
speraueri & non sunt confusi ·
Ego autem sum uermis & non homo · obpro
brium hominum & abiectio plebis ·
Omnes uidentes me deriserunt me · locuti sunt
labiis & mouerunt caput ·

X Cambridge, Corpus Christi College, MS. 411, fo 15r (see p. 108)

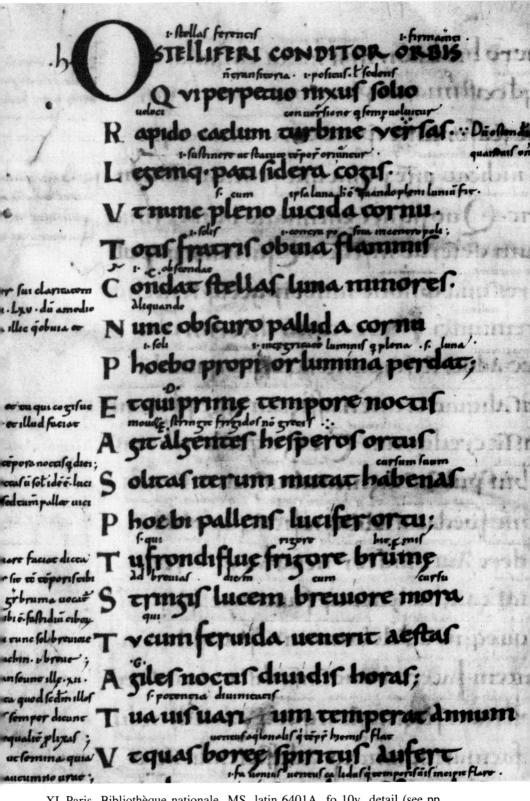

XI Paris, Bibliothèque nationale, MS. latin 6401A, fo 10v, detail (see pp. 131–2)

pseuenuerit usq: infinem . hicsaluuserit .

INSTERELITATE PLUUIAE . Scdm
Nitt. Dixithc discipulissuis .   MATHEUM .
Misereor turbe . quiaiam triduo pseuerant .
mecum . &nhabent qd manducent . Et dimittere
eosnolo . nedeficiant inuia . Et dicunt ei discipli
Undeergo nob indeserto panes tantos . utsaturem
turba tanta? &aitillishc . Quot panes habeatis?
Atilli dixer . Septem . &paucos pisciculos . Etprece
pit turbe . utdiscuberent sup terra . Etaccipiens
septem panes . &pisces . &gratias agens . fregit &dedit
discipulissuis . Etdiscipuli deder populo . &come
der omis . &saturati sunt . Etqd supfuit defragmentis .
tuler septem spostas plenas . Erant aute quiman
ducauer quattuor milia hominu . exter paruulos
&mulieres . Etdimissaturba ascendit innauicula .
&discipuli eiuscum eo .   ITEM PRO UBER
TATE PLUUIAE . Scdm LUCAM .
Nitt. Factum+ inuna dieru . &hic ascendit in
nauiculam &discipuli eius . &ait adillos. Transfre
temus trans stagnum . &ascender. Nauigantibus
aute illis. obdormiut . Et descendit pcella uenti
instagnu . &coplebatur fluctibus &periclitabantur.
Accedentes aute . suscitauer eum dicentes. Precep
tor . perimus. Atille surgens . increpauit uentum
&tempestate aque . &cessauit . Et facta e tranquilli

XII Firenze, Biblioteca Medicea Laurenziana, MS. Plut. XVII.20
[unfoliated] (see pp. 117–20)

INCIPIT EVANGELIUM SECUNDUM MATHEUM ·

LIBER GENERA

TIONIS IHŪ XPI FILII DAUID · FILII ABRAHAM ·
Abraham genuit isaac . Isaac autem genuit iacob · Iacob
autem genuit iudam &frs eius · Iudas autem genuit pha _
_ res & zaram dethamar · Phares autem genuit esrom .
Esrom autem genuit aram · Aram autem genuit ami _
_ nadab · Aminadab autem genuit naason · Naason autē
genuit salmon · Salmon autem genuit booz derachab ·
Booz autem genuit obech ex ruth · Obech autem genuit
iesse · Iesse autem . genuit dauid regem · Dauid autē
rex genuit salomonem . ex ea que fuit urię · Salomon
autem genuit roboam · Roboā autem genuit abiā ·
Abia autem genuit asa · Asa autem genuit iosaphath ·
Iosaphath autem genuit ioram · Ioram autem genuit
oziam · Ozias autem genuit ioatham · Ioathā autē
genuit achaz · Achaz autem genuit ezechiam · Ezechi _
as autem genuit manassen · Manases autem genuit
amon · Amon autem genuit iosiam · Iosias autem
genuit iechoniam &frs eius · in transmigratione baby _
_ lonis · Et post transmigrationem babylonis · iecho _
_ nias genuit salathihel · Salathihel autem genuit

QVI ECCL̃AE ANGLORꝰ MODERNO
tempore celeste fidus conferre digna
tus est · ut beatam alfegum · quem prius
habebat archipontificam · nunc se gaudeat
habere martyrem eius intercessione illagint
que ipsum coronauit in glo · uos conseruet & in
mundo.
Monas istius patris magnifica & martyris almi

XIV Paris, Bibliothèque nationale, MS. latin 987, fo 89r, detail showing a specimen of Style IV Anglo-Caroline minuscule from part 2 of the book (see pp. 139–40)

XVI.

XV (a) Cambridge, Corpus Christi College, MS. 57, fo 85r, detail showing mid-eleventh-century supply (in imitative script) to repair a damaged section (see pp. 153–4)

14
15
16
17
18

XV (b) Cambridge, Corpus Christi College, MS. 57, fo 101v, detail showing erasure and replacement in imitative script on lines 16–17 (see pp. 153–4)

minimē hēr anfiqua vt ce fanctie in hac htania
expeff apparēt.

S cē clemens	S cē remegi
S cē fixte	S cē germane
S cē corneli	S cē maure
S cē cipriane	S cē placide
S cē laurenti	S cē columbane
S cī uincenti · ii ·	S cē antoni
S cē apollonaris	S cē arfeni
S cē geruafi	S cē machari
S cē protafi	S cē laurentine
S cē xpophore	O mffcī confeffores
S cē georgii	O mffcī monachi & herem
S cē dionifii cum focuf	S cā felicitaf
S cī iustachii cū sociis	S cā perpetua
S cē berafme	S cā maria magdalene
S cē ofuuolde	S cā fcolaftica
O mffcī martyres orate	S cā agatha
S cī benedicte · ii ·	S cā agnef
S cē maiiine	S cā cecilia
S cē hilari	S cā lucia
S cē filuefter	S cā brigida
S cē gregori	S cā eugenia
S cē auguftine	S cā eulalia
S cē archberhte	S cā petronella

Hoc pfalteriū laminis argenteis deaurat
et gēmis ornatū, quondā fuit N. Cantuar
Archiepī, tandem venit in manus Thoma
Becket quondā Cant archiepī q̃ testatū
eft in veteri fcripto.

XVI Cambridge, Corpus Christi College, MS. 411, fo 140v, showing a
specimen of Style-IV Anglo-Caroline minuscule added to the book
illustrated in plate X (see pp. 60–1)

Worcester, Cathedral Library, MSS. Q.8 (fos 165–172) + Add. 7 (fos 1–6); El Escorial, Real Biblioteca, MS. E.II.1 (eleventh-century provenance Horton, in Dorset); Oxford, Bodleian Library, MS. Bodley 311 (*S.C.* 2122), giving the scribe's name as Iohannes (the book is of later eleventh-century Exeter provenance);[241] Rouen, Bibliothèque municipale, MS. U.107 (1385), fos 20–26. Finally, London, British Library, MS. Cotton Vespasian B.x (fos 31–124), apparently of late mediaeval Worcester provenance, and supposedly deriving from a late tenth-century exemplar written at St Augustine's Abbey, Canterbury, is usually thought to have been written *ca* 1000.[242] Its distinctive Caroline script – tending towards the elongated and narrowed forms found at Worcester in the early eleventh century – shares a generic likeness with London, British Library, MS. Cotton Nero A.i (fos 70–177),[243] a manuscript once used (and presumably owned) by Archbishop Wulfstan and normally assigned to the early eleventh century.[244] Also usually attributed to Worcester in the earlier eleventh century are London, British Library, MS. Royal 6.A.vii, and Oxford, Bodleian Library, MS. Tanner 3 (*S.C.* 9823),[245] as well as the Latin addition to BL MS. Cotton

---

Library, MS. Royal 15.C.x, of Rochester provenance but apparently written (Bishop, *English Caroline Minuscule*, p. 4) - at least in part - at St Augustine's, Canterbury; its (presumptively Continental) exemplar must also have been loaned into England for copying. Mr Bishop was ambivalent about BL MS. Royal 15.C.x: while attributing it to Canterbury, he said that this was 'not confirmed by the aspect of the script' (*ibid.*); he also compared its first hand (fos 1–79) with the script of a Worcester charter and with CCCO 197 (*ibid.*, p. xxii).

[241] This name may, of course, be derived from the exemplar.

[242] For some reproductions from this manuscript, see *Aethici Istrici Cosmographia*, facs. ed. Bishop (giving as plates A–B fos 34r, 122v). Cf. Ker, *Catalogue*, p. 268 (no. 206); Gneuss, 'A preliminary list', no. 386. Further development of this type of script is perhaps to be seen in the work of the scribe who wrote London, British Library, MSS. Harley 3376 (and its detached fragments) and Cotton Vespasian D.xv, fos 102–121 (as well as glosses in Cambridge, University Library, MS. Ff.4.42 [1285]: cf. also n. 239, above): Bishop, 'The Corpus Martianus Capella', p. 258; for a possibility of localising Harley 3376 at Worcester in the thirteenth century, see Franzen, *The Tremulous Hand*, pp. 11, 73–4, 81, 136; see also Dumville, 'The Harley Glossary: origin and provenance' (forthcoming).

[243] Fully reproduced in *A Wulfstan Manuscript*, facs. ed. Loyn.

[244] Ker, *Books, Collectors*, pp. 9–13, 15–18. Another such, part of which could have been written at Worcester, is the pontifical of Archbishop Wulfstan: cf. n. 282, below.

[245] Gneuss, 'A preliminary list', nos 465 and 667. To these should be added Cambridge, Corpus Christi College, MS. 190, part 1 (cf. n. 228, above). For a useful discussion of CCCC MS. 201, pp. 8–151 & 167–169 (Ker, *Catalogue*, pp. 82–90, no. 49.B), which contains Wulfstanian texts, see *The Benedictine Office*, ed. Ure, pp. 9–12; for reproductions, see Ångström, *Studies*, plates III–V (showing pp. 121, 147, 167), and *Wulfstan's Canons of Edgar*, ed. Fowler, frontispiece (showing part of p. 99). Glasgow, University Library, MS. Hunter V.5.1 (431) is usually assigned to Worcester in this period, at least in part: Ker, *English Manuscripts*, pp. 52–3 (cf.

Nero E.i, part 2, fos 185–186 (the remnants of what is now an Old English manuscript of *ca* A.D. 1000),[246] but their palaeographical affiliations have not yet been worked out in detail.

All these manuscripts are written in Anglo-Caroline Style I. While not numerous, they exhibit a range of subject-matter not paralleled by surviving specimens attributable to Winchester and therefore extend the range of Style-I usage beyond what is visible from that other principal centre of the style.[247] There is one further dimension to this. Although Worcester Cathedral had, by *ca* A.D. 1000, a large and well organised archive of episcopal land-charters, rather few single sheets have survived to the present.[248] Our knowledge of the chronological development of Worcester script is consequently attenuated (but it must be recorded that the position at Winchester is much worse).[249] Nevertheless, a charter issued by Bishop Oswald in 984 has been seen as marking a stage in the development of its practice of Anglo-Caroline Style I: Mr Bishop has noted that this document's Caroline script resembles that of Oxford, Corpus Christi College, MS. 197, our copy of Æthelwold's bilingual Rule of St Benedict. That observation has sometimes been seen as providing grounds for an attribution of CCCO 197 to Worcester, but the deduction is unnecessary, as we shall see.[250]

---

p. 8); Gneuss, 'A preliminary list', no. 261. Elsewhere, I have given reasons for taking a different view of its date and make-up: Dumville, 'Copying an exemplar'. Another pair of manuscripts in Style-I Anglo-Caroline (of *saec.* x/xi), associated by Bishop (*English Caroline Minuscule*, p. 20, n. 1) with Worcester but having later mediaeval provenances at Winchester Cathedral and St Peter's Abbey, Gloucester, respectively, is Cambridge, Corpus Christi College, MS. 448, fos 87–103 (contrary to what I said about date and origin in 'English Square minuscule script: the background and earliest phases', p. 176, following Bishop), and (sharing a scribe) London, British Library, MS. Royal 13.C.v (where fos 1–2 constitute a mid-eleventh-century supply in replacement for a single lost leaf); later dates sometimes given for these manuscripts are wide of the mark, it seems to me.

246 Ker, *Catalogue*, p. 217 (no. 166). Gneuss, 'A preliminary list', no. 345, has mistakenly run these leaves (whose Latin addition in fact belongs to the mid- or later eleventh century) together with fos 181–184 which are fragments of a quite different book, a cartulary written probably in the second half of the eleventh century (cf. Ker, *Books, Collectors*, pp. 49–51) and of which other fragments survive in London, British Library, MS. Additional 46204.

247 For a characterisation of the contents of books produced at Winchester after A.D. 963 (in contrast with those produced in the same period at Canterbury), see Bishop, 'Notes', p. 323.

248 For a survey, see Ker, *Books, Collectors*, pp. 31–59.

249 The arguments to the contrary by Pierre Chaplais have been refuted: Keynes, *The Diplomas of King Æthelred*, pp. 20–8; cf. Dumville, *Wessex and England*, pp. 78–83.

250 For the charter of A.D. 984 – London, British Library, Additional Charter 19794 (*Facsimiles*, ed. Bond, III.32) – see Sawyer, *Anglo-Saxon Charters*, no. 1347. On its scripts' resemblance to those of CCCO 197, see Ker, *Catalogue*, p. xxvi, and Bishop, *English Caroline Minuscule*, p. xxii. Bishop (*ibid.*) also compared the Latin

'It has been repeatedly pointed out that there was close collaboration between Winchester and Worcester during the period of the Benedictine reform':[251] quite so, and yet I must venture to suggest that no evidence has been adduced which would demonstrate this proposition for the period *ca* 960 to *ca* 1000. In view of that lack, it is necessary to ask why it was that the two centres came to share in the practice of Anglo-Caroline Style I. We have no evidence, and no particular reason to suspect, that Æthelwold's and Oswald's houses practised mutual colonisation.[252] The simplest explanation may reside in their Continental affiliations. Oswald was at Fleury in the years before 958. Æthelwold had hoped to go abroad in the mid-950s, but was prevented by the royal offer of the minster at Abingdon.[253] Instead he sent his disciple, Osgar (subsequently abbot of Abingdon), to Fleury: the precise dates of Osgar's sojourn there are not known, but it fell in the decade 954 x 964.[254] It is accordingly quite possible that the two men were monks there together in the period 954 x 958.[255] To these may be added a third, Germanus, who had a long and complicated career but who became (*inter alia*) abbot of Oswald's foundation at Winchcombe.[256] What they learned at Fleury may have been decisive in the history of script in England.[257]

---

script with the first hand of London, British Library, MS. Royal 15.C.x: for the complications which that comparison brings in its train, see above, n. 240.

[251] Gretsch, 'Æthelwold's translation', p. 133. Dr Alicia Corrêa is re-examining liturgical sources to see what evidence bearing on this issue may be discovered. On the literary culture of Worcester in the period, see Keller, *Zur Litteratur* and *Die litterarischen Bestrebungen*.

[252] In this context, one is bound to wonder what became of the minster (*monasterium*) which Oswald had purchased and ruled at Winchester before he went to Fleury: Byrhtferth, *Vita Sancti Oswaldi*, §2 (ed. Raine, *The Historians*, I.410–11). Oda 'munera perplurima concessit, cum quibus sibi monasterium quod est in Wintonia positum acquisiuit, donando digno pretio'. One ecclesiastic has been identified who may have changed affiliations: Foldbriht, monk of Glastonbury and Abingdon, who perhaps became abbot of Oswald's foundation at Pershore; cf. *Wulfstan of Winchester*, edd. & transl. Lapidge & Winterbottom, p. 20, n. 3.

[253] Wulfstan, *Vita Sancti Æthelwoldi*, §§10 and 14 (*Wulfstan of Winchester*, edd. & transl. Lapidge & Winterbottom, pp. 18–19, 26–7). The presumption is that Æthelwold would have gone to Fleury if he had succeeded in gaining royal permission to leave the country. Bishop ('Lincoln Cathedral MS 182', p. 73) was mistaken to place Æthelwold himself at Fleury.

[254] *Wulfstan of Winchester*, edd. & transl. Lapidge & Winterbottom, p. 26, n. 3.

[255] *Ibid.*, p. 27, n. 4.

[256] Lapidge, 'Abbot Germanus'; see also below, pp. 79–85.

[257] Before we go so far, we must take account of T.A.M. Bishop's thought that a single Continental style of Caroline minuscule might lie behind Anglo-Caroline Style I (cf. *English Caroline Minuscule*, p. xxii). If this is correct, we need to ask whether the ninth- and tenth-century script of Fleury can supply the model: there has as yet been no study of it, but the ground has been cleared in preparation by Mostert, *The Library of Fleury*; cf. Pellegrin, *Bibliothèques retrouvées*, pp. 129–297. The evidence for various English scribes at Fleury must also be considered: Bishop, *English Caroline*

It has long been common ground that monasteries of the Æthelwold connexion retained, at least throughout the founder's lifetime, a unity of purpose and practice which would have its reflex in scriptorial traditions. These houses therefore contained in fact or in principle ateliers from which issued books (and documents, no doubt) written in Anglo-Caroline Style I. In as much as the work of T.A.M. Bishop has made it clear that from Worcester came forth similar scribal productions,[258] one must extend the assumption made about Æthelwold's monasteries to those of the Oswald connexion. The most securely attributed manuscript from the first generation of these houses' existence is Orléans, Bibliothèque municipale, MS. 127 (105), a sacramentary of Winchcombe origin:[259] this is written in Style I, thus confirming the hypothesis. With the aid of one further manuscript the geographical range can probably be extended. London, British Library, MS. Harley 2904 is a lavish Gallican psalter

---

Minuscule, p. xii(–xiii), n. 2 (but cf. p. 16, n. 1), and p. 18; Vezin, 'Leofnoth'; Temple, *Anglo-Saxon Manuscripts*, pp. 59 (no. 32: Paris, Bibliothèque nationale, MS. latin 6401), 65 (no. 42: London, British Library, MS. Harley 2506), and 66 (no. 43: Orléans, Bibliothèque municipale, MS. 175 [152]). Francis Wormald ('L'Angleterre', p. 242) thought of these two last as exclusively tied to one another. But whether the association with Fleury can account wholly for Anglo-Caroline Style I is a nice question. Likewise, Mr Bishop (*English Caroline Minuscule*, p. xxii) wondered also whether Style-II Anglo-Caroline – which he described as 'well characterized' (rather too hopefully, I fear) and 'comparatively small and elegant' – had a single underlying model. The implication of its English distribution would be that it perhaps resulted from Dunstan's stay at Ghent. In chapter I, above, I saw fit to describe Style II as representing instead a particular attitude to Caroline script. One might also put the question whether the same could be true of Style I: the various forms are quite divergent while still being the result of a desire to produce a 'pure' Caroline style. Cf. also p. 143, below.

258 *Ibid.* For the corpus of manuscripts of known mediaeval Worcester provenance, including some of these specimens, see Turner, *Early Worcester MSS*, pp. lv–lxxi, and Ker, *Medieval Libraries*, pp. 205–15.

259 Temple, *Anglo-Saxon Manuscripts*, p. 58 (no. 31) and plate 139 (showing part of p. 8); Homburger, 'Eine spätkarolingische Schule von Corbie', p. 426 and fig. 184 (opposite p. 419: showing part of p. 150); Leroquais, *Les Sacramentaires*, I.89–91; Gremont & Donnat, 'Fleury, Le Mont Saint-Michel'; Lapidge, 'Abbot Germanus'. Unless it can be shown to have been written later than 975, I see no reason to distance its execution from Winchcombe Abbey. This important manuscript deserves a thorough palaeographical analysis. For a palaeographical and liturgical link with London, British Library, MS. Harley 2904, see O. Homburger, *Art Bulletin* 10 (1927/8) 401. For further reproduction see Samaran & Marichal, *Catalogue des manuscrits*, VII.219 and plate IX (it is there dated '985[?] x 1009', the former for reasons which will not bear scrutiny). Its script appears to be of the variety of Style-I Anglo-Caroline assigned (mistakenly) by T.A.M. Bishop to Abingdon Abbey. This opens up the possibility that manuscripts written in such a script-form should be attributed to houses of the Oswald connexion: examples would be Lincoln, Cathedral Library, MS. 182 (cf. n. 117, above); and Malibu (Cal.), J. Paul Getty Museum, MS. 9 (cf. Boutemy, 'Les feuillets de Damme').

accompanied by a litany of the saints:[260] it was written in the later tenth century in a monumental Style-I Anglo-Caroline minuscule, probably by a single scribe. An attribution of this book to the Old Minster, Winchester, was accepted by T.A.M. Bishop, but unwisely – for the evidence adduced in support of that localisation will not withstand critical scrutiny.[261] On the other hand, a case has been argued for this manuscript's origin at Ramsey,[262] Oswald's principal monastic founda-tion, established in 968/9. While not watertight,[263] the theory does account for features of the litany which are left unexplained by the hypothesis of the volume's creation at Winchester. The following aspects of this text are worthy of remark. The invocation of martyrs concludes with five from Britain: SS. Alban, Oswald (of Northumbria), Cenhelm (Kenelm of Winchcombe), Edmund (of East Anglia and Bury St Edmunds), and Æthelberht (of East Anglia). There is a striking relationship with texts of comparable geographical origin or party-filiation.[264]

---

[260] *Anglo-Saxon Litanies*, ed. Lapidge, pp. 203–9 (no. XXIV); cf. pp. 74–5 for a brief introduction. Where, in what follows, my readings differ from Lapidge's, they result from re-collation with the manuscript.

[261] *English Caroline Minuscule*, p. 14, relying on the evidence presented in *The Salisbury Psalter*, edd. Sisam & Sisam, p. 5 (with nn. 1 and 3); there and at p. 75, n. 2, this manuscript is said to belong 'fairly certainly' and 'probably' to Winchester. Cf. *ibid.*, p. 48: '*c.* 975–1000, Winchester (?)'. But the support is unimpressive: it consists of two textual oddities which MS. Harley 2904 shares with three Winchester psalters; however, these all belong to the mid-eleventh century or later and can therefore hardly be determinative of the origin of a book written as much as a century earlier. The Winchester case was admitted by Temple, *Anglo-Saxon Manuscripts*, pp. 64–5 (no. 41). For remarks on the artistic relationship of Harley 2904 with the psalter in Cambridge, University Library, MS. Ff.1.23 (1156), see Wormald, 'Decorated initials', pp. 107–10.

[262] Niver, 'The psalter'. Sisam & Sisam, *The Salisbury Psalter*, p. 5, n. 2, quoted Byrhtferth, *Enchiridion* (ed. Crawford, p. 184), to show that the Gallican was the psalter-text used at Ramsey (in A.D. 1011, at least). Lapidge, 'Abbot Germanus', pp. 107–8, has attributed Paris, Bibliothèque municipale, MS. latin 7299, fos 3–12, a kalendar coeval with BL MS. Harley 2904, to Ramsey. Boutemy ('Influences carolingiennes', p. 433) argued that a Ramsey artist worked in both Harley 2904 and Orléans, Bibliothèque municipale, MS. 175 (152) – cf. Temple, *Anglo-Saxon Manuscripts*, p. 66, no. 43 –, written at Fleury during the abbacy of Abbo (988–1004).

[263] Niver's case does seem conclusive, however, for an origin in the circle of Oswald. Cf. below, p. 63.

[264] Comparable, that is, if we accept that the book was written in one of Oswald's houses, most naturally Ramsey. In the three tables which follow, the roman numerals after the shelf-marks refer to those in *Anglo-Saxon Litanies*, ed. Lapidge. His litanies nos IX (London, British Library, MS. Additional 28188) and XXIII (London, British Library, MS. Harley 863), both from later eleventh-century Exeter, are clearly dependent ultimately on no. XXII. The litany (XII) in London, British Library, MS. Arundel 60, has most of these saints, but dispersed and in subordinate positions. We

TABLE I

Harley 2904 (XXIV)	Cotton Vit. A.vii (XXII)	Vat. Reg. lat. 12 (XLV)	CUL Ff.1.23 (I)
Albane	[Albane]		*Kenelme*
Osuualde	Oswolde (Saluii)		Osuuolde
Kenelme	Kenelme		
Eadmunde	Eadmunde	Eadmunde ora .ii.	Eadmunde
	Eadwarde	Eadwarde	
	Ælfheah		
	Æðelrede		
Aeþelbyrchte	Aðelbrihte	Æþelbyrhte	
		Albane	Albane
		(Georgii)	
		(Proiecti)	
		Kynelme	

The list of confessors invoked tells another story. That in Harley 2904 begins 'SANCTE BENEDICTE .iii.'. Benedict alone appears in capitals and with a triple invocation. It is not uncommon for him to head the list of confessors, but such a prominent invocation may be found elsewhere in Anglo-Saxon litanies only in Orléans, Bibliothèque municipale, MS. 127 (105), attributed to Oswald's house at Winchcombe.[265] When we reach the British confessors, we find the following.

---

find Oswald-Æthelberht-Cenelm in no. XVI.ii (London, British Library, MS. Cotton Galba A.xiv, fos 90r–97v), but in a different context. In these tables, square brackets containing a saint's name indicate editorial supply, while round brackets indicate invocations of international saints irrelevant in the present context; italics show that in that text a saint's name has been highlighted in some way.

[265] For Harley 2904 see *Anglo-Saxon Litanies*, ed. Lapidge, p. 205 (Benedict is also specially mentioned in an *Oratio post psalterium* on fos 213r–214v: cf. Deshusses & Hourlier, 'Saint Benoît dans les livres liturgiques', for the liturgical context); for Orléans 127 (105) see *Anglo-Saxon Litanies*, ed. Lapidge, p. 221. Benedict heads the list of confessors in nos I (Sancte BENEDICTE ora), II (Sancte Benedicte. .ii.), III.i and ii, VII.ii (SANCTE BENEDICTE. .ii.), VIII.i and ii, IX.ii, X, XI (Sancte Benedicte. .ii.), XII, XV (SANCTE BENEDICTE), XVI.i, XVIII, XXI, XXII.i and ii (SANCTE BENEDICTE), XXX, XXXII, XXXIII, XXXIV, XXXVI, XL, XLI.iii, XLII.i and ii (Sancte Benedicte. .ii.), XLV (Sancte Benedicte ora. .ii.), XLVI. In nos VI, XIII, XXVII, XXXVIII, he is low on the list, but gets a double invocation. Various different levels may be discerned here. In no. VII.ii (an addition, made either at Canterbury or at Abingdon, in Cambridge, Corpus Christi College, MS. 411) he is capitalised and invoked doubly. In nos II, XI, XLII.i and ii, and XLV he is invoked twice (the first two are from Canterbury, the third from Winchester, and the last from Bury St Edmunds but perhaps written at Canterbury). In nos I, XV, XXII.i and ii he is

TABLE II

Harley 2904 (XXIV)	Cotton Vit. A.vii (XXII)	Vat. Reg. lat. 12 (XLV)	CUL Ff.1.23 (I)
		Augustine cum sociis tuis	
		Pauline	
Cudberchte		Cuthberhte	Cuthberhte
Guðlace	Guðlace	Byrine	Machu
Uuilfride	Neote	Botulfe ora .ii.	Budoce
Iohannes	(Arseni)	Hiurmine ora .ii.;	
		Guthlace	Samson
Ceadda		Dunstane	Patrici
Aerconwolde	Erconwoldi	Eorconwolde	Guthlace
		Aþelwolde	Wilfrede
Swiðhune	Byrine	Oswolde	Swithune
Birine	Swyðune	Swiðune	Birine
Iudoce	Iudoce	Iudoce	Iudoce
	Grimbalde	Grimbalde	
Machu(te)	Botulfe	Machu	
	Aðulfe		
	Yuo	Hyue	
	Felix	(Antoni)	
	Dunstane		
	Aðelwolde		
	[+2 lost]		

What struck Charles Niver about this group, apart from the obvious addition of Winchester saints at the end, was the domination of the list by six saints from north of the Thames – the Northumbrians Cuthbert, Wilfrid, and John of Beverley; Ceadda (a Northumbrian) of Lichfield and Guthlac of Crowland, both in (Greater) Mercia, and Erconwald of London.[266] In spite of the Winchester tail,[267] this is not what one would expect to see in a litany in a book of Winchester origin.

---

simply capitalised: no. XV is from Canterbury, while the origins of nos I and XXII are under discussion in this chapter. Of those litanies where Benedict is low on the list of confessors but invoked doubly, VI is now a twelfth-century Worcester text, XIII certainly and XXVII probably come from Canterbury, while XXXVIII is from a lost book of uncertain origin.

[266] Niver, 'The psalter', pp. 667–72. One wonders whether the presence of St Erconwald symbolises the important role which the see of London had played in East Anglia for much of the tenth century.

[267] Swithhun, Birinus, Iudoc, Grimbald, Machu(tus).

The list of virgins invoked returns us to the locality, introducing us to
SS. Ætheldryth, Sexburh, Wihtburh, and Werburh (in the guise of
'Penburg' or 'Wenburga') and thus to a strong connexion with Ely.

TABLE III

Harley 2904 *(XXIV)*	*Cotton Vit.* *A. vii (XXII)*	*Vat. Reg.* *lat. 12 (XLV)*	*CUL Ff.1.23* *(I)*
Æþeldriða	Æþeldryða	Æþeldryða	Æþeldryða
Sæxburg	Wihtburh	Wihtburh	Sexburga
Wictburg[268]	Sexburh	Sexburh	
Penburg[269]			
	Eormenhild	Eormenhyld	Eormenhilda
		Eadburh	Eadburga
		Æþelburh	(Eugenia)
	(Anastasia)	Ælfgyfu	(Anastasia)
			(Sabina)
			(Potentiana)
			(Praxedis)
			(Petronella)
			Wenburga
			(Theodosia)
			(Eufraxia)
	(Iuliana)		(Iuliana)
	(Marina)		(Eulalia)
		Toua	Toua
	Myldreð	Myldryða	Mildryth
	Æglflæð[270]		
	Edgyð		
	[+ 1 illegible]		

---

[268] Wihtburh appears again in MS. Arundel 60 (XII: cf. n. 264, above), in the 'Douce
Psalter' (XXXII) from Crowland, and in the sacramentary of Robert of Jumièges
(XL).

[269] No St Penburh or Wenburh is known, and (from the context) one must presume that
this is the more familiar Werburh. The errors (which must have arisen when an
ancestor in Insular script was being copied) imply that a single source-text lies
ultimately behind nos I and XXIV and that the text in which the error occurred was
not executed at Ely. The omission of Werburh from nos XXII and XLV may indicate
that their scribes (or the scribe of a hypothetical hyparchetype) did not recognise
'Wenburg(a)', much less 'Penburg', and dropped her name. St Werburh recurs in nos
VI (a rewritten, twelfth-century text from Worcester), XII, and XXXII.

[270] St Æglflæd (*sic*) recurs, alone of English virgins, in the second, short litany in this
manuscript. She appears otherwise only in the derivative IX.i and ii and in BL MS.

The name-forms in Harley 2904 are more archaic, but clearly the same list of local virgins underlies all of these. Of all the surviving Anglo-Saxon litanies St 'Penburg'/'Wenburga' is found only in Harley 2904 and CUL Ff.1.23. St Wihtburh was translated from East Dereham (Norfolk) to Ely before 984.[271]

The deduction that MS. Harley 2904 was written at Ramsey is not absolutely certain; but, if it was not executed there, we have to appeal to another house in the Mercian-Northumbrian-East Anglian circle of Archbishop Oswald. There can be little doubt, in the light of this evidence, that Harley 2904 is not a Winchester book.[272]

What also emerges with great clarity from this investigation is the close relationship with London, British Library, MS. Cotton Vitellius A.vii, fos 1–112. The mid-eleventh-century provenance of this (now badly burned) pontifical was Exeter Cathedral: two derivatives of it were written there at that time, BL MSS. Additional 28188 and Harley 863, and the Cottonian manuscript itself bears additions in Exeter script (fos 1r–15r, 54v–71r; and perhaps 71r–112 in another hand).[273] But Neil Ker long ago deduced from its first litany that it was written at Ramsey;[274] and T.A.M. Bishop has pointed out that fos 15v–54r (including the litanies) are in script not identified as a product of the Exeter scriptorium.[275]

Arundel 60 (XII: cf. above, nn. 264, 268). Æthelflæd was perhaps the abbess of Romsey (Hants.), perhaps in the 990s: Knowles *et al.*, *The Heads*, p. 218; however, Ker (*Catalogue*, p. 279) has taken her to be a saintly queen buried at the Fenland abbey of Ramsey (cf. n. 274, below).

271 Rollason, *Saints and Relics*, pp. 209–11. On Wihtburh in her Ely context, see Ridyard, *The Royal Saints*, pp. 176–210.

272 If one were to wish, for whatever reason, to save the hypothesis of an origin in a house of the Æthelwold connexion, Ely would seem to be the only credible choice. But one would then have to explain the invocation of St *P*enburh.

273 Bishop, *English Caroline Minuscule*, p. 24, n. 1, has given a brief analysis of the scripts. For MS. Harley 863, a glossed psalter whose litany is the element derivative of MS. Cotton Vitellius A.vii, see Ker, *Catalogue*, pp. 306–7 (no. 232), and cf. *Anglo-Saxon Litanies*, ed. Lapidge, p. 74. For BL MS. Additional 28188 see *ibid.*, p. 67, and Gneuss, 'Liturgical books', pp. 131–4.

274 *Catalogue*, pp. 278–9 (no. 213). Since Ker wrote, the British Library authorities have divided Vitellius A.vii (the whole, composite, codex) into ten volumes. In Ker's notice, the date '1130' for the death of St Olaf (named in the litany: *Anglo-Saxon Litanies*, ed. Lapidge, p. 189) should read 1030; he took St Æglflæd to be not the abbess of Romsey but a queen buried at Ramsey. The only other litany in an Anglo-Saxon manuscript in which St Olaf is named (apart from the derivatives of Vitellius A.vii) is that in London, Lambeth Palace Library, MS. 427 (*ibid.*, p. 215), but that text is a fifteenth-century addition (*ibid.*, p. 76).

275 *English Caroline Minuscule*, p. 24, n. 1. The manuscript requires a thorough palaeographical analysis.Cf. Dumville, *Liturgy*, p. 79. For further remarks on it, see M. Lapidge in *The Anglo-Saxon Chronicle*, gen. edd. Dumville & Keynes, XVII.xci, n. 49. The core of the book (fos 15v–54r) is in script which would suit a date earlier

That part of the book is usually attributed to the first half of the eleventh century. Certainly its Old English name-forms are linguistically more modern than those in MS. Harley 2904. It also takes note of recent martyrs – Edward (978), Ælfheah (1012) –, of recently dead confessors – Æthelwold (984), Dunstan (988) –, and of recently translated saints – Æthelred (968 x 992, a Ramsey translation), Swithhun (971), Neot (975 x 1013), Botulf and Athulf (see above), Yvo (Ramsey, 1001) and Felix (Ramsey, 1026), and Mildred (last in 1030).[276] (This pattern is continued further in Vat. Reg. lat. 12 – Botulf and Iurmin; Yvo; Toua, at Thorney.)[277]

Vitellius A.vii can perhaps be attributed with more confidence to Ramsey (after 1030),[278] but the case for Harley 2904 is not to be neglected; it may certainly, in any case, be taken to have emerged from a house of the Oswald connexion. Its date can perhaps be more precisely reckoned by establishing as a *terminus ante quem* the earliest of the

---

than 1030 but which cannot be shown to contradict a dating in the 1030s or 1040s: it is not Style-IV Anglo-Caroline (on which see chapter IV, below). Cf. n. 283, below.

[276] On St Neot, see Lapidge, *ibid.*, pp. lxxxvi–lxxxix. On Æthelred (and Æthelberht), see Lapidge, 'Byrhtferth of Ramsey and the early sections', pp. 119–20; cf. Hunter Blair, 'Some observations', pp. 78–82. On Yvo, cf. Rollason, *Saints and Relics*, pp. 187, 227, 229, relying on the *uita* by Goscelin of Saint-Bertin. On Felix, see Niver, 'The psalter', p. 680, following the Ramsey house-history. On Æglflæd, see above, nn. 270 and 274. For a study of the complex history of the cult of St Mildred, see Rollason, *The Mildrith Legend*, as qualified by Sharpe, 'The date'.

[277] On St Toua see Clark, 'Notes on a *Life*'. Toua is invoked in litanies (other than the two last in Table III) in London, British Library, MSS. Arundel 60 (*Anglo-Saxon Litanies*, ed. Lapidge, no. XII) and Harley 863 (no. XXIII: her presence here suggests that she once occurred in MS. Cotton Vitellius A.vii where text has been lost to fire-damage); in Oxford, Bodleian Library, MS. Douce 296 (*S.C.* 21870) (no. XXXII); in Paris, Bibliothèque nationale, MS. latin 8824 (no. XXXVI). Vat. Reg. lat. 12 seems to have some sort of a relationship with the 'Paris Psalter': cf. Harris, 'An illustration', p. 257; but it is not very clear from the litanies that there is such a link.

[278] The date depends wholly on the presence of St Olaf in the longer litany. On him see Hoffmann, *Die heiligen Könige*, pp. 58–89; I do not know whether there is any evidence for the cult of Olaf Haraldsson's christian predecessor, Olaf Tryggvason (995–1000). But if the date (1026) of the translation of St Felix is historically accurate, his presence in the litany is perhaps further evidence to much the same effect. This first appearance of St Olaf in an English liturgical book raises questions about the sources of the tenth- and eleventh-century English missions in Scandinavia: on these in general, see Godfrey, *The Church in Anglo-Saxon England*, pp. 350–61. Important evidence will increasingly come from examination of Anglo-Saxon liturgical manuscript fragments which have survived in Norwegian and Swedish repositories: cf. Gneuss, 'A preliminary list', nos 777, 789, 870–875, 936. For first studies of these see Gjerløw, 'Fragments' (but cf. Dumville, 'On the dating', p. 49) and *Adoratio Crucis*; Alicia Corrêa and I have further investigations in hand. In so far as Style-I Anglo-Caroline specimens are preserved thus, scholars' early attributions to Winchester (rather than to houses of the Oswald connexion) may on palaeographical grounds prove to be wide of the mark.

Fenland translations.[279] As T.A.M. Bishop showed, the scribe of MS. Harley 2904 also wrote the pontifical in Cambridge, Sidney Sussex College, MS. 100 (D.5.15), part 2;[280] we are thus allowed to attribute another Style-I book to Oswald's circle.[281] Such an origin may help to explain why the Sidney Sussex manuscript found its way to Northumbria.[282]

It is necessary also to ask how long Style-I Anglo-Caroline continued to be written in houses associated with Oswald. In this matter the direct evidence must, it seems, be drawn from Worcester, for manuscripts of the early eleventh century are lacking which are attributable to other houses founded by Oswald.[283] Fortunately, we possess in the cartulary known as *Liber Wigorniensis* – London, British Library, MS. Cotton

---

[279] Because of the absence of most of them from the litany in MS. Harley 2904. This would perhaps suggest a date before 992 (or 1001). A *terminus post quem* depends on the cults of the saints invoked. Among the martyrs there, Æthelberht may be the East Anglian king killed by Offa rather than the Kentish martyr translated to Ramsey. Among the virgins, SS. Sexburh and Wihtburh were translated by Bishop Æthelwold (*ob.* 984), Ely's ecclesiastical patron. The evidence of the litanies (clouded though it is by scribal error: cf. n. 269, above) makes it clear that St Werburh must have been culted at Ely in the later tenth century, thus invalidating the conclusions drawn by Ridyard, *The Royal Saints*, p. 209(-10), n. 151. If Ely was reformed in 964 x 971, perhaps in 970 (*Wulfstan of Winchester*, edd. & transl. Lapidge & Winterbottom, pp. xlviii and 39, n. 3), then we should – on this argument – see 970 x 1001 as offering the outermost limits for the execution of MS. Harley 2904.

[280] *English Caroline Minuscule*, p. 14 (no. 16) and plate XIV (showing part of fo 3r and of the additions on fo 14v). For the text see *Two Anglo-Saxon Pontificals*, ed. Banting, pp. xxxix–li, 155–70 (with a plate of fo 6r on p. 156).

[281] One may wonder why Ramsey Abbey would have produced a pontifical, a bishop's service-book. Before 992 the answer would have been that its ecclesiastical patron was Oswald, an archbishop. On Oswald, see Nelson, *Politics and Ritual*, pp. 301–2, 372–4, and 399, n. 130. MS. Cotton Vitellius A.vii, if produced at Ramsey in the 1030s or later, must have been a commission – as Rouen, Bibliothèque municipale, MS. Y.7 (369) must have been from Winchester's New Minster (cf. Dumville, *Liturgy*, pp. 87–8). On Vitellius A.vii see further Nelson, *Politics and Ritual*, pp. 363 and n. 12, 382 and nn. 33–36.

[282] On the Northumbrian additions on fos 13v13–14v10, see Bishop, *English Caroline Minuscule*, p. 14 and plate XIV(*b*): the script is perhaps best characterised as a version of Style-I Anglo-Caroline. Mr Bishop identified the Northumbrian hand also in neumed marginalia in Cambridge, Corpus Christi College, MS. 183, fo 93r/v. These additions were effected at Durham Cathedral. *Ex hypothesi*, the Sidney Sussex manuscript was written at Ramsey for Oswald's use at York; after his death, it passed by gift of a subsequent archbishop to the latter's suffragan at Durham. From the same administrative context, of the union of the sees of Worcester and York, comes the pontifical of Archbishop Wulfstan – London, British Library, MS. Cotton Claudius A.iii, fos 31–86 and 106–150 (ed. Turner, *The Claudius Pontificals*, pp. v–xxviii, 1–88; cf. Ker, *Catalogue*, pp. 177–8, no. 141). For textual links between these two pontificals, see *Two Anglo-Saxon Pontificals*, ed. Banting, p. xli.

[283] The first is the 'Ramsey Pontifical', probably written soon after 1030 (see n. 278) in Style I. For further evidence of some sort of scriptorial continuity at Ramsey, see Bishop, 'Notes', pp. 434 and 185, where he remarked that in some 'Ramsey script of

Tiberius A.xiii, fos 1–118 – a precisely datable book.[284] The latest document (in the original portion) was issued in 996, one of the series of episcopal leases for which the archive is famous;[285] the manuscript is augmented in the hand of Archbishop Wulfstan (*ob*. 1023).[286] These dates of 996 x 1023 can perhaps be narrowed to 996 x 1016 by reference to the apparent resumption of lease-giving in A.D. 1016, involving documents which were not included in the cartulary and which yet superseded charters therein.[287] The Latin script of *Liber Wigorniensis*, in five principal hands, breaks completely with the foregoing tradition of Latin script at Worcester. The scribes wrote similar hands which, in Neil Ker's words,[288] 'suffer mostly from a lack of proportion in height between the ascenders and descenders and the letters on the line'. (In this it was adumbrated in the script represented by some related books mentioned above.)[289] In as much as a group of scribes wrote in this manner, we may be confident that here we see the scriptorium-style of the moment. Ker continued by observing that their script's 'affinities are with the hands employed in English manuscripts in the first half of the eleventh century'.[290] While this is indeed the case, the relationship is with vernacular rather than with Latin script. The earliest datable specimen of Old English script with such proportions belongs to the years 1001 x 1013 and was probably written at the Old Minster, Winchester.[291] In as much as script with such proportions does not seem to represent a sustained and more generally English development of Anglo-Caroline (whereas it perhaps had a wider and longer impact in the vernacular context), we may suppose that it represented a brief phase at Worcester, not outliving (and perhaps entirely coincident with) the

---

the early twelfth century . . . many letter forms recall those of the late tenth' (p. 185). For manuscripts of mediaeval Ramsey provenance see Birch, 'Historical notes'; 'MS Sloane 3548', ed. Bressie; Ker, *Medieval Libraries*, pp. 153–4.

[284] On the two Worcester cartularies in MS. Cotton Tiberius A.xiii, see Ker, *Books, Collectors*, pp. 31–59; the name of this section was given by Finberg, *The Early Charters of the West Midlands*, pp. 15–18.

[285] Sawyer, *Anglo-Saxon Charters*, no. 1381, on fo 89r/v: the hand (iv) was illustrated by Ker, *Books, Collectors*, p. 32.

[286] Ker, *ibid*., pp. 18–20, 54–6.

[287] *Ibid*., pp. 52–4. The documents in question are Sawyer, *Anglo-Saxon Charters*, nos 1388 (A.D. 1016), 1384 (A.D. 1017), 1385 (A.D. 1002 x 1023).

[288] *Books, Collectors*, p. 34.

[289] See p. 55 (and cf. n. 242).

[290] *Books, Collectors*, p. 34. The same may be seen in London, British Library, MS. Cotton Vespasian A.xiv (fos 114–179) – Ker, *ibid*., pp. 20–1 – in which the script has moved towards the new proportions. Wulfstan's own script (see the plate, *ibid*., p. 25, from Copenhagen, Kongelige Biblioteket, MS. G.K.S. 1595.4°, fo 66v), informal as it is, nevertheless partakes very much of the new proportions.

[291] Cambridge, Corpus Christi College, MS. 173 (facs. edd. Flower & Smith, *The Parker Chronicle and Laws*), fos 29v–30r: cf. Dumville, 'Beowulf come lately', and *Wessex and England*, pp. 56–60.

pontificate of Wulfstan (1002–1016 x 1023),[292] who may in any case have been responsible for ordering the construction of the cartulary. It is in the nature of our sources that we have no information as to whether this style spread to other houses of the Oswald connexion: but no specific evidence has been advanced to suggest that Oswald's two successors at Worcester and York, Ealdwulf (992–1002, formerly abbot of Peterborough, a house of the Æthelwold connexion) and Wulfstan (formerly bishop of London, 996–1002), had any particular connexion with his family of monastic houses.[293] Nor is it clear when the unity of that family began to break down: Cyril Hart has suggested that the process began in 992, with the deaths of Oswald and Ealdorman Æthelwine and the transmission of their public offices into the hands of other families.[294] In the work of Byrhtferth, however, we do have some evidence for continuing connexions.[295] Nevertheless, the political events of 1016 are likely to have been responsible for significant changes in the relationships of churches with lay patrons and with one another.[296]

After 1023 the local charter-series from Worcester fails us until the mid- or late 1030s. Four documents – of A.D. 1033 x 1038 (in English), 1038 (in Latin and English), 1042 (in English), and 1053 (in Latin) – all attest to a lack of straightforward continuity of script-style.[297] Indeed the

---

[292] Although a new bishop of Worcester, Leofsige (abbot of Thorney), was appointed in 1016, charter-evidence seems to suggest that Wulfstan continued to be involved in the affairs of the see: Sawyer, *Anglo-Saxon Charters*, no. 1388 (Leofsige, A.D. 1016), no. 1384 (Wulfstan, A.D. 1017), no. 1459 (Wulfstan, perhaps A.D. 1017), no. 1847 (Wulfstan, A.D. 1017). There are other, less precisely dated, documents issued by Wulfstan which could belong to the period 1016 x 1023. Cf. *Sermo Lupi ad Anglos*, ed. Whitelock, pp. 9, 11–12.

[293] *Ibid.*, pp. 7–8, and 'A note on the career'.

[294] Hart, 'The East Anglian chronicle', pp. 276–9.

[295] See above, p. 48 and n. 210, for the transmission of Byrhtferth's hagiography uniquely in a Worcester manuscript. Byrhtferth's *Vita Sancti Ecgwini* was written for the community at Evesham which he visited to prepare for the work of composition: Lapidge, 'Byrhtferth and the *Vita S. Ecgwini*', pp. 341–2 (but his dating depends on conjecture from some disreputable source-material). On Oswald II (nephew of the archbishop) and the continuity of the Ramsey educational tradition, see Lapidge, 'The hermeneutic style', pp. 94–5, 106–7, and Dronke *et al.*, 'Die unveröffentlichen Gedichte', pp. 66–8. Ælfweard, monk of Ramsey, was abbot of Evesham 1013 x 1016–1044 (and bishop of London from 1035): Knowles *et al.*, *The Heads*, pp. 46–7; cf. Whitelock, *Some Anglo-Saxon Bishops of London*, pp. 32–4. After the Norman conquest, the link between Worcester and Ramsey survived or was reestablished, as is attested by a confraternity-agreement of A.D. 1092: *The Cartulary of Worcester*, ed. Darlington, pp. 160–1 (no. 304); cf. also Hunt *et al.*, *A Summary Catalogue*, II, pt 1, pp. 439–40, on Oxford, Bodleian Library, MS. Bodley 543 (*S. C.* 2588), fo 13v.

[296] Hart, 'Eadnoth', pp. 66–7, and 'The East Anglian chronicle', p. 279.

[297] Ker, *Books, Collectors*, pp. 34–5, referred to Worcester writing as 'unstable' before 1058, by which date we see the belated adoption of Anglo-Caroline Style IV (cf. chapter IV, below). The documents are Sawyer, *Anglo-Saxon Charters*, nos 1399, 1393, 1394, and 1407, respectively.

Latin document of 1053 is regressive in as much as it is written throughout 'in a rough imitation of tenth-century Anglo-Saxon [Square] minuscule'.[298] Suddenly, in the closing years of Bishop Ealdred's tenure at Worcester (1046–1062), we find a radical change, with the visible adoption of a reformed Anglo-Caroline minuscule (in the style associated with the name of Eadwig Basan) marked by a charter dated 1058 and written in a hand detectable in a major Worcester book of the period.[299] The last decade of the Anglo-Saxon period seems to see at Worcester a renewed flourishing of book-production, archival development, and literary activity – probably associable with Wulfstan, prior of Worcester, then bishop 1062–1095 – of a sort not seen since the days of Archbishop Wulfstan.[300]

Style-III Anglo-Caroline minuscule

On the face of it, the writing of Style-I Anglo-Caroline script had ceased at Worcester not later than the pontificate of Archbishop Wulfstan (from 1002). It was his work which Prior, then Bishop, Wulfstan took up in the later 1050s.[301] In the three or four intervening decades, cultural activity seems to have been at a low level and scriptorial standards consequently poor.[302] Four or five Old English manuscripts may be attributable to this period, but the matter requires much further study.[303] Although T.A.M. Bishop wrote cautiously that, 'considered as an index of intellectual activity, the script of some MSS., uncertainly dated and not all certainly attributed, might suggest that this continued vigorous at Worcester throughout the eleventh century',[304] the absence of Latin manuscripts

---

[298] Ker, *Books, Collectors*, p. 34, n. 2; it is not without parallels, however, and is therefore unlikely to be a forgery. It is London, British Library, Additional Charter 19800: *Facsimiles*, ed. Bond, IV.32.

[299] Sawyer, *Anglo-Saxon Charters*, no. 1405, in Latin and Old English; to the reproductions listed by Sawyer, add Denholm-Young, *Handwriting*, plate 8. The book in question is London, British Library, MS. Cotton Nero E.i (Ker, *Books, Collectors*, p. 34, n. 2), a massive, two-volume passional of which the charter-scribe was the principal copyist (cf. n. 210, above).

[300] On Wulfstan II as prior before 1062, see Knowles *et al.*, *The Heads*, p. 83. For intellectual revival at Worcester in his time, see Ker, *Books, Collectors*, pp. 27–30, 31–4, 39–52, 56, and *Catalogue*, *passim*; Bishop, *English Caroline Minuscule*, p. 20, n. 1; Mason, *St Wulfstan*.

[301] See immediately above, and nn. 299–300.

[302] *Ibid.*; see also chapter IV, below, especially pp. 136–7.

[303] The manuscripts available for consideration in this regard are the following: Gneuss, 'A preliminary list', nos 64, 117, 356, 359, 632/3, 656 (Ker, *Catalogue*, nos 48, 73, 178, 182, 328, 343). To these should probably be added the recently discovered Copenhagen binding strips from a manuscript of Ælfric's *Sermones catholici: Fifty-six Ælfric Fragments*, facs. ed. Fausbøll.

[304] *English Caroline Minuscule*, p. 20, n. 1.

deriving from the Worcester scriptorium in the second quarter of the eleventh century suggests that his conclusion is mistaken; a discontinuity of scriptorial tradition seems detectable.

One group of manuscripts remains to be considered, however. The principal clues to its development reside in two books rather different from one another. Cambridge, Corpus Christi College, MS. 178, part 2, contains a copy of Æthelwold's bilingual Rule of St Benedict.[305] It has been dated, on the evidence of its scripts, to the first half of the eleventh century.[306] It is perhaps ironic that in our search for criteria by which to evaluate one problematic manuscript of this text we eventually meet another. What is more, CCCC 178 is the manuscript whose text is most closely related to that of CCCO 197.[307] The vernacular script of CCCC 178, part 2, sits very well with the proposed dating. The Latin script has, however, been described by T.A.M. Bishop as 'outside the main categories of English Caroline';[308] he observed further that it appears to be 'of strong individuality'.[309] In this scribe's Anglo-Caroline we see some sharper angles than were customary in Style I (although the Worcester version of Style I, particularly in its monumental grade, seems to have been in part rather more angular than its Winchester counterpart),[310] some examples of pointed non-Caroline **a**, and proportions changing towards those found in the book's vernacular script and also (in more extreme form) in *Liber Wigorniensis*. On this information I should be tempted to date it fairly early in the first half of the eleventh century. As Bishop remarked,[311] the place of origin of CCCC 178 has been inferred from its mediaeval ownership: in this case, that deduction may be seen to be vindicated by a search for comparanda for its Latin script in particular.

An Anglo-Caroline script in which the art of hesitation has been carried to extremes is found in a remarkable copy of Vergil's works; a

---

[305] Gretsch, *Die Regula*, pp. 30–2; it is her MS. w.

[306] Ker, *Catalogue*, pp. 60–4 (no. 41.B); Bishop, *English Caroline Minuscule*, p. 20 (no. 22), where (on plate XX) p. 302 is illustrated.

[307] Gretsch, *Die Regula*, pp. 107–11, 118–21. CCCO 197 is her MS. x. Cf. Gretsch, 'Æthelwold's translation', pp. 125–43.

[308] *English Caroline Minuscule*, p. 20. However, if it has to be categorised, it is best described as a specimen of Style I.

[309] *Ibid*. On the evidence of Bishop's plate XX one might conclude that the strokes of which the script is composed were very hesitantly or shakily executed (and therefore that it was not inappropriate that the manuscript should have been glossed in the so-called 'Tremulous Hand'!). Consultation of the manuscript itself, however, shows that this appearance results from the nature of the surface of the membrane and that photography has magnified the effect.

[310] This is quite noticeable, for example, in the forms of **a** and **o** employed in Worcester and 'Oswald-connexion' Style-I Caroline manuscripts. Cf. also the general comments by Bishop, *ibid*., p. xxii.

[311] *Ibid*., p. 20.

royal diploma from the Worcester archive has provided both localisation and dating for this Vatican Anglo-Caroline Vergil. Roma, Biblioteca Apostolica Vaticana, MS. Reg. lat. 1671 was written by four scribes.[312] Between them, they practised two quite different styles of Anglo-Caroline minuscule. In this manuscript of 218 folios, scribes ii and iv were responsible for fos 2v13–89v and 158r–218: they wrote forms of Style I. Hands i and iii (fos 1r–2v12, 90r–157v)[313] show a remarkable script. Wherever strokes could be broken or turned suddenly at an acute angle, this seems to have been attempted. The result was described by T.A.M. Bishop as 'strongly mannered'.[314] In some letters – and very noticeably in **g** – the scribes' approach has produced sharp contrast of heavy and light, broad and narrow, strokes, almost in the manner of Gothic script. In **c, e, o**, and sometimes in **a**, the scribes have produced letters with radically angular bodies – with broken backs, indeed. The hands of scribes i and iii give a strongly confident impression: they profess an assured style, translating hesitation into a deliberate art-form. A strongly defined, easily recognisable style of Anglo-Caroline had been created. There are some other features of this script requiring comment. Ascenders, usually quite tall, are mostly wedged, though not aggressively so. Descenders are commonly turned back (leftwards) somewhat, a tendency which is generalised to **r** and **s** whose uprights travel slightly below the ruled line: in the case of **r**, that part of the letter can be accentuated by being quite sharply curved back; this is particularly noticeable when a deeply split form is written, almost in v-shape, with the strokes coming together at the ruled line. All these features combined to create a thoroughly distinctive form of Anglo-Caroline which seems to be the exclusive property of a single scriptorium.[315]

Mr Bishop identified scribe iii of the Vatican manuscript as also the scribe of a charter from the Worcester cathedral archive – now London, British Library, MS. Additional Charter 19793, whose text contains the

---

[312] *Ibid.*, p. 17 (no. 19).

[313] Hand iii has been illustrated by Bishop, *ibid.*, plate XVII (showing part of fo 90r).

[314] *Ibid.*, p. 17. Two details noted by Bishop concerning this manuscript are worth recording here, lest they be lost sight of. In connexion with his study of an early tenth-century manuscript, Cambridge, Trinity College, MS. B.15.33 (368), where the feature occurred, he reported that 'One of the scribes of Vatican, Reg. lat. 1671. . ., numbered the quires of his portion independently' (Bishop, 'An early example of the Square minuscule', p. 249, n. 1). On fos 69v–70r neumes of as yet unknown date are found 'pointing the declamation of' *Aeneid*, II.274–286: this is another example of a feature already identified elsewhere (Bishop, *English Caroline Minuscule*, p. 17, n. 3, for the Vatican Vergil; Liuzzi, 'Notazione', for the original identification of this practice). Temple, *Anglo-Saxon Manuscripts*, p. 55 (*s.n.* 28), has linked this manuscript's decoration to that of the Old English book now Vercelli, Biblioteca Capitolare, MS. CXVII (and cf. Turner, *Early Worcester MSS*, p. lxxi).

[315] Below (p. 75), I propose the name 'Style III' for the script of this group.

date 969.[316] Writing of this, Bishop observed that its script 'has a nerveless aspect and, by itself, might be taken for an archaizing late copy or forgery'.[317] This was how it was indeed taken by P.H. Sawyer and his palaeographical advisers in 1968, attributing it to the first half of the eleventh century, against the trend of preceding scholarly commentary in which the document had been generally regarded as original and genuine.[318] Bishop, however, who was probably the first palaeographer able to observe a range of writing in this style, concluded (albeit with appropriate reserve) that 'it may be an early experiment in the script and style'.[319] In other words, the charter would be an indication that in 969 the Worcester scriptorium was seeking to come to grips with Caroline minuscule and, in the attempt, was to produce a highly distinctive version yet still 'with Square aspect' and 'retaining many forms of an ornate Square minuscule'.[320] The ornate phase of Square minuscule was that now known as Phase III, written in the reigns of Edmund I, Eadred, and Eadwig (939–959),[321] but in the 1960s thought (mistakenly, as it seems) by Bishop to extend over the period *ca* 940–*ca* 970.[322] What Bishop evidently thought of as a heritage of the native Insular script, I have sought to explain instead as the stylisation of a mannerism. It is very unlikely indeed that the extant single-sheet charter dated 969 could be contemporary and original.[323]

---

[316] Sawyer, *Anglo-Saxon Charters*, no. 772: *Facsimiles*, ed. Bond, III.29. Cf. Gelling, *The Early Charters of the Thames Valley*, p. 18 (no. 3). See Bishop, *English Caroline Minuscule*, p. 17, for the identification.

[317] *Ibid.*

[318] Sawyer, *Anglo-Saxon Charters*, p. 246 (*s.n.* 772).

[319] *English Caroline Minuscule*, p. 17; in 'The Copenhagen gospel-book', p. 38, he described Style I as having 'competed for a time with a type of Caroline under the strong influence of the Square minuscule' and specifically referred to the Vatican Vergil as containing both types (*ibid.*, p. 38, n. 1).

[320] The descriptions (and cf. n. 319, above) are by Bishop, *English Caroline Minuscule*, p. 17, referring to scribes i and iii of the Vatican Vergil. On the year 969 at Worcester, cf. Robinson, *St Oswald*, pp. 14–21, 33–7; John, *Land Tenure*, pp. 80–167, and *Orbis Britanniae*, pp. 234–48 (reprinting a paper first published before *Land Tenure*); Sawyer, 'Charters of the Reform movement'; *The Cartulary of Worcester*, ed. Darlington, pp. xiij–xix.

[321] Dumville, 'English Square minuscule script: the mid-century phases', and *Wessex and England*, pp. 62–6.

[322] 'Notes', p. 325; cf. *English Caroline Minuscule*, p. xx, for a vaguer formulation. I have discussed the significance of Bishop's chosen dating below, in chapter III (see pp. 88–9).

[323] The first moves, outside the documentary context, towards the new proportions (on which see Dumville, 'Beowulf come lately') are perhaps to be placed in the 990s: see, for example, the Latin and Old English writing in Cambridge, University Library, MS. Gg.3.28 (1493), written at Cerne not earlier than A.D. 993 (for a facsimile of fo 255r, see *Aelfric's De temporibus anni*, ed. Henel, frontispiece). On proportions, see also below, p. 74.

There is a further complication in this assessment of that charter. It presents itself as a diploma of King Edgar conveying land to his thane Ælfwold at *Æpslea*, identified as Aspley Guise (Bedfordshire).[324] A generation ago many scholars thought that tenth-century royal diplomas were written by ecclesiastical scribes for the beneficiaries and therefore locally either to the land granted or to the principal seats of the donees or, perhaps, to the place where the king completed the transaction. Such a view would not now be normally held, for it is clear that royal diplomas of that period were usually produced in chancery by clerks acting on behalf of the monarch.[325] Therefore, if the diploma were original, it should not have been written by a Worcester scribe. Cyril Hart in 1975 was quick to see the unfortunate direction of Bishop's argument.[326] However, the burden of the evidence seems to be that this style of writing is found only at Worcester.

That the best palaeographical advice (usually that of N.R. Ker) available to Sawyer, and apparently independent of Bishop's views published a few years later, placed the writing of BL Add. Ch. 19793 in the eleventh century is a point not to be underrated.[327] It is the dating offered by Bishop, not the localisation of the scribe at Worcester, which produces the tension in interpretation of the evidence. Also in the Worcester archive was another diploma of Edgar in favour of Ælfwold (whose single sheet was unfortunately lost in the eighteenth century), issued on the same occasion in 969 in identical and unexceptionable formulation and with almost the same witness-list, conveying land at Kineton (Warwickshire).[328] Kineton lay within the sphere of influence of the bishops of Worcester, but Aspley well outside it. Neither estate was held by Worcester cathedral in 1066.[329] Hart has pointed out that Ælfwold

---

[324] On the question of this identification, cf. Mawer *et al.*, *The Place-names of Worcestershire*, p. xl, and Gelling, *The Early Charters of the Thames Valley*, p. 18 (no. 3).

[325] Keynes, *The Diplomas of King Æthelred*, pp. 14–83; on the implications for the study of books, cf. Dumville, 'English libraries before 1066'.

[326] *The Early Charters of Northern England*, pp. 81–2 (*s.n.* 62). However, his comments on the Vatican Vergil and Winchester are frivolous; on deductions from the initials, cf. the discussion by Elżbieta Temple cited above, n. 314.

[327] On Ker's role, see Sawyer, *Anglo-Saxon Charters*, pp. ix, x. It is noteworthy that, at that stage, Mr Bishop (who was also sometimes consulted by Sawyer) apparently did not see the need to dissent from the later dating, if he was asked about this particular specimen.

[328] Sawyer, *Anglo-Saxon Charters*, no. 773. On these two documents (nos 772, 773) see Keynes, *The Diplomas of King Æthelred*, pp. 76–9. Curiously, the discrepancy between the witness-lists is that Ealdorman Æthelwine is found attesting no. 773 but not no. 772. Kineton was in the King's hands in 1066 (Domesday Book, vol. 1, fo 238rb).

[329] And neither document is found in the eleventh-century Worcester cartularies, a state of affairs for which there are various possible explanations.

was a brother of Ealdorman Æthelwine, Bishop Oswald's colleague in the foundation of Ramsey Abbey, and has suggested that in view of Oswald's standing with the family of Ealdorman Æthelwine Ælfwold might have felt that Worcester Cathedral was a secure place to deposit his title-deeds.[330] Equally, however, that standing might have attracted grants or bequests to Oswald or his successors. It must also be noted that the two grants to Ælfwold have been attributed to the same occasion, conveying thus a substantial transfer – of twenty-five hides. It is a nice question how likely such an occurrence would be.[331] A simple hypothesis would be that the *Æpslea* diploma was forged on the basis of that for Kineton; but, until a credible motive can be established, we cannot proceed further in that direction. For the moment, it seems necessary to note that the extant copy of the *Æpslea* diploma was written at Worcester in the early eleventh century: the consequences of those deductions for the status of the document remain to be worked out.[332]

A final indication that the style of writing found in the diploma for Ælfwold (and its relative, the Vatican Vergil) belongs to Worcester comes from a codex of certain Worcester provenance: fos 107–166 of Worcester, Cathedral Library, MS. F.48 constitute, in T.A.M. Bishop's words, a 'degenerate specimen in the same style'; he was prepared to admit that it should probably be dated in the eleventh century, thus attributing quite a long life to this mannered form of Anglo-Caroline.[333]

The question of dating this last group of manuscripts must now be reviewed. Its origins should perhaps be placed early in the eleventh

---

330 'Athelstan', pp. 131–2, and *The Early Charters of Northern England*, pp. 81–2 (no. 62). One is bound to wonder whether Bishop Oswald had a role in securing a grant or grants for Ælfwold, in view of this archival history. Sawyer, *Anglo-Saxon Charters*, nos 1750 and 1763 (Glastonbury Abbey's archive) are lost diplomas of Eadwig and Edgar in favour of an Ælfwold who may have been the same person. However, there may have been another Ælfwold, domiciled in the South-west: *ibid.*, no. 596 (archive of the Old Minster, Winchester) is a diploma of Eadwig granting land in Somerset to his faithful thane Ælfwold; the same estate was granted to one Cenwulf in A.D. 961 (*ibid.*, no. 697, from the same archive), a circumstance which suggests that the previous owner's career had ended by that date.

331 Dr Susan Kelly tells me that there are sufficient like occurrences for this not to be a factor which could by itself cast doubt on either diploma.

332 If BL Additional Charter 19793 were to be deemed original and contemporary, we should have to suppose that it is a rare example of an unofficial original. There is a group of such documents apparently emanating from Worcester in the episcopate of Cenwald (cf. Keynes, 'King Athelstan's books', pp. 158–9; cf. pp. 141–2, below) and it is not impossible that the practice could have been revived in Oswald's time. But we should hesitate greatly, on a number of counts, before proceeding down this path.

333 *English Caroline Minuscule*, p. 17 (by a misprint, the reference to this manuscript was given as 'F.148'). For a brief notice of its later history, see Ker, *Books, Collectors*, p. 29.

century. The Vatican Vergil provides evidence which can be taken in the same sense. The four scribes were working in collaboration with one another (as the evidence of fo 2v demonstrates beyond doubt for scribes i and ii):[334] the two quite different styles of Anglo-Caroline which they represent must therefore be recognised as being practised contemporaneously at Worcester. In as much as scribes ii and iv were writing Style I, we may suppose that they represent the last appearances there of a script-form which had probably been the practice of the scriptorium (albeit alongside Square minuscule) since Oswald became bishop in 961. A further piece of evidence for this chronology is provided by the proportions of the script of hand iii. In the height of the ascenders we see clear evidence of a shift away from the proportions characteristic of Style I towards those found in early eleventh-century vernacular minuscule and in specimens of Caroline script influenced by that development: at Worcester we have associated Latin writing in that style with the pontificate of Archbishop Wulfstan (from 1002).[335]

It seems likely, therefore, that we must put the development and practice of this form of Anglo-Caroline within the first quarter of the eleventh century. Elsewhere, earlier styles of Anglo-Caroline were being replaced from the late 1010s onwards by the style created by 'Eadwig Basan'.[336] As we have seen, that was not adopted at Worcester until the 1050s;[337] in the meantime, from the 1020s or 1030s, there is no evidence of a clear direction in Worcester scriptorial practice. All this leaves us with no reason to prolong the life of Style I beyond what was applicable elsewhere[338] and little reason even to think that it survived long into the time of Archbishop Wulfstan, when experiments with and adoption of different proportions were clearly the fashion of the day. We should perhaps deduce that the style represented by the group of manuscripts just

---

[334] Bishop, *English Caroline Minuscule*, p. 17, for the division of stints on this page (cf. above, p. 70). The evidence of one scribe's independent quire-signatures (cf. n. 314, above) does not militate against this. For the use of non-Caroline, non-Insular **a** in this manuscript (cf. n. 240, above), see Bishop, *ibid.*.

[335] See above, pp. 65–7, 69. In principle, there are three dating options when we consider Style III: (i) it was written at Worcester before the adoption of Style I; (ii) Style III was chronologically coincident with part of the period in which Style I was written there, being an unsuccessful passing fashion; (iii) it superseded Style I at Worcester. Given the specific palaeographical context, only the third option is a likely approximation to the historical development.

[336] See chapter IV, below.

[337] *Ibid.*; see also above, pp. 67–8.

[338] The relationship of this Worcester script-history to that of other houses which had been set up as Benedictine monasteries by Oswald remains unclear: cf. above, pp. 65–6. The evidence of the Ramsey pontifical in London, British Library, MS. Cotton Vitellius A.vii suggests, for what it is worth, that Style-IV Anglo-Caroline had not triumphed there in the 1030s (or even later, depending on the book's specific dating).

discussed was developed as a formal-grade replacement for Style I; the new fashion may have been too mannered to prove successful at that time and place, giving way fairly quickly therefore to more rapid, less formal styles. The last gasps of one of its practitioners, working in unfavourable circumstances, may perhaps be represented by the cited folios of Worcester MS. F.48.

Mr Bishop placed CCCC 178 outside his 'main categories of English Caroline'.[339] The Vatican Vergil and its relatives stand at a yet greater distance. Although this style may have been practised for a relatively short time and by relatively few scribes, it remains as a distinctive, local contribution to the development of Anglo-Caroline minuscule. In recognition of this, and of its place – chronologically – after the creation of Styles I and II, I propose to refer henceforth to this peculiar Worcester fashion as Anglo-Caroline Style III.

Conclusions on the date and origin of
Oxford, Corpus Christi College, MS. 197

Mechthild Gretsch's studies of Æthelwold's bilingual Rule of St Benedict have indicated that the closest textual relative of CCCO 197 is provided by the Worcester manuscript CCCC 178.[340] Palaeographical analysis of the Oxford book has shown its script to be a representative of Style-I Anglo-Caroline written by a scribe who had been trained first in English Square minuscule but who had nevertheless successfully mastered the pure Caroline style.[341] In T.A.M. Bishop's account of Anglo-Caroline the script of CCCO 197 represents 'a variety of Style I in which a rough energy prevails over the monumental quality' usually associated with the liturgical books produced in houses of the Æthelwold connexion. In Bishop's view this, when compared with the other and better known variety of Style I, is 'equally plain and severe, less rounded, slightly compressed'; it 'begins to take on a distinct identity' with a Worcester episcopal document of A.D. 984.[342] That is London, British Library, Additional Charter 19794, by which Archbishop Oswald leased a parcel

---

[339] *English Caroline Minuscule*, p. 20. His observation that this manuscript shows no sign of a 'decorative treatment of the *rt*-ligature found in some Worcester MSS., some certainly of the middle or late eleventh century' is to be taken as indicating that its script does not show features of Worcester Style IV (whose history begins in the later 1050s).

[340] 'Æthelwold's translation', p. 332 (cf. above, nn. 305 and 307).

[341] See above, pp. 19–30.

[342] *English Caroline Minuscule*, p. xxii. In his paper on 'The Copenhagen gospel-book', p. 38, Bishop might appear to be attributing Copenhagen, Kongelige Biblishoteket, MS. G.K.S. 10.2° to Worcester, but careful scrutiny of the passage shows that to be a mistaken reading: he is merely calling it a Style-I manuscript.

of land to his thane Cynelm, and about whose contemporaneity and genuineness no doubts have been expressed.[343] Dr Ker and Mr Bishop both noted that the script of this charter (the bottom portion of a chirograph) 'resembles' (Bishop) or (Ker) 'has a certain resemblance to' that of CCCO 197,[344] and the conclusion has therefore been drawn that that manuscript may have been written at Worcester.[345] To deduce this is probably to travel too fast. Anglo-Caroline Style I was written also in others of the houses associated with Oswald. The mid-eleventh-century provenance of CCCO 197 is Bury St Edmunds. To the extent that St Edmund's minster seems to have been drawn into that circle of reformed houses not later than the 980s,[346] we need to consider a range of options for the origin of the Oxford manuscript.

In as much as CCCO 197 is a specimen of Anglo-Caroline Style I, it is unlikely to have been written later than the opening decade or two of the eleventh century; at Worcester, evidence that that style was practised much beyond A.D. 1000 is wanting,[347] while testimony from other houses of the Oswald connexion is quite absent for this period. That it is also (in respect of its Old English) a specimen of Square minuscule renders wholly improbable a date more than a few years after the millennium.[348] At Worcester (unlike Winchester) we have evidence for the continuing use of Square minuscule alongside Anglo-Caroline in the second half of the tenth century for Latin texts,[349] even those closely connected with Benedictine usage – in this last respect, the marginal additions (in informal Square minuscule) to London, British Library,

---

[343] Sawyer, *Anglo-Saxon Charters*, no. 1347: *Facsimiles*, ed. Bond, III.32. The place-name is probably an insertion, however.

[344] Ker, *Catalogue*, p. xxvi; Bishop, *English Caroline Minuscule*, p. xxii.

[345] Gneuss, 'A preliminary list', no. 672. In her attempt to tie CCCO 197 to Winchester or its dependent houses, Gretsch ('Æthelwold's translation', p. 133) has over-interpreted Bishop's remarks on Style-I Anglo-Caroline in *English Caroline Minuscule*, pp. xxi–xxii. Bishop (*ibid.*, p. xxii) seems rather to have spoiled the apparent effect of his remark by his further reference to the resemblance of the script of CCCO 197 to that of London, British Library, MS. Royal 15.C.x; on the attendant complexities, see above, n. 240.

[346] See above, pp. 35–48.

[347] See above, pp. 53–6 and 63–75.

[348] Cf. Dumville, 'Beowulf come lately'.

[349] See, for example, London, British Library, MS. Royal 13.A.xv (cf. above, pp. 53–4); and perhaps Oxford, Bodleian Library, MS. Lat. theol. c.4 (*S.C.* 1926*), on which see above, p. 54. Gretsch ('Æthelwold's translation', p. 134, on her MSS. O and g) has even hinted that Cambridge, Corpus Christi College, MS. 57 (of mid-eleventh-century Abingdon provenance: see above, p. 8, n. 4; below, p. 136, n. 106, and pp. 153–4) might have originated at Worcester (cf. Meyvaert, 'Towards a history', pp. 100, 110); if, however, it was written at Abingdon, it would provide evidence that that house was like Worcester and Canterbury in allowing the latinate use of Square minuscule.

MS. Royal 2.A.xx should be noted –;[350] but from other houses of the Oswald connexion no identified Square-minuscule specimens of Latin writing are known.[351]

What should perhaps weigh most heavily in discussion of the possible places of origin of CCCO 197 is the evidence that its scribe had been trained first in Anglo-Saxon Square minuscule and had apparently come to Caroline writing only recently.[352] We must, it seems, place the manuscript in the last quarter of the tenth century.[353] While we cannot rule out the possibility that Worcester cathedral priory received a new scribal recruit from another, and perhaps unreformed, house in that period, it would be simpler to think of CCCO 197 as having been written at a more recently reformed church.[354] In the diocese of Worcester, Westbury-on-Trym, Winchcombe, Pershore, and Evesham were all reformed or refounded under Oswald's auspices.[355] In Ealdorman Æthelwine's area of control, Ramsey Abbey was a new creation (albeit first staffed in large part by monks drawn from Westbury-on-Trym) but Bury St Edmunds was an older house reformed before the end of the 980s. In these circumstances there seem to be no reasons which would compel us to deny that CCCO 197 could have been executed at Bury

---

[350] Dumville, 'English Square minuscule script: the background and earliest phases', p. 149, n. 6; Warner & Gilson, *British Museum Catalogue*, I.33–6 and IV, plate 18(*a*), showing Old English in the annotating hand on part of fo 12r; Thompson, *Catalogue of Ancient Manuscripts*, II.60–1 and plate 21, showing a range of additions on fo 14v. This series of marginally entered liturgical texts (by a scribe who wrote Latin, Greek, and Old English) deserves scholars' attention: I cannot find that it has attracted comment since 1921. This scribe collaborated with one who, appearing only on fos 37v and 38v, wrote a mixed Anglo-Caroline which included non-Insular, non-Caroline **a** (cf. nn. 228 and 240, above). The only parallel which I can offer for such systematic marginal *liturgica* is provided by CCCC MS. 41, of the first half of the eleventh century: see *Cambridge, Corpus Christi College 41: the Loricas and the Missal*, ed. Grant; the original manuscript (a copy of the Old English Bede) was attributed to Winchester by Miller, *Place Names in the English Bede*, pp. 4–5 (his MS. B: cf. Grant, *The B Text*, p. 445, 'Winchester is a possibility'); for subsequent description and comment, ignoring Miller, cf. James, *A Descriptive Catalogue*, I.81–5; Ker, *Catalogue*, pp. 43–5 (no. 32); Wormald, *English Drawings*, p. 60 (no. 5); Temple, *Anglo-Saxon Manuscripts*, pp. 98–9 (no. 81).

[351] However, Old English continued to be written in Square minuscule in southern and midland England for as long as that script was used: cf. Dumville, 'Beowulf come lately'. If Cyril Hart's association of various aspects of the history of the Anglo-Saxon Chronicle with Byrhtferth of Ramsey were acceptable (see, for example, Hart, 'The B text'), we should have some more specimens associable with that house.

[352] See above, pp. 23–8.

[353] See above, pp. 28–30.

[354] And perhaps, by implication, that as part of his re-education he was made (a) to learn the Caroline script and (b) to copy out the Rule which he was now to follow!

[355] For their antecedents see Sims-Williams, *Religion*, pp. 174–6. The previous status of Pershore is not at all clear.

itself in the late tenth century where copies of that text would have been a necessary adjunct to the process of reform. It could of course have been imported thither from another house of the Oswald connexion, but there is no need to make that our starting point.[356] Among the manuscripts of pre-Conquest date but post-Conquest Bury provenance, there is sufficient evidence – if it be allowed to speak for itself – for an active scriptorium, library, and readership from the mid-tenth century.[357] Most studies of manuscripts with a Bury St Edmunds provenance have proceeded from the assumption that before the middle of the eleventh century the house had no scriptorial capacity.[358] Study of that church's pre-Conquest history suggests that this assumption is at best unwise. If Bury was, as seems probable, linked from the first to the ealdormen of East Anglia and then to Ramsey Abbey, it needs to be accepted into the group of churches whose tenth- and eleventh-century manuscripts must still be tracked down.[359] Perhaps CCCO 197 can be accepted as a first contribution.[360]

---

356 Gretsch ('Æthelwold's translation', p. 133) has hypothesised Ely as the source of this manuscript. But Ely as the agent of reform at Bury St Edmunds has long been discredited (cf. the remarks of Gransden, 'The legends', pp. 17–18) and in any case it belonged to the Æthelwold connexion.

357 In view of the picture drawn here, I have withdrawn my remarks about Bury in 'English libraries before 1066', p. 162, from the second edition of that paper.

358 Temple, *Anglo-Saxon Manuscripts*, pp. 71, 93, 101; O'Keeffe, 'The text of Aldhelm's *Enigma* no. c', p. 67. Cf. Bishop, 'Notes', pp. 187 and 414; 'An early example of Insular-Caroline', p. 399; *English Caroline Minuscule*, pp. xvi, 2. For a different view see Millar, *English Illuminated Manuscripts*, p. 15, who placed the writing of Vat. Reg. lat. 12 at Bury (see his plate 20 for two further reproductions from that manuscript).

359 As listed by Bishop, *English Caroline Minuscule*, p. xvii.

360 The other manuscripts of pre-Conquest date but with post-Conquest Bury provenance are Gneuss, 'A preliminary list', nos 128, 132–137, (*not* 147: Cambridge, St John's College, MS. B.13 [35], dated simply '*saec.* xi' by Gneuss, is to be rejected as post-Conquest and is perhaps datable *saec.* xi/xii), 285, 339, 413, 477, 503, 511, 529 (Ker, *Catalogue*, p. 350, no. 290), 661, 912. Including CCCO 197 (Gneuss, no. 672), this gives a total of eighteen manuscripts of very varied dates, origins, and contents. Eight or nine are Continental imports: nos 128, 133–137, 477(?), 529, 661, ranging in date from the seventh century (no. 529) to the early eleventh (no. 477). Two Square-minuscule manuscripts (no. 503, palimpsest, lower script; no. 511, Phase-I Square minuscule – cf. Wormald, 'The Insular script', pp. 161–2) probably pre-date Edmund I's foundation at Bury in A.D. 945, and three eleventh-century books have been attributed to Canterbury (no. 132 certainly – Bishop, 'Notes', pp. 187 and 414 –, nos 413 and 912 less so), but there is no obvious reason why the other manuscripts should not have been written at Bury: nos 147, 285, 339, and (if English) 477. Of Latin books, the illustrated copy of the works of Prudentius in London, British Library, MS. Additional 24199 (Gneuss, no. 285 – cf. Wieland, 'The Anglo-Saxon manuscripts of Prudentius's *Psychomachia*') is of some importance (see below, p. 145, n. 25). Of Old English, the interpolated copy of Ælfric's Lives of Saints in London, British Library, MS. Cotton Iulius E.vii (Gneuss, no. 339) deserves attention (for a reproduction see Turner *et al.*, *The Benedictines in Britain*, p. 68,

APPENDIX

The foundation of Cholsey Abbey, the fate of Abbot Germanus, and the cult of St Kenelm of Winchcombe

In recent publications, both Michael Lapidge and I have studied late tenth- and early eleventh-century liturgical manuscripts showing a particular interest in St Kenelm, the patron-saint of Winchcombe Abbey.[361] Winchcombe was one of the group of houses founded, refounded, or reformed by Oswald during his tenure of episcopal office.[362] In charge of Winchcombe he placed Germanus, a man of unknown antecedents, who had been trained in the monastic life at Fleury. The Reform-community at Winchcombe had a short life for, on the death of King Edgar, Germanus and his monks were expelled thence by Ealdorman Ælfhere. They eventually settled at Oswald's principal Reform-foundation, Ramsey Abbey, which was protected by the might of Ealdorman Æthelwine. This arrangement appears not to have been a comfortable one, for Germanus was senior to the prior of Ramsey, Eadnoth I, having himself held that office before being translated to Winchcombe.[363] There is some reason, as Lapidge has shown, to think that Germanus lost neither his devotion to St Kenelm nor his attachment to abbatial office.[364] The three manuscripts which can be associated with Winchcombe on liturgical evidence – Orléans, Bibliothèque municipale, MS. 127 (105); Cambridge, University Library, MS. Ff.1.23 (1156), and MS. Kk.5.32 (2074) – nevertheless have complex features and histories which in some measure inhibit us from simply assigning them an origin at that house. Lapidge has particularly indicated the manuscripts' personal associations with Abbot Germanus; for my part, I have preferred to stress primarily the palaeographical (but also the textual and liturgical) evidence which associates the two Cambridge

---

plate 46): cf. Ker, *Catalogue*, pp. 206–10 (no. 162), and Dumville, 'Beowulf come lately', pp. 59–60. If all these books, and some of those dated '*saec*. xi²' (Gneuss, nos 35, 129–131, 143, 514, 549), were at Bury in 1066, they would have constituted an interesting and useful collection. On the house's library in that period, see Thomson, 'The library of Bury St Edmunds Abbey'. Cf. Ker, *Medieval Libraries*, pp. 16–22.

361 Lapidge, 'Abbot Germanus'; Dumville, 'On the dating', pp. 40–1, and *Liturgy*, chapter II.

362 See above, pp. 44–5 (cf. 77) and n. 192. For some discussion of the fate of these Reform-houses in A.D. 975, see Williams, '*Princeps*'; for Evesham see further Dumville, *Wessex and England*, p. 34, n. 21, and p. 41(–2), n. 58.

363 Lapidge, 'Abbot Germanus'; Knowles *et al.*, *The Heads*, p. 61 (cf. p. 78).

364 Lapidge, 'Abbot Germanus'.

manuscripts with Canterbury, and rather (it has seemed to me) with St Augustine's than with Christ Church. Evidence may now be at hand which allows these perceptions to be brought wholly into line with one another.

It is possible to suppose that, in the years after 975, the Reform-monks expelled from Winchcombe retained a sense of community even while they lived among their brethren of Ramsey.[365] At the very least, as I have just remarked, Abbot Germanus seems not to have renounced past associations. In 992, following the deaths of Ramsey's spiritual and lay patrons, Oswald and Æthelwine, new arrangements had to be made for the governance of that abbey. For whatever reason, it seems not to have been possible for Germanus to remain there. According to the Ramsey house-history, Germanus was made abbot of Cholsey (Berkshire) in that year.[366] From his attestations of royal diplomas, we can see that Germanus had a long career in his new post: he is still heard of in documents of A.D. 1012 and 1013;[367] an attestation in 1019 occurs in a diploma of uncertain merit.[368]

Cholsey Abbey has seemed to have no Anglo-Saxon history save in respect of its association with Germanus. That it might have survived beyond his time is perhaps implied by William of Malmesbury's account of the revival of Reading Abbey in 1121 by King Henry I, in as much as Cholsey Abbey was still identifiable at that date.[369]

Radingis fuit quondam cenobium sanctimonialium, sed iam multis annis abolitum. Illud rex Henricus pro indicta sibi penitentia restaurare intendens, duo alia olim diruta monasteria Lefminstre et Celsi adiunxit . . .

At Reading there was once a community of nuns, but it was done away with many years ago now. King Henry, intending to restore it by way of a penance for himself, attached to it two other long-destroyed abbeys, Leominster and Cholsey . . .

---

[365] *Ibid.*

[366] §62 (LXV): ed. Macray, *Chronicon Abbatiæ Rameseiensis*, pp. 110–11. The text reads: 'Sub eodem quoque tempore prefatus rex Æthelredus uenerabilem uirum Germanum . . . ecclesie Celesige orbate pastore prefecit, ubi et plurimis postea annis usque ad communis debiti exactionem in bonorum exercitiis operum studia semper continuauit honesta'. Knowles *et al.*, *The Heads*, pp. 39–40, thought that A.D. 992 was too late for this event, but no reason was stated. For Cholsey Abbey as a physical object see Gem, 'Church architecture in the reign of King Æthelred', especially pp. 105–9.

[367] For the documents named here see Sawyer, *Anglo-Saxon Charters*, nos 927 and 931.

[368] *Ibid.*, no. 954, a confirmation of privileges to St Mary's Abbey, Exeter, in the name of King Cnut.

[369] *Gesta pontificum Anglorum*, II.89 (ed. Hamilton, p. 193).

Leominster, a nunnery, was suppressed only in 1046, after a scandal; but that at Reading has not been thought to have outlived Æthelred's reign.[370] Domesday Book has no notice of Cholsey Abbey: in 1066 the King held the manor of Cholsey,[371] and we have to assume that the abbey's endowments had been incorporated in the royal demesne.[372]

It is accordingly clear that Cholsey Abbey had a short history. How was it that Germanus came to be given a site there for a monastery? Only one piece of direct evidence seems to survive, and that from a thirteenth-century St Albans source. An anonymous autograph-chronicle of Anglo-Saxon history, incorporated by John of Wallingford into his historical miscellany written at St Albans Abbey in 1247 x 1257, contains much matter whose sources have still not been traced, as well as material whose credentials – some worthy, some not – are certain.[373] Among the items of unknown origin is a notice of the foundation of the monastery at Cholsey.[374]

Circa hec tempora rex Ethelredus fundauit monasterium Celisige, suggestione archiepiscopi Sirici; et, paterna pietate constructum et ditatum, tradidit ad ordinandum Germano abbati Winchelcumbie, quem Edgarus pater eius a Floriacensi monasterio transtulerat illuc. Ubi cum bene omnia ordinasset, transtulit eum ad suam abbatiam nouam Celisige. Fundauit autem eam pro anima fratris sui E<d>wardi predicto modo occisi.

Circa hec tempora Ethelwinus alderman, exortatione Oswaldi Eboracensis archiepiscopi, fundauit Ramense monasterium, et transtulit illuc duos reges et martires Ethelbrittum et Ethelredum qui ibidem intechantur.[375]

About this time King Æthelred founded Cholsey Abbey, at the suggestion of Archbishop Sigeric; and, having with fatherly devotion built and enriched it, he

---

[370] Knowles *et al.*, *The Heads*, p. 218 (with cross-reference to p. 219), on Reading; on Leominster see *ibid.*, p. 214, and Kemp, 'The monastic dean'.

[371] Domesday Book, vol. 1, fos 56vb–57ra.

[372] Cholsey's history as an estate was in royal hands: Sawyer, *Anglo-Saxon Charters*, nos 354 and 1494. Hart, 'Two queens', p. 15, has hinted that Queen Ælfthryth was involved in the foundation of the abbey.

[373] It is in London, British Library, MS. Cotton Iulius D.vii; for a published text see *The Chronicle*, ed. Vaughan. This work does not seem to have been discussed by Gransden, *Historical Writing*, I.

[374] *The Chronicle*, ed. Vaughan, pp. 59–60: the material occupies fo 31rb of the manuscript. The editor has caused confusion by his method of presentation of the text: fos 30r23–33v28 are laid out in two parallel columns of varying width containing texts in parallel sequences; single-column format resumes only with fo 33v28, 'De filiis Æthelredi regis . . .'. The text in the b-columns was neither marked nor intended for insertion into that of the a-columns.

[375] On *intechare*, which the editor regarded as unique to this text (occurring on his pp. 57, 58, 60) and as derived from *entheca*, 'a coffin', see the comments in *The Chronicle*, ed. Vaughan, p. xiv and n. 3. Is this not, however, simply an aberrant spelling of *integare*?

gave it to Germanus, abbot of Winchcombe, whom his [Æthelred's] father, Edgar, had brought thither from Fleury Abbey – to organise. When he [Germanus] had arranged everything there well, he [Æthelred] translated him to his new abbacy at Cholsey. He founded that for the soul of his brother Edward, killed in the way described above.

About this time, Ealdorman Æthelwine, at the urging of Oswald, archbishop of York, founded Ramsey Abbey, and translated thither two royal martyrs, Æthelberht and Æthelred, who are enshrined there.

The internal chronology of this anonymous chronicle is not precise at all, as the juxtaposition of these two items will show.[376] In the narrative they follow a lengthy notice of St Dunstan.[377] If we take the reference to Archbishop Sigeric as a precise indication of chronology, the foundation (or intention to found) can be placed within the years 990–994. This would sit well with the Ramsey historian's assertion that King Æthelred had given Cholsey to Germanus in 992.[378]

It is, however, the involvement of Archbishop Sigeric which is of greater interest in the present context. Not only does he provide the link with Canterbury which the manuscript evidence requires[379] – and he was abbot of St Augustine's before he became archbishop –,[380] but his involvement probably helps to explain the choice of site for the new monastery. From 985 to 990 Sigeric was bishop of Ramsbury (Wiltshire) and he may have retained that position for some while after his translation to the archiepiscopal see: his successor is not found in office until 991 x 993.[381]

These events may serve to account for another association which has until now remained unexplained. Ælfric, archbishop of Canterbury (995–1005), in 1003/4 made a will of which a copy survives from the archives of Abingdon Abbey.[382] Among his bequests are some to ecclesiastical institutions: Christ Church, Canterbury; St Albans Abbey; Abingdon Abbey; Cholsey Abbey. Ælfric is thought to have been originally a monk of Abingdon and subsequently abbot of St

---

[376] Æthelwine founded Ramsey in 968/9 but translated the royal martyrs there possibly as late as 991. Perhaps the latter event provides the chronological connexion with the process of foundation of Cholsey which must have begun (on the information provided here) in A.D. 990 x 994.

[377] *The Chronicle*, ed. Vaughan, pp. 57–9. Dunstan died in A.D. 988.

[378] See above, p. 80.

[379] Cf. pp. 79–80, above.

[380] Sigeric may have been abbot of St Augustine's and bishop of Ramsbury at the same time: cf. Knowles *et al.*, *The Heads*, p. 35.

[381] S. Keynes *apud* Fryde *et al.*, *Handbook*, p. 220.

[382] Sawyer, *Anglo-Saxon Charters*, no. 1488. But the dating depends on the separation of two bishops Wulfstan. See the references given in n. 293, above, for discussion of some of the problems.

Albans.[383] But his association with Cholsey has remained obscure. In fact, he was Sigeric's successor at both Ramsbury and Canterbury; and, in spite of his translation to the archbishopric, he retained the see of Ramsbury until his death a decade later.[384]

All these pieces of information seem to fit together. Sigeric persuaded King Æthelred to use royal land to endow an abbey at Cholsey.[385] The monastery was situated in Sigeric's old diocese of Ramsbury. Germanus was made abbot, thus relieving a difficult situation at Ramsey. Sigeric became Germanus's ecclesiastical patron and King Æthelred his lay patron: one might think that the abbot had done rather well out of this development. Germanus's diocesan was Ælfric and links with him remained until 1005: it may be the case that, after 994, Ælfric simply took Sigeric's place as Germanus's spiritual patron. Germanus no doubt took from Ramsey to Cholsey some surviving monks of those who had constituted the Winchcombe community to A.D. 975. They retained their devotion to St Kenelm of Winchcombe and the new abbey was probably dedicated partly to that royal boy-martyr.[386] However, this sequence of events had removed Germanus from the family of Reform-monasteries instituted by Oswald. In so far as Germanus was now indebted first to an archbishop of Canterbury who had also until recently been abbot of St Augustine's, we may suppose that the cultural affiliations of Cholsey Abbey would be with the Canterbury houses. This is precisely what we see in the two eleventh-century manuscripts showing particular concern for the cult of St Kenelm.[387] They may have been written at Canterbury or

---

383 See Knowles *et al.*, *The Heads*, p. 65, for the reasons for this history. On the obscurity of the origins of the Reform-monastery at St Albans, see *Wulfstan of Winchester*, edd. & transl. Lapidge & Winterbottom, p. 1, n. 46.

384 S. Keynes *apud* Fryde *et al.*, *Handbook*, p. 220.

385 The chronicle in MS. Cotton Iulius D.vii reports that King Æthelred founded Cholsey Abbey for the soul of his brother Edward, king and martyr: one wonders whether Sigeric used moral blackmail on Æthelred to secure this foundation. However, no such dedication of the abbey to St Edward is known. Whitelock, *Anglo-Saxon Wills*, p. 162, wrote that the foundation was made 'according to tradition in expiation of the murder of his brother Edward': 'tradition' turns out to be the chronicle cited here!

386 For the evidence see Dumville, *Liturgy*, chapter II. There must be some suspicion that promotion of the cult of St Kenelm was in some way associated with that of St Edward: for comparable possibilities, see Fell, 'Edward, king and martyr, and the Anglo-Saxon hagiographic tradition', pp. 8–10, and Rollason, 'The cults of murdered royal saints', pp. 17–22. Winchcombe Abbey under Abbot Germanus may have been dedicated to St Peter and St Kenelm, although at a later date St Mary and St Kenelm were the patrons (cf. Knowles *et al.*, *The Heads*, p. 78). The evidence of the kalendar in Cambridge, University Library, MS. Kk.5.32 (2074) may be taken to mean that Cholsey Abbey was dedicated to SS. Mary and Kenelm. One might also hypothesise that Germanus (and any followers) brought some books to Cholsey from Ramsey.

387 Cambridge, University Library, MSS. Ff.1.23 (1156) and Kk.5.32 (2074). Cf. Clemoes, *Manuscripts from Anglo-Saxon England*, pp. 5–6 (no. 8) and

at Cholsey but they belong palaeographically to the Canterbury orbit, as well as having textual and liturgical links with that city.[388]

What happened to Cholsey Abbey after 1005? In 1006 a Danish army spent the night there, according to what is probably an Abingdon addition to the Anglo-Saxon Chronicle of Æthelred's reign.[389]

7 þa to ðam middan wintran eodan him to heora gearwan feorme, ut þuruh Hamtunscire into Bearrucscire to Readingon; 7 hi a dydon heora ealdan gewunan, atendon hiora herebeacen swa hi ferdon. Wendon þa to Weal-ingaforda 7 þæt eall forswældon (7 wæron him ða ane niht æt Ceolesige) 7 wendon him þa andlang Æscesdune to Cwicelmes hlæwe . . .

And then towards Christmas they betook themselves to the entertainment awaiting them, out through Hampshire into Berkshire to Reading; and always they observed their ancient custom, lighting their beacons as they went. Then they turned to Wallingford and burnt it all (and were one night at Cholsey) and then turned along Ashdown to Cuckamsley Barrow . . .

The bracketed words are found only in MS. C and its derivative, MS. D. Their absence from MSS. EF suggests that they entered the text during its sojourn at Abingdon in the mid-eleventh century.[390] It has been speculated that this episode marked the end of the nunnery at Reading.[391]

---

15 (no. 25). Probably to this period belongs a forged charter in favour of Christ Church, Canterbury, in which St Kenelm appears as a witness and which is dated on his day, 17 July: London, British Library, MS. Cotton Augustus ii.96 (Sawyer, *Anglo-Saxon Charters*, no. 156: *Facsimiles*, ed. Bond, IV.7); cf. Brooks, *The Early History*, pp. 102–3.

[388] Cf. pp. 79–80, above. When Abbo of Fleury was at Ramsey (A.D. 985–987) he seems to have enjoyed close links with Archbishop Dunstan, as is evident both from the fact and from the content of his letter to Dunstan which is prefixed to his *Passio S. Eadmundi* (ed. Winterbottom, *Three Lives*, pp. 67–8; cf. n. 187, above). In a Worcester manuscript of the second half of the eleventh century (cf. n. 210, above) – London, British Library, MS. Cotton Nero E.i – are found three poems by Abbo to Dunstan (*Memorials of Saint Dunstan*, ed. Stubbs, pp. 410–12). After Dunstan's death in 988, and particularly in the period 995–1012, there seems to have been a frenzy of hagiographic activity, centred on Canterbury, which serves as testimony to the development of cult. At this time, between 995 and 1004, Abbo was sent a copy of B's prose Life of Dunstan to versify. It is striking that this was done, not by the archbishop of Canterbury, but by Wulfric, abbot of St Augustine's (see Stubbs, *ibid.*, pp. xxvii–xxviii, 409, for the evidence of Sankt Gallen, Stadtbibliothek, MS. 337; cf. p. 147, n. 39, below). One is tempted to wonder whether the relationship of Canterbury with Abbot Germanus had strengthened its ties with Abbo and Fleury.

[389] I give the text from MS. C(DEF), accompanied by the translation by Whitelock, *English Historical Documents*, p. 240.

[390] On this see Dumville, 'Some aspects of annalistic writing', pp. 27–8.

[391] This is the implication to be drawn from Knowles *et al.*, *The Heads*, p. 218; Whitelock, *Anglo-Saxon Wills*, p. 162, speculated that Cholsey Abbey 'was perhaps destroyed by the Danes in 1006'.

Whatever the impact on Cholsey, Abbot Germanus remained active for several years yet and we must suppose that the abbey enjoyed a continuing history. Its end is presumably to be placed in the half-century before the Norman conquest, the endowment reverting to the royal demesne. Whether it survived the death of its first abbot is perhaps doubtful; and what happened to its monks is unknown.[392]

---

[392] The later history of Cambridge, University Library, MS. Kk.5.32 (2074), fos 49–60, may be relevant here. In *Liturgy*, chapter II, I have pointed to the unusually detailed additions concerning St Edward which it attracted (probably in the later eleventh century).

III

THE EARLY HISTORY OF CAROLINE WRITING
AT CHRIST CHURCH, CANTERBURY

The evidence presented in the last chapter indicates that Style-I Anglo-Caroline script was practised in the approximate half-century 960–1010 by scribes at churches founded by or associated with St Oswald. The appearance of this style in surviving manuscripts of the 960s – emanating from the royal chancery and from Winchester – has indicated a threefold spread from a presumed point of origin.[1] I have wondered, in the previous chapter, whether the determining factor may not have been the sojourns of Oswald and Osgar at Fleury in the immediately preceding period.[2]

At the end of the half-century just mentioned, as the third Reform-generation in the English Church was coming into its inheritance, we see developments in English Caroline minuscule which led to the creation of what has with justice been described as a national script-style.[3] That process will be studied in the next chapter. The principal scribe at that point of departure was, or became, a monk of Christ Church, Canterbury. His work was essentially in the Style-I tradition, but modified by borrowings from Style-II practice. In the present chapter I propose to look at some aspects of the Canterbury background to developments after A.D. 1012, reserving to the next, however, consideration of one difficult and controversial group comprising mostly liturgical manuscripts written in Style I.[4]

Canterbury may be seen as the home of a scriptorium responsible for the best-defined group of Anglo-Caroline books outside the Style-I tradition. It has usually been said that Glastonbury was the point of origin for Anglo-Caroline Style II, but reasons have emerged for some

---

[1] On the question of that point of origin, a Continental model, see Bishop, *English Caroline Minuscule*, pp. xx–xxii. On the threefold dissemination, see pp. 18, 52–3, above.

[2] See above, p. 57; cf. pp. 142–3, below.

[3] See pp. 125–6, 135–8, below.

[4] This group centres on London, British Library, MS. Royal 1.D.ix and Rouen, Bibliothèque municipale, MS. Y.6 (274): see below, pp. 116–20, 134–5, and 139–40.

scepticism on this account.[5] A case was made by T.A.M. Bishop for seeing St Dunstan as a practitioner of a hybrid Insular-Caroline minuscule recognisably antecedent to mature Style-II Anglo-Caroline.[6] The undoubted development of the style at St Augustine's Abbey, Canterbury, has therefore led to some uncertainty about the history of this script-form. One solution would be to uncouple its development from the career of Dunstan. As I remarked above – in disagreement with Mr Bishop –, Style II seems to represent a tendency, an attitude or state of mind, rather than a tightly defined and artistically exclusive script-form.[7] In those circumstances we might, if we were so inclined, attribute the practice of Style II at St Augustine's to an independent creativity within a larger, southern English, context of polygenetic development of an Insular-influenced Anglo-Caroline minuscule.[8]

There are other possibilities of interpretation, however. Much turns on the nature of relationships between Christ Church and St Augustine's Abbey in the tenth century, and, in particular, on what connexions Archbishop Dunstan (959–988) might have had with the abbey. Unfortunately the tenth century is one of the cloudiest in that house's history.[9] There is not much doubt that the abbey had a continuous existence through the First Viking-Age and until the time of Dunstan's appointment to the archbishopric; however, it must be admitted that the documentary basis for this assertion is slight.[10] Early in the tenth century we find a mid-ninth-century vernacular document being copied into the 'Gospels of St Augustine' in a primitive form of Square minuscule.[11] Such slender threads of testimony do not prepare us for the important book-production which has been attributed to that house's tenth-century history.[12]

---

[5] See above, pp. 3, 17–18, 50–1, and below, pp. 89–90, 96–98, 142–4, 153.

[6] 'An early example of Insular-Caroline'; cf. *English Caroline Minuscule*, pp. xviii, xxii–xxiii.

[7] See chapter I, above.

[8] Bishop, 'Notes', pp. 332–4.

[9] I am indebted to Dr Susan Kelly for advising me on matters concerning the history and archives of St Augustine's.

[10] Sawyer, *Anglo-Saxon Charters*, nos 394, 518, 1506 provide some relevant material for A.D. 925, 946, and 958 respectively. And if the Abbot Eadhelm who was killed at Thetford in 952 (Anglo-Saxon Chronicle, *s.a.* 952 D) was indeed abbot of St Augustine's (Knowles *et al.*, *The Heads*, p. 35 and n. 1), we have a little more evidence for the house in the mid-tenth century.

[11] Sawyer, *Anglo-Saxon Charters*, no. 1198: Cambridge, Corpus Christi College, MS. 286, fo 74v (on which see Dumville, *Wessex and England*, pp. 94–5 and plate VI, and 'English Square minuscule script: the background and earliest phases', pp. 169–73 and plate V).

[12] For a Breton gospel-book (London, British Library, MS. Royal 1.A.xviii) possibly given to St Augustine's by King Æthelstan (A.D. 924–939), see Keynes, 'King Athelstan's books', pp. 165–70.

However, a number of significant difficulties attends the received cultural history of tenth-century Canterbury. Only some of these can be tackled here, for my main purpose in this chapter is to examine that history for evidence as to the influence of the Style-I Anglo-Caroline tradition on scriptorial activity there in the approximate period A.D. 960–1010. According to the existing scholarly account, there was no such influence. Nevertheless, Mr Bishop's writings on the script of Christ Church *ca* 1000 have left various loose ends: if they are gathered up and pulled, only part of his design remains intact. Two such hostages to fortune may be mentioned: his illustrations of hands allegedly written at Christ Church at that period clearly show Style-I influence on their scribes;[13] and various passing observations of his on the Canterbury background to the style pioneered in the years around 1020 by 'Eadwig Basan' indicate that Mr Bishop saw Style-I influence there in the preceding years, even though that awareness did not find a place in his history of the development of Anglo-Caroline minuscule.[14]

To Mr Bishop's outline-history of scriptorial activity at Canterbury from the mid-tenth century to the early years of the eleventh we may now turn. For him, revival began in the generation *ca* 940 x *ca* 970, and first at St Augustine's Abbey. In this period was placed a number of books – sharing a late mediaeval provenance at that house – written in generally very well executed Square minuscule. Among these specimens he distinguished between relatively earlier and later productions.[15] The date-range was provided by Bishop's sense that a style of Square minuscule is found in royal diplomas of that period and that that style is replicated in these manuscripts.[16] Unfortunately, neither part of that observation is accurate. The diplomas to which he referred must be those written in Phase-III Square minuscule, issued in the reigns of Edmund I, Eadred, and Eadwig (939–959), after which there is an abrupt change of style.[17] Phase-III Square minuscule is not that generally represented in the books attributed to St Augustine's, however. What is more, there is greater chronological and stylistic depth represented among these books than Mr Bishop allowed. For example, the copy of Amalarius's *Liber officialis* in Cambridge, Trinity College, MS. B.11.2 (241) is a specimen of Phase-II

---

[13] Bishop, 'Notes', pp. 413–23 and plates XIII(*c*) and XV on London, British Library, MS. Harley 1117, for example; see also *English Caroline Minuscule*, p. 8 (no. 10) and plate VIII, on Oxford, Bodleian Library, MS. Bodley 708 (*S.C.* 2609).

[14] *English Caroline Minuscule*, pp. xxi–xxiii (unless it be hidden in the phrase, p. xxiii, 'Possibly influenced by continuing or new contacts with other centres').

[15] Bishop, 'Notes', pp. 323–36 (cf. pp. 93 and 412–13).

[16] *Ibid.*, p. 325.

[17] For some discussion of these styles and transitions, see Dumville, *Wessex and England*, pp. 61–7, albeit without the numbering of phases; I have treated them more fully in 'English Square minuscule script: the mid-century phases'.

Square minuscule and may be attributed with confidence to the 930s:[18] if it originated at St Augustine's we may suppose that there was continuity of development of Square-minuscule writing there from Phase I, in the 920s, from which time there survives a copy of a St Augustine's document;[19] the Amalarian manuscript is an outstanding piece of book-production. Square minuscule seems to have continued in use at St Augustine's until the late tenth century, although it must be admitted that the evidence is distributed discontinuously.[20]

During the course of this history, Caroline began to be practised at St Augustine's. Mr Bishop placed this development within the second half of the tenth century,[21] but hinted strongly that the earliest possible date might be acceptable for the first specimens from the house.[22] The tenth-century Caroline manuscripts thought to have been written at St Augustine's show script, decoration, and physical features retaining a strongly Insular character. In so far as a decisively definable style of Anglo-Caroline has been associated with tenth-century Canterbury, it is the strongly hybrid form seen in manuscripts attributed to St Augustine's. In 1957 Mr Bishop hinted further that Caroline minuscule might have been received and developed at St Augustine's independently of its history at Glastonbury, Abingdon, Winchester, and elsewhere.[23] By 1971 another and more precise model had replaced that hypothesis in his mind: 'its Caroline minuscule seems to be allied, to be in not exactly immediate succession to a specimen of Caroline minuscule written at Glastonbury'.[24] He continued: 'The evidence that Glastonbury was the first home of Style II is less substantial than could be wished; numerous and securely attributed MSS. show that it was successively adopted, in the second half of the tenth century, by St. Augustine's and by Christ Church Canterbury'.[25] Finally, he observed,

---

[18] *Ibid.*; cf. also Dumville, *Britons and Anglo-Saxons*, chapter XIV, and 'On the dating', p. 43.

[19] See above, n. 11.

[20] In addition to the references given in n. 15, above, see *Aethici Istrici Cosmographia*, facs. ed. Bishop, introduction. The detailed periodisation of these manuscripts requires further discussion: see Dumville, 'English Square minuscule script: the mid-century phases'.

[21] *English Caroline Minuscule*, pp. 4 (no. 6), 5 (no. 7), 7 (no. 9). For the fullest available reproduction of a Style-II Anglo-Caroline manuscript – Leiden, Bibliotheek der Rijksuniversiteit, MS. Scaliger 69 – see *Aethici Istrici Cosmographia*, facs. ed. Bishop; for further relatives of that scribal performance, see Vezin, *Bibliothèque de l'École des Chartes* 124 (1966) 532–5.

[22] For this (potentially more radical) point of view, see Bishop, 'Notes', pp. 333–4.

[23] *Ibid.*

[24] *English Caroline Minuscule*, p. xx.

[25] *Ibid.*, p. xxii. On the numbers of manuscripts attributed to these houses, see p. xv.

'How long Style II was practised at St. Augustine's is unknown, for want of attributed and dated MSS.'.[26]

The caution about Glastonbury must be taken; and the model which brings such influence from Glastonbury to Canterbury is one constructed in another discipline, where it is uncertain that it can be sustained.[27] For this hypothesis to be upheld, two requirements must be met. First, it must be shown beyond doubt that Style-II Anglo-Caroline was written at Glastonbury Abbey before Dunstan's expulsion in A.D. 956; at present, evidence which would demonstrate the point has not been discovered.[28] Secondly, an explanation is needed as to why a script which is supposed to have come to Glastonbury in Dunstan's train should be practised at St Augustine's before it was taken up at Christ Church. One might go some way towards meeting this condition by noting scattered items of evidence which show or suggest a connexion between Dunstan, Glastonbury, and St Augustine's Abbey: for example, in B's Life of St Dunstan, one finds the archbishop at the abbey;[29] and the double-acrostic poem, INDIGNVM ABBATEM DVNSTANVM XP̄E RESPECTES, evidently composed by Dunstan as abbot of Glastonbury (A.D. 940 x 956), is found in a manuscript attributed by T.A.M. Bishop to St Augustine's on the evidence of the other connexions of its two scribes.[30]

But it is probably unnecessary to attempt to meet this condition, for evidence which suggests that Style-II Anglo-Caroline had already been developed at Christ Church has now come to hand as a result of study of the so-called 'Leofric Missal'. That conclusion itself would appear to

[26] *Ibid.*, p. xxiii. By a curious coincidence, his following footnote (p. xxiii, n. 1) contains a remark about Cambridge, University Library, MS. Kk.5.32 (2074), fos 49–60, which he attributed to post-1023 Glastonbury Abbey: both localisation and dating are mistaken, as I have shown in *Liturgy*, chapter II; the most plausible attribution (which, I said there, 'would be quite satisfactory') seems to be to St Augustine's, Canterbury. Cf. also my remarks above, pp. 79–85.

[27] For discussion of this problem, see Dumville, *Liturgy*, chapter II.

[28] See my remarks above, pp. 86–7.

[29] §36: *Memorials of Saint Dunstan*, ed. Stubbs, pp. 48–9. Cf. Pantin, 'The pre-Conquest saints of Canterbury', p. 157. It is striking how rapidly the cult of St Dunstan seems to have developed at St Augustine's: in 995 x 1004 we see a copy of B's *Vita S. Dunstani* being received at the abbey, revised, sent to Abbo of Fleury for versification (Sankt Gallen, Stadtbibliothek, MS. 337), and revised once again (London, British Library, MS. Cotton Cleopatra B.xiii, fos 59–90, which on the evidence of its script must have been written at St Augustine's very close indeed to the date of composition); on all this see Stubbs, *Memorials of Saint Dunstan*, pp. xxvi–xxix. For the possibility that all the surviving copies of B's work were written at St Augustine's, see p. 147, n. 39, below.

[30] The poem has been edited and translated by Lapidge, 'The hermeneutic style', pp. 95–7, 108–11 (for further discussion of its literary context see Lapidge, 'St Dunstan's Latin poetry'). On the manuscript – Cambridge, Trinity College, MS. O.1.18 (1042) – see Bishop, 'Notes', pp. 326–34 (cf. 412–13), and Keynes, *Anglo-Saxon Manuscripts*, pp. 20–1 (no. 10) and plates Xa–Xb (illustrating fos 12r and 112v).

negate at least the next chronological inference in Mr Bishop's outline-history of Style II:[31]

> about the turn of the tenth century the search for a perfected minuscule was pursued in the scriptorium of Christ Church Canterbury, where scribes may be seen modifying and refining their work from book to book and almost from page to page. Here the Square minuscule seems to have been given up all at once, and some scribes seem to have intentionally purged all traces of the native script from their Caroline minuscule. Possibly influenced by continuing or new contacts with other centres, the script of Christ Church developed and diverged from the St. Augustine's type; accurately cut pens were used to achieve a controlled but decisive shading in rather larger forms; the drawing, firm and consistent but still free and assured, created forms excellently differentiated and spaced; in the script of Christ Church at the beginning of the eleventh century the Caroline minuscule attained a possible limit of perfection.

It is possible that there was a moment at which the Anglo-Caroline of St Augustine's Abbey provided a decisive influence upon the work of the Christ Church scriptorium. But the cathedral scriptorium had already been experimenting with and developing Style-II Anglo-Caroline. For us to be able to comment satisfactorily on the interaction of the two houses' scripts, we should need to know more about the general state of relationships between the cathedral and the abbey. Mr Bishop has shown that manuscripts travelled between the two houses, and that books in the library of one served as exemplars in the scriptoria of the other.[32] It is not known whether the same was true of scribes. Might the accession of Sigeric, abbot of St Augustine's from 970 x 975 (and bishop of Ramsbury 985–990), to the archbishopric in 990 have provided a decisive moment of the sort referred to, above?[33] If, in general, the relationship of the cathedral and the abbey remained in this period as close as it had been in earlier centuries,[34] to make too sharp a separation of the activities and products of their scriptoria may be mistaken. The danger is compounded by the fact that the primary evidence for localisation is usually provided by late mediaeval provenance, reinforced by the association of collaborating scribes in several manuscripts of that same provenance; but the fit is not perfect and, for the moment at least, much caution should be counselled.[35]

---

[31] *English Caroline Minuscule*, pp. xxii–xxiii.

[32] *Ibid.*, pp. 6, 7, for example. Cf. Bishop, 'Notes', pp. 413–14, 417–18.

[33] For the career of Sigeric, see Knowles *et al.*, *The Heads*, p. 35; Brooks, *The Early History*, pp. 278–83; Ortenberg, 'Archbishop Sigeric's journey'. See also above, pp. 79–83, and below, pp. 103–4.

[34] On this, see (for example) Brooks, *The Early History*, pp. 87–92, 163–4. The change may come in the period after A.D. 1011/12: *ibid.*, p. 265.

[35] Compare, for example, the histories of Oxford, Bodleian Library, MS. Auct. F.1.15 (*S.C.* 2455), part 1, and London, British Library, MS. Cotton Otho E.i: Bishop, 'Notes', p. 418.

We must accordingly turn back to the evidence for tenth-century practice of Caroline writing at Christ Church. It begins in a Continental gospel-book given to Canterbury Cathedral by King Æthelstan (924–939): London, British Library, MS. Cotton Tiberius A.ii.[36] On fo 15r is a poem, 'Rex pius AEÐELSTAN', which serves as an inscription of gift, recording the king's donation of the book to Christ Church.[37] The poem was composed, if its present tenses may be taken at face-value, during Æthelstan's lifetime; Simon Keynes has deduced from it that it was written in 937 x 939.[38] There is no obvious reason to doubt that this copy is original and belongs to the time of composition. However, his further conclusion that it 'provides valuable evidence for the presence of a continental scribe at Canterbury in the late 930s' is rather uncertain,[39] for it is in principle more likely to have been written by a royal scribe.[40] Michael Lapidge indeed, in his study of the poem, has gone so far as to argue that it was composed at Christ Church, that its scribe was active there and that he was 'possibly' the king's secretary Petrus who had in 927 composed another set of documentary verses on Æthelstan's behalf.[41] These propositions are uncertainly consistent with one another. That the Continental scribe belonged to the *familia* of Christ Church in the 930s must remain doubtful.[42]

More promising evidence is provided by the manuscripts of Frithegod's *Breuiloquium uitae sancti Wilfredi*, an extraordinary poem written at Canterbury in A.D. 948 x 958.[43] Frithegod was a Frankish cleric who entered the service of Archbishop Oda (941–958) and who seems to have left England after the latter's death in mid-958. The story of Frithegod's career and the development of his literary work have recently been elucidated by Michael Lapidge.[44] The text in the earliest of

---

[36] Keynes, 'King Athelstan's books', pp. 147–53. Francis Wormald (*English Drawings*, pp. 22–3) argued that it provided the direct model for the Anglo-Saxon artist who drew the portrait of St Matthew added to Oxford, St John's College, MS. 194, a Breton gospel-book then in the possession of Canterbury Cathedral.

[37] Edited and translated by Lapidge, 'Some Latin poems', pp. 93–7.

[38] Keynes, 'King Athelstan's books', pp. 150–1 and plate IV.

[39] *Ibid.*, p. 151; cf. Brooks, *The Early History*, pp. 219–20.

[40] This is the conclusion which Keynes has drawn about the other inscription recording Æthelstan's gift – a prose notice on fo 15v written in Phase-III Square minuscule (Keynes, 'King Athelstan's books', pp. 149–50 and plate III). Either that is one of the very earliest Phase-III specimens or it should be dated a little later than the last years of Æthelstan's reign, namely to the period 944x949 in which the scribe is known to have been active.

[41] 'Some Latin poems', pp. 96, 95, 97. For the other poem see *ibid.*, pp. 83–93, 98.

[42] For a similar muddle see Brooks, *The Early History*, pp. 219–20.

[43] ed. Campbell, *Frithegodi Monachi Breuiloquium*; cf. Lapidge, 'The hermeneutic style', pp. 77–81.

[44] 'A Frankish scholar'.

the three manuscripts of the *Breuiloquium* – London, British Library, MS. Cotton Claudius A.i, fos 5–36 – is written in a single hand in Continental Caroline minuscule.[45] The second manuscript – St Petersburg, Public Library, MS. O.v.XIV.1 – is a copy of the first, and was made by five collaborating scribes, one of whom (scribe IV), according to Lapidge, had written the Cottonian manuscript.[46] Two of the scribes wrote a minuscule which must be described as a hybrid of Continental Caroline and English Square minuscule.[47] Finally, the third manuscript – Paris, Bibliothèque nationale, MS. latin 8431, fos 21–48 – was written by a single scribe in what can perhaps be described as English Caroline minuscule; it too is a copy of the Cottonian manuscript.[48] Palaeography and textual history combine to demand that these manuscripts were all produced in a single scriptorium in close proximity to the author: that was assuredly located at Canterbury. It is also likely from what may be reconstructed of Frithegod's career that all three would have been written before Frithegod's hypothesised departure from England in or soon after 958.[49]

[45] On this manuscript, cf. Ker, *Catalogue*, pp. 176–7 (no. 140); Lapidge, 'A Frankish scholar', pp. 51–3 and plates I–II. It should be noted that this was subsequently in the library of Glastonbury Abbey (Lapidge, *ibid.*, p. 53, n. 34, and p. 57, n. 56). Two later Christ Church manuscripts – London, British Library, MSS. Harley 3020 and Royal 12.C.xxiii – had a similar history: Dumville, *Liturgy*, pp. 110–11; Carley, 'Two pre-Conquest manuscripts', pp. 201–4 (cf. Stork, *Through a Gloss*, frontispiece, for a reproduction of Royal, fo 83r). For the importance of such transmission, see above, pp. 50–1.

[46] Lapidge, 'A Frankish scholar', pp. 53–5 and plates III–IV. It is to be noted that this was at one time bound with an Anglo-Saxon manuscript – now St Petersburg, Public Library, MS. O.v.XVI.1, of the first half of the tenth century (cf. Dumville, 'English Square minuscule script: the background and earliest phases', pp. 173–8). It would be a remarkable coincidence if these two manuscripts had reached Corbie independently.

[47] Scribe I even wrote **t** with turned-down toe, a ninth-century feature found in some of the oldest specimens of Square minuscule (*ibid.*, p. 165); for a facsimile of St Petersburg Scribe I, see Lapidge, 'A Frankish scholar', plate III.

[48] *Ibid.*, pp. 55–6 and plate V.

[49] This is the indefeasible deduction from Lapidge's account of the textual history of the poem and the palaeography and history of the manuscripts. If the Paris manuscript went to the Auvergne with Frithegod, it must have been written in the mid-tenth century: its apparent shelf-mark '.Lan.' (fo 21v) must therefore be a tenth- as well as an eleventh-century usage (cf. *ibid.*, p. 56 and n. 49, where the reference is presumably to Paris, B.N., MS. latin 6401A, not 6401). Likewise, the comparison of the opening chrismon of St Petersburg Scribe I (*ibid.*, p. 54 and n. 39) with a royal diploma of A.D. 984 (Sawyer, *Anglo-Saxon Charters*, no. 853) must be misleading, given both the textual history and the palaeography. That these points were not taken by Lapidge in his paper (see 'A Frankish scholar', p. 58, where he allowed datings of 948 x *ca* 1000 for all three witnesses) has unfortunately given an impression of self-contradiction in what is otherwise a beautifully lucid account. One other matter touching on chronology requires comment. The narrow dating for Frithegod's sojourn at Canterbury (coextensive with Oda's pontificate, 941–958) relies on the assumption

The evidence of the St Petersburg manuscript is critical here. It shows a scriptorium at work, presumably in the 950s, with one Continental scribe working alongside two probably English scribes (and another as yet unattributed). If the Continental scribe was Frithegod himself, we are left with one scribe in that manuscript and the scribe of the Paris manuscript writing minuscule not obviously attributable to a national origin: both were working at Canterbury.[50] It is hard not to allow that the scriptorium, presumably at Christ Church, had adopted Caroline minuscule with determination, and probably under the direction of a Frankish master (who may or may not have been Frithegod himself).

It is perhaps no surprise that such activity should occur during Archbishop Oda's tenure of the see of Canterbury. This reform-minded prelate is known to have taken monastic vows (perhaps in 936) and to have been in contact with Continental Benedictine houses.[51] He despatched his nephew Oswald to Fleury to study the monastic life in a Benedictine context: shortly after his uncle died, Oswald returned to England where he secured the patronage of Dunstan[52] (who succeeded as archbishop of Canterbury sixteen months or more after Oda's death)[53] and found himself appointed by King Edgar to the see of Worcester in succession to Dunstan. There is some evidence from A.D. 957 that Oda had intended to found a monastery at Ely, perhaps in the Reform-tradition and headed by Oswald: but the plan came to nothing when Oda died soon afterwards, before Oswald's return.[54]

A further and important body of evidence may apply to these years. Oxford, Bodleian Library, MS. Bodley 579 (*S.C.* 2675) is a substantial Continental sacramentary (known from its later history as 'the Leofric Missal') which was imported into England after 910 and before about 930.[55] Once in England it began to receive a remarkable series of

---

that he was personally dependent on the archbishop (*ibid.*, p. 62); otherwise, we could allow him a much longer career in England.

[50] Brooks, *The Early History*, p. 231, has made an interesting speculation based on the evidence of these hands: 'if there is any historical truth in Eadmer's story that the four *clerici* who had brought the relics of Audoenus to England subsequently joined Oda's community at Christ Church, then we could well understand how there should be several scribes with Continental Caroline hands at Christ Church in the mid-tenth century'.

[51] *Ibid.*, pp. 222–3. Cf. Dumville, *Wessex and England*, chapter V.

[52] See chapter II above, especially p. 52.

[53] On the events of this period see Whitelock, 'The appointment', and Brooks, *The Early History*, p. 244.

[54] *Ibid.*, p. 226; Sawyer, *Anglo-Saxon Charters*, no. 646; *Facsimiles*, ed. Keynes, no. 5.

[55] *The Leofric Missal*, ed. Warren, for a complete edition of the contents of the codex. In view of the possibility that the manuscript travelled from Arras to Aquitaine before it came to England (cf. Dumville, *Liturgy*, p. 82), an entertaining possibility as to the agent of transmission to England may be mentioned, if perhaps only to be dismissed. This

additions which enable us to say something of its history.[56] From the 920s (when the earliest English addition was made)[57] to the early years of the eleventh century, some thirty scribes augmented this manuscript, whether in Anglo-Saxon Square minuscule or in Anglo-Caroline. In spite of the large number of tenth-century English hands and the different scripts visible in this book, it is possible to argue that they are the products of a single scriptorium during a period of somewhat under a century. The earliest hands are all specimens of Square minuscule in Phases I, II, and III, belonging therefore to the years *ca* 920 x *ca* 960.[58] While some later Square minuscule is found, hybrid Insular-Caroline minuscule is used in additions on a good many occasions. The tenth-century Anglo-Caroline additions belong, almost without exception, to the Style-II tradition. Only the very latest of this series of supplements can be described otherwise: a couple of additions may be considered to have been written in Style I verging on Style IV, a transitional type belonging to the early years of the eleventh century;[59] one specimen describable as Style IV, albeit with some non-standard features, may be the last of this series.[60] Only one house is known at which all these scribal fashions may be admitted to have been practised, and that is Christ Church, Canterbury. Furthermore, it is clear that this was a book suitable principally for a bishop or an archbishop: that it was used at an episcopal church in England is made clear by additions specifically for a bishop's use.[61] If the added blessings – on the king, and on the king in the time of a synod – are English, then they may point in the same direction.[62] The short litany added by an English scribe contains the invocations 'Vt regem Anglorum et exercitum eius conseruare digneris. Vt eis uitam et sanitatem atque uictoriam dones, te rogamus.'[63] What is more, two

---

is the journey which Lapidge ('A Frankish scholar') has supposed Frithegod to have made. If we are obliged, with Lapidge, to bring Frithegod to England in Archbishop Oda's train, that would probably be too late to satisfy the demands of the palaeography of the English additions. On the other hand, if we allow Frithegod to have arrived earlier, joining Athelm (923–926) or Wulfhelm (926–941), the option is open!

56 I hope shortly to publish studies of the structure of the codex and of the palaeography of the tenth-century additions.

57 Dumville, 'English Square minuscule script: the background and earliest phases', pp. 173–8, referring to fo 12; for fo 154v see Pächt *et al.*, *Illuminated Manuscripts*, III.3 (no. 20). See also fo 267v.

58 For Phase II see n. 57, above; specimens of Phase III may be seen on 15v–16r and 245v, for example.

59 See fos 210r18–19 and 259v12–260r.

60 Fo 58v1–22: it is just possible that this could be one of the Exeter additions.

61 Fos 276v–278v.

62 Fos 13v11–14r.

63 Fos 257r–258r: *Anglo-Saxon Litanies*, ed. Lapidge, p. 225 (no. XXIX [i]); cf. *ibid.*, pp. 76–7, where this litany is mistakenly treated as part of the original, Continental text. Its immediate liturgical context is not clear to me.

alterations were made by an English scribe to votive masses which the original, Continental book contained:[64] these indicate that the change was effected in the reign of a married king; Edmund I, Eadwig, Edgar, or Æthelred must be the ruler in question.

The book eventually left Canterbury for the South-west, reaching Exeter by the time of Bishop Leofric (1046–1050 at Credition, 1050–1072 at Exeter), and perhaps having sojourned for a while at Tavistock Abbey.[65] Under Leofric's supervision it received a further and extensive series of additions.[66] We must suppose either that it was replaced at Christ Church by more modern liturgical manuscripts, becoming surplus to requirements and able to be passed on to a bishop of a poorer see (we know that Leofric gained many of his books from Canterbury[67]), or (more excitably) that it was snatched from Canterbury by vikings and ransomed in the South-west. It has in fact usually been argued that the book's whole tenth-century English history was spent in the South-west, at Glastonbury Abbey: but neither the palaeography nor the episcopal nature of the original book and its English additions will permit this history; elsewhere I have shown the liturgical argument (from the added kalendar) for a Glastonbury attribution to be misconceived and an attribution to Canterbury well within the bounds of possibility.[68]

What may be seen to be particularly important once the book has been attributed to Canterbury is the practice there of hybrid Insular-Caroline minuscule of a type recognised otherwise only in manuscripts associated (whether directly or by an extended and less plausible chain of reasoning) with Dunstan. First, this evidence allows an argument for continuity in the writing of Caroline minuscule at Christ Church from the pontificate of Oda to that of Dunstan. Secondly, it reinforces the doubts which have already arisen about the necessary attribution of Dunstan's Caroline writing to his time as abbot of Glastonbury (A.D. 940 x 956).[69] Only

---

64 Fos 231v19–20 ('regi nostro famuleque tuę regine') and 232r21 ('regem nostrum famulamque tuam reginam'). These alterations were made to the mass-prayers of a votive *pro amico*, affecting the collect and postcommunion respectively.

65 For discussion, see Dumville, *Liturgy*, chapter II.

66 The most thorough treatment is that by Drage, 'Bishop Leofric', chapter III.

67 This matter deserves a separate study; cf. Bishop, *English Caroline Minuscule*, pp. xvi, 5 (no. 7), 7 (no. 9), 8 (no. 10).

68 Dumville, *Liturgy*, chapters I–II. From rewritten passages on fos 111v–112r (pointed out by H.M. Bannister), E.W.B. Nicholson (*apud* Hunt *et al.*, *A Summary Catalogue*, II, pt 1, pp. 487–9) argued that, given the reading '[cum] archiepiscopo nostro atque rege nostro' (112r8–9), 'In that case (as no *bishop* is included in this *Exultet*) it looks as if [Leofric A] was in use at Canterbury before Leofric obtained it'. Unfortunately Nicholson spoiled the effect of this inspired deduction by arguing that this Arras manuscript must be dated 'not before 1040'. The phrase in question belongs to the collect which concludes the *Exultet* preface.

69 See above, pp. 86–7 and references in n. 5. For a false augmentation of the corpus of manuscripts attributed to Dunstan, see Galloway, 'On the medieval and post-medieval collation', p. 107.

two manuscripts are known to contain matter in Dunstan's own hand: Oxford, Bodleian Library, MS. Auct. F.4.32 (*S.C.* 2176), of late mediaeval Glastonbury provenance;[70] Roma, Biblioteca Apostolica Vaticana, MS. lat. 3363, a Loire-Valley product with extensive marginalia in Anglo-Saxon Square minuscule and in Dunstan's Insular-Caroline.[71] Similar script has also been noted in corrections to four other manuscripts, only one of which has a known mediaeval provenance – thirteenth-century Bury St Edmunds was the home of the Continental book, Oxford, Bodleian Library, MS. Rawlinson C.697 (*S.C.* 12541); other corrections (in Anglo-Saxon Square minuscule) have suggested the presence of this manuscript at St Augustine's Abbey, Canterbury, in the mid-tenth century.[72] Only one of the books thus corrected is tenth-century and English – Cambridge, University Library, MS. Ee.2.4 (922) + Oxford, Bodleian Library, MS. Lat. theol. c.3 (*S.C.* 31382), fos 1–2: its text-hand, like the correcting hand, is a specimen of Style-II Anglo-Caroline displaying in its Insular elements some Celtic features.[73] A Celtic dimension is variously recorded for St Augustine's in the mid-tenth century.[74] It may be that at both the Canterbury houses we see evidence from early in Dunstan's

---

[70] Fos 1r (verses), 20r (last four lines), 36r, 47r: *Saint Dunstan's Classbook*, facs. ed. Hunt.

[71] Troncarelli, *Tradizioni perdute*; Parkes, 'A note on MS Vatican, Bibl. Apost., lat. 3363'; cf. Dumville, 'English Square minuscule script: the background and earliest phases', pp. 173–8.

[72] Ker, *Catalogue*, p. 427 (no. 349); Bishop, 'Notes', p. 93, and *English Caroline Minuscule*, p. 2 (cf. 'An early example of Insular-Caroline'); Lapidge, 'The revival', pp. 18–20, and 'Some Latin poems', pp. 72–83; Keynes, 'King Athelstan's books', p. 144 and plate I; O'Keeffe, 'The text of Aldhelm's *Enigma* no. c'.

[73] Bishop, 'An early example of Insular-Caroline' and *English Caroline Minuscule*, p. 2 (no. 3) and plate II. Particularly notable in this regard are forms of abbreviation of *est*, *qui*, and the syllable *-ra(-)*.

[74] This is shown, for example, by the reception of the Welsh codex, Cambridge, Corpus Christi College, MS. 153, and of the hypothesised Welsh exemplar of MS. 352: Bishop, 'The Corpus Martianus Capella' and *English Caroline Minuscule*, p. 3 (no. 4). The same may be true of the copy of Gildas's *De excidio Britanniae* in London, British Library, MS. Cotton Vitellius A.vi (for a reduced plate of fo 16v, see Brown, *Anglo-Saxon Manuscripts*, p. 7, no. 3), but the evidence of this manuscript (of which I am preparing a full study) has not yet been thoroughly evaluated. The tenth-century Brittonic miscellany, Oxford, Bodleian Library, MS. Bodley 572 (*S.C.* 2026), fos 1–50, also reached St Augustine's. It is a nice question whether we might now include 'St Dunstan's Classbook' on this list. If so, a Breton element must be added to the picture: another Breton manuscript in tenth-century Canterbury (apparently at Christ Church) was Oxford, Bodleian Library, MS. Hatton 42 (*S.C.* 4117), containing *Collectio canonum Hibernensis*, a text used already by Archbishop Oda (cf. Dumville, *Wessex and England*, chapter V, and 'Wulfric cild').

pontificate for reception of, adaptation to, and experiments with Caroline minuscule, leading rapidly to the creation of Style-II Anglo-Caroline.[75]

It is no doubt significant, as T.A.M. Bishop observed, that the text carried in CUL MS. Ee.2.4 (922) is Smaragdus's Commentary on the Benedictine Rule.[76] (At Christ Church in the later middle ages a closely related copy of that text was attributed to Dunstan himself.)[77] A high proportion of the books now associated with St Augustine's Abbey in the tenth century comprises works on monasticism, including two copies of the Rule itself.[78] Such a strain is also found among Christ Church books, but is there greatly outnumbered by more generally literary texts.[79] There can, I think, be little doubt that the mid-century generations of ecclesiastics at Canterbury were much concerned with monastic theory and practice, and notably that of St Benedict of Nursia. At St Augustine's Abbey this seems to be a phenomenon which antedated the adoption of Caroline minuscule by native scribes.

Because none of the Anglo-Caroline manuscripts from St Augustine's has been independently dated on non-palaeographical criteria, it is not easy to be certain how the development of what has seemed to be that

[75] One may compare what was happening in the 960s in the royal chancery (on the evidence of the scribe known as 'Eadgar A': cf. Bishop, *English Caroline Minuscule*, p. 9, no. 11, and plate IX) and at Winchester Cathedral (on the evidence of Cambridge, Corpus Christi College, MS. 173: cf. Dumville, *Wessex and England*, p. 61); these specimens of Phase-IV Square minuscule show another, but quite different, example of such experimental adaptation of the two scripts to one another.

[76] Bishop, 'An early example of Insular-Caroline', p. 396.

[77] London, British Library, MS. Royal 10.A.xiii (cf. p. 8, n. 4, above), containing an originally anonymous copy of that text. On fo 2v is a full-page illustration of a monk beginning to write out the Benedictine Rule: it was reproduced by Warner & Gilson, *British Museum Catalogue*, IV, plate 65. A legend (of unspecified date) identifies the figure as St Dunstan. On fo 1r, in a fourteenth-century hand, we read 'Exposicio sancti Dunstani super regulam sancti Benedicti', to which is added 'Quidam uero dicunt quod est exposicio Smaradi monachi; alii dicunt quod est exposicio Eligii, et ita est'. The book belonged to Christ Church by at least the fourteenth century.

[78] Cambridge, Trinity College, MS. O.2.30 (1134), fos 129–172, in Square minuscule; London, British Library, MS. Harley 5431, in Anglo-Caroline minuscule (I cannot see why Wormald, 'Æthelwold and his Continental counterparts', p. 31, n. 74, has described this manuscript as Continental).

[79] For example, Cambridge, University Library, MS. Ff.4.43 (1286), containing Smaragdus's *Diadema monachorum*; Roma, Biblioteca Apostolica Vaticana, MS. Reg. lat. 489, fos 61–124, containing monastic works by Sulpicius Seuerus (as also in London, British Library, MS. Additional 40074, but I am doubtful about the attribution to Christ Church given by Gneuss, 'A preliminary list', p. 21, no. 296, and repeated by Brooks, *The Early History*, p. 268, for the script seems to be of the type characteristic of St Augustine's). For a list of manuscripts (with their contents) variously ascribed to late Anglo-Saxon Christ Church (but with no attempt to discriminate between degrees of probability of attribution), see Brooks, *ibid.*, pp. 266–70; for useful comment on the contents, *ibid.*, pp. 270–8.

abbey's distinctive style of the script relates to the work of the Christ Church scriptorium. The kalendar and *computistica* of the 'Leofric Missal' (MS. Bodley 579, fos 38–59) at least give an approximate date (probably 979 x 987) for one important stratum within the tenth-century work on that codex.[80] Crucially, T.A.M. Bishop saw 'some resemblance' between the script of this part of the 'Leofric Missal' and one of the hands in Cambridge, University Library, MS. Ff.4.43 (1286), a copy of Smaragdus's *Diadema monachorum*, another work on the Benedictine Rule:[81] in both manuscripts the membranes are arranged HFHF, a criterion employed by Mr Bishop as an indicator of relative dating among manuscripts attributable to the Christ Church scriptorium.[82]

In Mr Bishop's history of the Christ Church scriptorium, CUL MS. Ff.4.43 (1286) occupied an important place. His view was that it 'seems to be the earliest extant product of the Christ Church scriptorium to show the Continental script'. Four of its six scribes seem to have been trying, with very varying degrees of success, to learn the script, while two expert scribes practised widely divergent forms of Anglo-Caroline. Various difficulties, both internal and external, attend Mr Bishop's reconstruction of the history of Caroline writing at Christ Church. As he himself noted, one of the scribes is found in a manuscript – Roma, Biblioteca Apostolica Vaticana, MS. Reg. lat. 489, fos 61–124 (monastic writings of Sulpicius Seuerus) – which occupies a relatively much later place.[83] Secondly, those scribes who are seen as beginners in MS. Ff.4.43 (1286) are by no means all to be reckoned as calligraphers experienced in Square minuscule: there are absolute beginners here, trying to come to grips with Caroline models; they cannot therefore be used as precise evidence for the point of transition from Insular to Caroline writing.[84] Thirdly, scribes 5 (fos 49–64) and 6 (fos 73–88) practised very different versions of Anglo-Caroline minuscule; something of the same contrast may be seen between scribes 2 and 1 of Oxford, Bodleian Library, MS. Bodley 708 (*S.C.* 2609), a copy of Gregory the Great's *Regula pastoralis*, whose third scribe offered a different style again, his 'ugly but proficient work' being 'unlike that of contemporary Christ Church scribes'.[85] What the contemporaneous practice of these divergent styles means for the development of Anglo-

---

[80] For the dating see Dumville, *Liturgy*, chapter II.

[81] *English Caroline Minuscule*, p. 1 (no. 2) and p. 6 (no. 8).

[82] 'Notes', pp. 420–1 (cf. *English Caroline Minuscule*, pp. xxv–xxvi).

[83] *Ibid.*, p. 6 (quotation) and pp. xxv–xxvi.

[84] Contrast the remarks of Clemoes, *Manuscripts from Anglo-Saxon England*, p. 14 (no. 24).

[85] *English Caroline Minuscule*, p. 8. For another plate from this manuscript see Thompson, *An Introduction*, p. 433 (no. 173).

Caroline writing at Christ Church is a nice question, one to which we must shortly return.

Mr Bishop held, in derivation from the views of David Knowles,[86] that the Benedictine Rule had not been adopted by the Christ Church community until it was imposed in A.D. 997 by Archbishop Ælfric. But this history depends on unreliable eleventh-century sources and responds to concerns of a later period.[87] It is specifically controverted, for example, by the Benedictine character of the 'Bosworth Psalter'[88] – London, British Library, MS. Additional 37517 – written under Dunstan's auspices in a monumental Square minuscule similar to that of another book associated with Dunstan, his pontifical, now Paris, Bibliothèque nationale, MS. latin 943.[89] Indeed, there is an argument that the Rule was known and followed at Christ Church as early as the time of Archbishop Wulfred (805–832).[90] However, to see the community as becoming fully Benedictine only in 997 was to gain a fixed point for the full adoption of Caroline minuscule script. This was reinforced by Mr Bishop's identification, in Canterbury books, of the scribes of two apparently original royal diplomata, belonging to A.D. 995 and 1002.[91]

---

[86] Bishop, *English Caroline Minuscule*, p. 6. Knowles's views were fashioned in the course of a three-way controversy: Robinson, 'The early community'; Symons, 'The introduction of monks'; Knowles, 'The early community'. For a different emphasis, cf. Knowles, *The Monastic Order*, pp. 696–7. See now also Brooks, *The Early History*, pp. 243–82, on the period of reform at Christ Church.

[87] *Ibid.*, pp. 255–61 (cf. 149). For a palaeographical correction to Brooks's account (in respect of 'Eadwig Basan'), see below, p. 126 and n. 75.

[88] Gasquet & Bishop, *The Bosworth Psalter*, pp. 3–14, 126–30; Korhammer, 'The origin', pp. 173–4; Temple, *Anglo-Saxon Manuscripts*, pp. 48–9 (no. 22); *Die monastischen Cantica*, ed. Korhammer; *The Canterbury Hymnal*, ed. Wieland; Brooks, *The Early History*, pp. 252–3; Dumville, 'On the dating', p. 45.

[89] Temple, *Anglo-Saxon Manuscripts*, pp. 60–1 (no. 35), and cf. pp. 48–9 for the relationship: the original scribe of the Paris manuscript wrote also Oxford, Bodleian Library, MS. Bodley 718 (*S.C.* 2632) and Exeter, Cathedral Library, MS. 3507 (cf. Ker, *Catalogue*, p. 437). If one wished to deny the argument made here about the value of the evidence from the 'Bosworth Psalter' for the Benedictine character of Christ Church in Dunstan's time, it would be necessary to suppose that it applied to Dunstan's monastic refoundation at Westminster. For the nature of the interpretation which would have to be made of Bosworth's testimony, see Korhammer, 'The origin', pp. 182–7. The 'Dunstan Pontifical' is found in the possession of Wulfsige, prior and (perhaps after Dunstan's death) abbot of Westminster, then (991 x 993–1002) bishop of Sherborne (cf. Knowles *et al.*, *The Heads*, p. 76, on Wulfsige).

[90] I am indebted to Brigitte Langefeld for pointing this out to me; she hopes to publish on this matter soon.

[91] Taunton, Somerset County Museum, DD/SAS.PR.502 (Sawyer, *Anglo-Saxon Charters*, no. 884; Bishop, *English Caroline Minuscule*, pp. xxvi, 7; *Facsimiles*, ed. Keynes, no. 11); London, British Library, Stowe Charter 35 (Sawyer, *Anglo-Saxon Charters*, no. 905; Bishop, 'Notes', pp. 420–1; Whitelock, 'A note on the career', p. 461; *Facsimiles*, ed. Sanders, III.36). It has been noted that the correct date for the charter is 11 July, 1002, even though the manuscript reads *M.III.*; Keynes (*The*

One may feel some considerable doubt about the second of these identifications,[92] but the pattern seemed clear enough at the time when Mr Bishop defined it. He was able to suppose that Caroline writing began at Canterbury cathedral late in the pontificate of Dunstan (*ob.* 988) as 'a suitable exercise for a benedictinizing element in the Christ Church community'.[93] After 997, in his reconstruction of events, development was rapid. Some forty manuscripts have been described by Mr Bishop as the survivors of books produced in the cathedral scriptorium during a period spanning little more than the last decade of the tenth century and the first decade of the eleventh.[94] He also took the view that 'Unlike the rival Canterbury scriptorium the Christ Church scribes seem to have abandoned the insular script all at once';[95] this conclusion must be understood as applying only to Latin writing but, even so, its accuracy is uncertain. Further, he has suggested that 'Some, though not all, of the scribes seem to have tried to eliminate, in writing the caroline, the last vestiges of the square minuscule'.[96]

The presence in CUL MS. Ff.4.43 (1286) of developed hands in divergent styles could be reconciled with its supposed position at the beginning of the history of Caroline writing at Christ Church if, and only if, we were to suppose that the two scribes in question were both imported from other scriptoria. In principle, this is not an impossible proposition; in practice, however, if it is associated with Mr Bishop's relative chronology, it creates a more severe difficulty than that which it is designed to solve. What is more, this whole exercise raises questions about the nature and definition of Style-II Anglo-Caroline minuscule.

Mr Bishop and I have taken different positions on this last question. At the beginning of this book I described Style II as an 'attitude', a willingness to admit an admixture of Insular elements into Caroline book-production.[97] On the other hand, Mr Bishop saw Style II as a series of attempts, by a variety of scribes, to imitate an as yet unidentified Continental model: these scribes nonetheless accepted eclecticism as a

---

Diplomas of King Æthelred, p. 259) has seen in this a reason for doubting the strict contemporaneity of this single sheet and therefore for admitting that this was a Christ Church scribe. In fact, examination of the manuscript shows the last minim of the date to be additional: one would do better to accept the scribe as being in the king's employ. Both of these diplomas are written in Style-I Anglo-Caroline; in the latter case, in some respects the script is verging on Style-IV usage (for this development, cf. chapter IV, especially pp. 134–5, below).

[92] Cf. below, pp. 109–10.
[93] *English Caroline Minuscule*, p. 6.
[94] *Ibid.*, pp. xx, xxii–xxiii, 6–8, and 'Notes', p. 420.
[95] *Ibid.*, p. 419.
[96] *Ibid.* This suggests that a pure Caroline (represented in England by Style-I Anglo-Caroline) was perceived by these scribes as having especial merit.
[97] See above, p. 2.

principle of script-creation.[98] If we return to CUL MS. Ff.4.43 (1286), these points may be illustrated from the two expert scribes (5 and 6) whose work has already been mentioned.

Hand 6 was illustrated in Bishop's *English Caroline Minuscule* and has come to seem the very embodiment of Christ Church Anglo-Caroline in this era.[99] It may be held to represent a development of the form of Style II which had been pioneered at St Augustine's Abbey. If so, MS. Ff.4.43 cannot represent the origins of Christ Church Anglo-Caroline unless we suppose that this particular variety had already been developed at St Augustine's and was now being imported into and somewhat modified at Christ Church. Questions are raised thereby about the integrity of the scriptorial forms associated with each of the Canterbury minsters. In the work of Scribe 6 of MS. Ff.4.43 we see a very regular and disciplined type of Anglo-Caroline, purged of consistent use of Insular letter-forms and ligatures, but retaining in its angularity some reminder of the Insular background. By comparison with the still hybrid script of St Augustine's – whose general aspect is determined above all by the slanting strokes of single-compartment **a** and of split **r** with (short) descender[100] – that represented here by Hand 6 is regimented and (from the Caroline point of view) sanitised. One might argue, however, that it remains recognisably within the Style-II tradition. On the other hand, if one turns to the Caroline script of books which Mr Bishop has attributed to a place within the Style-I tradition and, almost certainly erroneously, to an origin at Abingdon Abbey,[101] one finds writing of remarkably similar aspect: 'mere aspect' (as Mr Bishop might put it) this may be,[102] but it would not be unimaginable to posit this as the result of continuing to 'cleanse' the practices of one such as Scribe 6 of MS. Ff.4.43.[103]

The disciplined and regular calligraphy of that scribe is indeed reminiscent in some respects – while yet having been purged of more of its Insular features – of the *computistica* in MS. Bodley 579, fos 38–59.[104]

---

[98] 'Notes', pp. 331–2. On eclecticism, see *ibid.*, p. 412, and *Aethici Istrici Cosmographia*, facs. ed. Bishop.

[99] *English Caroline Minuscule*, plate VI (no. 8).

[100] This may be seen most easily *ibid.*, plate V (no. 7). For other plates illustrating Anglo-Caroline from St Augustine's, see *ibid.*, plates IV (no. 6) and VII (no. 9), and 'Notes', plates XIII–XIV (between pp. 330 and 331).

[101] *English Caroline Minuscule*, p. 13 and plate XIII (no. 15); 'Lincoln Cathedral MS 182' (with plates). To my mind these attributions are based on a false premise: cf. Dumville, 'English libraries before 1066', pp. 163–4. I have discussed all the evidence relating to manuscripts associated with that house in the late Anglo-Saxon period in 'The scriptorium and library of Abingdon Abbey, A.D. 954–1066' (forthcoming).

[102] For the usage, see (for example) Bishop, 'Notes', p. 334, and *English Caroline Minuscule*, p. xvi.

[103] On the other hand, one might resort to an explanation of comparable pressures concerning regularity and size of script with both Style-I and Style-II traditions.

[104] For a reproduction, see Bishop, *ibid.*, plate I.2, showing fo 40v (kalendar for April).

If the latter can be attributed to the last decade of Dunstan's pontificate, then Mr Bishop's dating of CUL MS. Ff.4.43 (1286) must be approximately correct, though for different reasons. The importance of the evidence of the 'Leofric Missal' is that it shows a mature Style-II Anglo-Caroline to have been developed at Christ Church by the 980s. At that date the cathedral scriptorium still arranged its parchment in the Insular fashion.[105]

On the other hand, the work of Scribe 5 of MS. Ff.4.43 and Scribe 2 of MS. Bodley 708[106] – starkly divergent from that of his collaborators – one might think to belong to quite another tradition of Anglo-Caroline minuscule. This was not Mr Bishop's view, for he treated these performances as within the tolerances of Style II. While one of the scribe's forms of the letter **e** does remind the reader that there was an Insular context, it seems to me that – taking Mr Bishop's hint about a script 'possibly influenced by continuing or new contacts with other centres'[107] – one might think of his work as falling within the tradition of Style I with its large, round, and pure Caroline shapes. Two further points arise in connexion with this scribe's hand. To one (the use of small majuscules) we shall have to return later, for it impinges on a matter discussed in chapter IV.[108] Secondly, in MS. Ff.4.43 Scribe 5 wrote fos 10v15–11v, 12r17–16v, and 49r–64v: towards the end of his last stint, his hand verges on a form of Style II which one might most readily associate with the scriptorium of St Augustine's Abbey. The question must be put whether this is a lapse from a standard laboriously achieved or rather an attempt to write more in the local scribal idiom, perhaps in preparation for junction with the stint of Scribe 6. Possible contexts for the movements or attitudes of scribes require some discussion before a determination can be approached.

A scribe or scribes may have been brought to (or may otherwise have arrived at) Christ Church from a centre where Style I was then practised. Consideration of the successors of Archbishop Dunstan may display some possibilities. In the period from 923 to 1013 the usual practice was to translate to Canterbury one of the bishops of Ramsbury, Wells, or Winchester.[109] This habit was broken by the translation of Dunstan in the

---

[105] For the change to the Continental mode, see *ibid.*, p. xx, and 'Notes', pp. 420–1; he dated that development closely *ca* 1000.

[106] *English Caroline Minuscule*, plate VIII (p. 8, no. 10).

[107] *Ibid.*, p. xxiii; quoted above, p. 88, n. 14.

[108] See below, p. 128 and n. 84.

[109] Four bishops of Wells were promoted (Athelm in 923, Wulfhelm in 926, Byrhthelm in 959, Lyfing in 1013), three bishops of Ramsbury (Oda in 941, Sigeric in 990, Ælfric in 995), and two bishops of Winchester (Ælfsige in 958 and Ælfheah in 1006). Seniority does not seem to have been the factor which determined choice; rather, these three sees of the West Saxon heartlands were favoured in this succession. Indeed, even among these three, seniority seems not to have been the determinant:

extraordinary circumstances of 959 and of Dunstan's immediate successor, Æthelgar, from Selsey in 988.[110] The pattern was reasserted by the next three appointments, however. In 990 Sigeric, formerly monk of Glastonbury and abbot of St Augustine's, was brought from Ramsbury, as was in 995 Ælfric, formerly abbot of St Albans; in 1006 Ælfheah was translated from Winchester, while in 1013 Lyfing (formerly abbot of Chertsey) came from Wells.[111] The next two elections, completing the first half of the eleventh century, were of internal candidates. Unfortunately we know nothing of the script practised at Ramsbury or Selsey in this period.[112] At Wells we have possible evidence only from the eleventh century, from the 'Lanalet Pontifical', but its origin is disputed.[113] Archbishop Ælfric, perhaps once a monk of Abingdon, Æthelwold's foundation, was translated ultimately from a house (St Albans) which has been attributed to the Æthelwoldian connexion.[114] Ælfheah definitely came from the principal location of Style I, Winchester, and Lyfing, as a former abbot of Chertsey, certainly emerged from the same circle. We can therefore imagine a scribe or scribes coming to Canterbury in the train of either Æthelgar in 988 or Ælfheah in 1006, who would have been accustomed to write Style-I Anglo-Caroline.[115]

---

although the most senior of the three succeeded in 941, 1006, and 1013, it was the most junior who was promoted in 990 and 995 (and perhaps in 926).

[110] Dunstan had been translated from London where (as previously at Worcester) King Edgar had placed him during the period of divided royal sovereignty. Before Æthelgar had become bishop of Selsey in 980, he had been abbot of the New Minster at Winchester (from its reform in 964), and there is some suspicion that he retained the abbacy until 988 (or indeed 990): Knowles *et al.*, *The Heads*, pp. 80–1.

[111] For the view that Sigeric was abbot of St Augustine's, Canterbury, in the 970s and 980s, see Knowles *et al.*, *The Heads*, p. 35. On Ælfric's previous career, see *ibid.*, p. 65 (cf. also n. 114, below). For Lyfing, abbot of Bishop Æthelwold's reformed house at Chertsey (Surrey), see *ibid.*, p. 38. On all these, cf. Brooks, *The Early History*, pp. 278–80.

[112] But the more complex possibility presents itself, that Æthelgar could have brought a scribe with him from Selsey who had previously been at the New Minster; indeed, in view of Æthelgar's probable retention of the abbacy of the New Minster during his episcopate (and perhaps his archiepiscopate), such a scribe might have been brought directly from Winchester.

[113] An origin at Wells would be the most economical, but various other options (Crediton, Tavistock, etc.) have been suggested. Cf. Dumville, 'On the dating', pp. 51–2, and *Liturgy*, pp. 86–7.

[114] Knowles *et al.*, *The Heads*, p. 65. It must be acknowledged, however, that the alleged Æthelwoldian origin of St Albans is unattested: cf. *Wulfstan of Winchester*, edd. & transl. Lapidge & Winterbottom, p. l, n. 46 (and note also p. cxli); if Ælfric had previously been a monk of Abingdon, that might supply some support for such a view. For Ælfric's interest in the monastery at Cholsey (Berkshire), as evidenced by his will (Sawyer, *Anglo-Saxon Charters*, no. 1488), see above, pp. 82–4.

[115] One monk of Winchester who might have made the transition with Bishop Ælfheah in

The alternative possibility is that a decision was taken in the Christ Church scriptorium, for whatever reason, to train one scribe or more in the practice of Style-I minuscule. If this decision was reached as late as the years after 988, then – given that Christ Church had a distinctive and successful style of its own, within the tradition of Style II – a motive for the change would have to be hypothesised. There is little evidence, however, that the script-form recognised by modern scholarship as the house-style of Christ Church was regarded there as the only permissible style. One may imagine that the relatively relaxed attitude which allowed the creation and practice of Style II would permit also the writing of Style I, if scribes could achieve it. Indeed, this would seem to be a theme of Anglo-Caroline scribal activity at Christ Church in the years to 1010. While some scribes remained firmly within the tradition of Style II, others – in a variety of ways – sought an accommodation with Style I.

One extraordinary book – Cambridge, Corpus Christi College, MS. 23, part 1, containing an illustrated copy of the works of Prudentius – may bear witness to the complexity of the process by which Style I came to be written in the Christ Church scriptorium. Of mid-eleventh-century Malmesbury provenance, this manuscript has been attributed to Christ Church, Canterbury, on rather specific art-historical evidence. The artist appears to be the second of those whose work is found in the 'Cædmon Genesis' or 'Junius Manuscript of Old English Poetry' – Oxford, Bodleian Library, MS. Junius 11 (*S.C.* 5123) – on pp. 73–88 and is probably very much influenced by the 'Utrecht Psalter', that illustrated manuscript written at Reims *ca* A.D. 820 (now Utrecht, Bibliotheek der Universiteit, MS. 32) but then recently arrived at Canterbury. This evidence would place the origin of this Cambridge copy of Prudentius's works *ca* A.D. 1000. If the dating and localisation are correct, the interest of the book is that it shows three scribes, apparently a master and two pupils, writing the text in three Caroline-minuscule styles none of which is that usually encountered in products of the Christ Church scriptorium. The membranes are arranged in the Insular fashion, HFHF. The principal hand (fos 1–40, 64r1–13, 65–104) is, I think, probably that of a foreigner. His two collaborators (Scribe 2 on fos 41–56; Scribe 3 on fos 57–63 and 64r14–64v) imitate not the principal hand, but scripts of the sort usually recognised as antecedent to Style-I Anglo-Caroline. In hand 2 the result is an awkward, stiff, and hybrid large minuscule with huge-bowled **g**, frequent majuscule **N**, and very large **x**. In hand 3, a generally smaller script (unstable in size, however) shows repeated

---

1006 was Wulfstan *cantor*, precentor of the Old Minster: see *Wulfstan of Winchester*, edd. & transl. Lapidge & Winterbottom, pp. xxx–xxxix. He would presumably have been too senior and too old to be pressed into service as a scribe at Christ Church but the influence of such a considerable figure might have been significant in the scriptorium.

changes of aspect on each page. The principal hand offers every sign – save in the colour of ink used – of foreign training. Noteworthy features of that hand are single-compartment **a**, an unusual form of the **r** + **a** ligature, and a distinctive form of **t** written before **e** or **i**. In general, hand 1 is forward-leaning. It would appear, then, that among the possible elements in the development of Style I at Christ Church were the presence of a foreign writing master and the availability of pure (and perhaps early) Caroline models for imitation by new scribes.[116]

The impression which one must gain, on surveying all the Christ Church manuscripts of this period, is that Style-I Anglo-Caroline enjoyed extraordinary prestige in the eyes of members of the Canterbury cathedral scriptorium. For example, at the upper end of the hierarchy of book-production, we find a monumental grade of Style II practised (and perhaps created) by the scribe of the 'Anderson Pontifical' (London, British Library, MS. Additional 57337) and the 'Arenberg Gospels' (New York, Pierpont Morgan Library, MS. M.869),[117] usually attributed

---

[116] On CCCC 23 see James, *A Descriptive Catalogue*, I.44–6; Ker, *Catalogue*, pp. 42–3 (no. 31); Temple, *Anglo-Saxon Manuscripts*, pp. 69–70 (no. 48). It is not textually linked with copies known to have been written at Canterbury. It is, however, associated (in respect of another text) with Oxford, Bodleian Library, MS. Marshall 19 (*S.C.* 5265), written at Soissons in the ninth century, at Malmesbury in the late tenth century, and by the thirteenth at Christ Church, Canterbury. On all this, cf. Thomson, *William of Malmesbury*, pp. 78, 113–16, and Wieland, 'The Anglo-Saxon manuscripts of Prudentius's *Psychomachia*'. For the art of MS. Junius 11, see Temple, *Anglo-Saxon Manuscripts*, pp. 76–8 (no. 58). There is a huge literature on the 'Utrecht Psalter' and its influence on late Anglo-Saxon art: see Wilson, *Anglo-Saxon Art*, pp. 180–90, for a brief introduction to the subject; cf. Dodwell, *Anglo-Saxon Art*, p. 171, Backhouse, 'The making of the Harley Psalter', and Gameson, 'The Anglo-Saxon artists'. CCCC 23 by no means presents the sole difficulty from this period: if York, Minster Library, MS. Add. 1, fos 24r–156r, and London, British Library, MS. Harley 76 were also written at Christ Church, as is usually held, we see a variety of discrepant interpretations of Caroline minuscule, all containing Style-I elements, written there in close chronological proximity to one another and to manuscripts more readily recognisable as products of the cathedral scriptorium; on York MS. Add. 1, cf. Dumville, 'On the dating', pp. 53–4, and on MS. Harley 76 see above, p. 33(–4), n. 117.

[117] On the 'Arenberg Gospels' see Temple, *Anglo-Saxon Manuscripts*, pp. 74–5 (no. 56): T.A.M. Bishop, quoted by Temple, assigned it to Christ Church, Canterbury, in the last decade of the tenth century. Cf. Ker, 'A supplement', p. 127 (no. 416). For these two manuscripts' shared scribe, see Heslop, 'The production', pp. 169–70. However, Heslop has argued for a quite late date (after 1023) on the grounds that a short litany in the 'Anderson Pontifical' (*Anglo-Saxon Litanies*, ed. Lapidge, pp. 67–8, 140–1) contains St Bartholomew among the apostles: he has linked this to an alleged gift of relics to Christ Church by King Cnut and Queen Emma in that year; this is subject to the same objection as affects his dating of the 'Missal of Robert of Jumièges' (cf. Dumville, 'On the dating', p. 52), that it is based on non-contemporary, post-Conquest source-material of very uncertain value.

rather to Christ Church than to St Augustine's.[118] Given that these books stand somewhat apart from their contemporaries, the only certain basis for localisation within Canterbury is provided by the function of the pontifical. The text in this manuscript has been shown to depend on transmission from Winchester,[119] as is the case also with another pontifical written in Style II (and with membranes arranged HFHF) – Cambridge, Corpus Christi College, MS. 146, pp. 61–318.[120] The impact of the use of Winchester at Canterbury Cathedral is in effect summarised and canonised (as Edmund Bishop observed long ago)[121] in the kalendar in London, British Library, MS. Arundel 155, written at Christ Church in A.D. 1012 x 1023.[122] The monumentality of the script of the 'Anderson Pontifical' no doubt derives from imitation of the script of its Style-I, Winchester, model.

The same attitude is found in manuscripts of less exalted status. As Mr Bishop has remarked, we can see scribes seeking progressively to eliminate Insular features from their hands.[123] We observe various hybrids of Style I and Style II, mostly at the upper end of the hier-archy.[124] At a more workaday level we see Style I, or what aspires to it, being written by scribes with an undoubted Style-II background.[125]

---

[118] The attribution rests on Bishop's view of the script of both volumes. If Heslop's late dating were to be sustained, the manuscripts' production would have to be attributed to St Augustine's from which we have some evidence for the continuity of Style-II traditions. But this would be second best to an attribution to Christ Church a quarter-century earlier.

[119] Prescott, 'The structure', pp. 121–3. This has led him, most unwisely, to suggest (apparently following unpublished comments by D.H. Turner) that the manuscript itself was written at Winchester. But Style-II Anglo-Caroline is not known to have been written there. He has also suggested a date soon after the completion (A.D. 963 x 984) of the 'Benedictional of St Æthelwold' – London, British Library, MS. Additional 49598. For further comment, cf. Dumville, *Liturgy*, p. 77.

[120] Ker, *Catalogue*, pp. 50–1 (no. 37). Lapidge (*Anglo-Saxon Litanies*, p. 63, no. III) has firmly attributed this book to the Old Minster, Winchester, but that decision rests on deduction from the text, not the script. There are in fact textual reasons too for an attribution to Canterbury Cathedral: see, for example, the *ordo* for the mutual consecration of archbishops of York and Canterbury, §XIIII, on pp. 136–138. For further discussion, see Dumville, *Liturgy*, chapter III.

[121] Gasquet & Bishop, *The Bosworth Psalter*, pp. 27–34, 66–8; cf. Brooks, *The Early History*, pp. 264–5.

[122] On this book see Ker, *Catalogue*, pp. 167–71 (no. 135); Temple, *Anglo-Saxon Manuscripts*, pp. 84–5 (no. 66); and chapter IV, below.

[123] 'Notes', p. 419.

[124] For example, in London, British Library, MS. Harley 603, fos 1–27 and 50–73: on this book see Backhouse, 'The making of the Harley Psalter', with reproductions of fos 8r, 13v, 25r, 54v, 65v (and details of 2r, 62v), sections best attributable to the beginning of the eleventh century. Cf. Gameson, 'The Anglo-Saxon artists'.

[125] As seen for example in MS. Bodley 708 (cf. p. 103, above): Bishop, *English Caroline Minuscule*, plate VIII. Cf. also London, British Library, MS. Cotton Tiberius A.xv,

And, as we approach the major changes which took place in the Caroline minuscule of Christ Church *ca* 1020, with the development of Style IV,[126] we meet various transitional scripts – transitional, that is, between Styles I and IV,[127] between Styles II and IV,[128] and between Styles I, II, IV.[129] Style II may have persisted, for a few years after 1020,[130] at the hands of older scribes but, at least at Christ Church, the future lay with Style-IV Anglo-Caroline.[131]

In as much as Style-IV Anglo-Caroline represented a development essentially from Style I, but as modified by some Style-II features, the background to this effective triumph of Style I in Canterbury – a city perceived by scholars as the bastion of Style-II usage – deserves scrutiny. Mr Bishop, in recognising and demonstrating the origin of Style IV, said little about its antecedents. For example, he wrote that 'the work of some of the later scribes of [Christ Church] stemma A seems to mark them as the close precursors of [the inventor of Style IV]. . ., and whose clear, carefully formed, slightly denatured script is . . . outside the limits of this survey'.[132] This is undoubtedly the case: for example, adoption of the characteristically Style-I r+a ligature may be seen in a number of specimens of earlier Christ Church work; tall **a** is also found sporadically.[133] However, no very clear progression has yet been traced through these manuscripts. Mr Bishop thought that he had found the link between Style-II and Style-IV manuscripts, but did not lay any great

---

fos 1–173 (for a description see Brett, 'A Breton pilgrim', pp. 50–7, 65–70), written after A.D. 990.

[126] On this, see chapter IV, below.

[127] For example, in the 'Royal group' of liturgical manuscripts: below, pp. 116–20. A more problematic example is Cambridge, Corpus Christi College, MS. 411, whose attribution (cf. Wormald, 'Late Anglo-Saxon art', p. 20, and 'Continental influence', pp. 8–9) to St Augustine's defies belief (cf. Temple, *Anglo-Saxon Manuscripts*, pp. 63–4, no. 40). It should be assigned to Christ Church in the early years of the eleventh century.

[128] This is the development which we see at St Augustine's. Cambridge, University Library, MS. Gg.5.35 (1567), usually dated after 1039 (but perhaps not necessarily all of a piece), is a classic example of this combination. Earlier, in 1021/2, there is some modest evidence from Cambridge, University Library, MS. Kk.5.32 (2074) for Style-IV influence on Style-II writing: cf. Dumville, *Liturgy*, chapter II.

[129] For example: London, British Library, MS. Additional 37517, fos 2r–3r (cf. Dumville, 'On the dating', p. 45). For a much more problematic case – that of York, Minster Library, MS. Add. 1 –, see my discussion *ibid.*, pp. 53–4; see also n. 116, above.

[130] Bishop, 'Notes', p. 420, n. 2, on Paris, Bibliothèque nationale, MS. latin 10062, fos 162–163: cf. Delisle, 'Vers et écriture', pp. 437–8; Heslop, 'The production', pp. 169–70 (but cf. nn. 117–118, above).

[131] See chapter IV, below.

[132] 'Notes', p. 420; for his stemmata of scribes, see pp. 422–3.

[133] These features, along with small majuscule N, may be seen in (for example) London, British Library, MS. Harley 1117, fo 45r, as illustrated by Bishop, *ibid.*, plate XV (facing p. 419).

stress on it in his work: 'It is [London, British Library, MS. Royal 7.C.iv which] both sums up the calligraphic tendencies of several of the later MSS. in [Christ Church] stemma A and is evidently the precursor of the script found in Christ Church MSS. of the second and third decades of the eleventh century'.[134]

Unfortunately, this seems to be a false trail. Among the Anglo-Saxon books belonging to Christ Church in the later middle ages were two Style-I manuscripts: London, British Library, MS. Royal 1.E.vii–viii, a large-format Bible of some four hundred folios,[135] and MS. Royal 7.C.iv, a copy of an ascetic work, the *Liber scintillarum* of Defensor of Ligugé (which in the mid-eleventh century had received a continuous interlinear Old English gloss).[136] These had already been noted by Mr Bishop in 1959 as 'certainly or probably attributed to Christ Church' when he considered them to be parallels to large, round Caroline-minuscule specimens from eleventh-century St Augustine's.[137] The attribution of a Christ Church origin to these books has become fixed,[138] but it needs (I think) to be dislodged. The arrival of the Style-I Bible at Christ Church would nicely parallel the reception of Style-I liturgical books from Winchester, now attested only by their derivatives. We have no reason to think that later tenth-century Christ Church had the scribal resources to produce a massive and wholly Style-I manuscript. The case of the holograph manuscript of Defensor's work is somewhat more compli-cated. Mr Bishop attributed it to his Christ Church scribe xviii, adducing three other specimens of the hand.[139] London, British Library, MS. Harley 1117, fos 45–62 are very clearly not by the same scribe;[140] MS. Harley 603, fos 50r–54ra23 are written in an Anglo-Caroline hybrid of Style I and Style II which seems unlike the script of Royal 7.C.iv.[141] Finally, a royal diploma, *scripta* at Canterbury in A.D. 1002 (London, British Library, Stowe Charter 35), is in quite similar but perhaps not identical script;[142] in any case it is unnecessary to think in terms of a

---

[134] *Ibid.*, p. 415.
[135] Cf. Dumville, 'On the dating', pp. 47–8 (given the arguments advanced in chapter II, above, houses of the Oswald connexion would also have to be considered as possible sources).
[136] Ker, *Catalogue*, pp. 323–4 (no. 256). For a facsimile (of fo 70v) see Warner & Gilson, *British Museum Catalogue*, IV, plate 51. Hofstetter (*Winchester*, pp. 433–6) has shown that this gloss is lexically of Canterbury, not Winchester, type.
[137] Bishop, 'Notes', p. 94.
[138] Temple, *Anglo-Saxon Manuscripts*, pp. 119–20 (no. 102), on BL Royal 1.E.vii–viii.
[139] 'Notes', p. 423.
[140] For a reproduction, cf. n. 133, above.
[141] Fo 51v of BL Harley 603 has been reproduced by Brown, *Anglo-Saxon Manuscripts*, p. 74; for a detail, see Wormald, *English Drawings*, plate XI(*a*). For part of 51r see Gameson, 'The Anglo-Saxon artists', plate VA.
[142] Sawyer, *Anglo-Saxon Charters*, no. 905: see n. 91, above. Backhouse ('The making of the Harley Psalter', p. 112, n. 14) has reacted properly (but unnecessarily, in view

Christ Church scribe writing what a royal official would more naturally have undertaken.[143] There is no reason to think that MS. Royal 7.C.iv was written at Christ Church.

We cannot doubt the availability of Style-I models at Christ Church in the late tenth and early eleventh centuries. The question therefore naturally arises as to when members of the cathedral scriptorium might have felt able to turn their hands to a full-scale essay in the 'Æthelwoldian' style. The answer to that question is deeply controversial. For there exists a group of lavish liturgical books in Style-I Anglo-Caroline of the early eleventh century. These manuscripts – which include the 'Missal of Robert of Jumièges' – have various connexions with Christ Church and have often been given an origin there. But there are rival views, in favour of Winchester's New Minster or Peterborough Abbey. If these de luxe volumes were created at Christ Church the work was done immediately before, or before and after, Canterbury's trial by vikings in 1011/12. The issues surrounding these books will be discussed in the next chapter.[144]

The present chapter must end, as it began, on a note of frustration. It has been possible here only to sketch some of the difficulties which hold back our perception of the book-production of tenth-century Canterbury. Crucial questions remain unanswered, manuscript material still awaits attribution, and a large mass of palaeographical data remains to be reexamined and analysed. What seems clear, however, is that Caroline writing at Christ Church has a longer and more continuous history in the tenth century than would often be admitted. The Benedictinising of the Canterbury houses seems likely to have been undertaken by Dunstan at the latest and it is to his pontificate that we should date the beginning of the surge of book-production first studied by T.A.M. Bishop.[145] At Christ Church A.D. 1011/12 probably marks the effective end of the Style-II Anglo-Caroline tradition.

---

of the information given in my note) to the chronological implications of Keynes's doubts about the authenticity of the diploma.

[143] Here (as in Sawyer, *Anglo-Saxon Charters*, no. 884: cf. n. 91) we perhaps have evidence towards developing a paradigm of the life of an Anglo-Saxon royal-chancery scribe: cf. Dumville, 'English libraries before 1066', p. 175, n. 41.

[144] See below, pp. 116–20.

[145] Bishop himself did not exclude that possibility: *English Caroline Minuscule*, p. 6, on CUL MS. Ff.4.43 (1286). For subsequent interpretation, downplaying its likelihood, see Brooks, *The Early History*, pp. 266–7, 276–8.

IV

'EADWIG THE FAT' AND THE ORIGINS
OF ANGLO-CAROLINE MINUSCULE, STYLE IV

The years 1011 and 1012 were traumatic indeed for the church and city of Canterbury. The Anglo-Saxon Chronicle, in annals written soon afterwards,[1] has a stark account of the succession of events. I quote Dorothy Whitelock's translation.[2]

[1011]   In this year the king and his counsellors sent to the army and asked for peace, and promised them tribute and provisions on condition that they should cease their ravaging. They had then overrun: (i) East Anglia, (ii) Essex, (iii) Middlesex, (iv) Oxfordshire, (v) Cambridgeshire, (vi) Hertfordshire, (vii) Buckinghamshire, (viii) Bedfordshire, (ix) half Huntingdonshire, [(x) much of Northamptonshire]; and south of the Thames all Kent, Sussex, the Hastings district, Surrey, Berkshire, Hampshire, and much of Wiltshire. All those disasters befell us through bad policy, in that they were never offered tribute in time [nor fought against]; but when they had done most to our injury, peace and truce were made with them; and for all this truce and tribute they journeyed none the less in bands everywhere, and harried our wretched people, and plundered and killed them.
    And then in this year, between the Nativity of St Mary and Michaelmas, they besieged Canterbury, and they got inside by treachery, for Ælfmær, whose life Archbishop Ælfheah had saved, betrayed it. Then they captured there Archbishop Ælfheah, and the king's reeve Ælfweard, and Abbess Leofrun,[3] and Bishop Godwine;[4] and they let Abbot Ælfmær[5] escape. And they took captive there all the ecclesiastics,

---

[1] Attested by MSS. CDEF. See Keynes, 'The declining reputation', pp. 229–36; cf. Dumville, 'Some aspects of annalistic writing', pp. 24–30.

[2] *English Historical Documents*, pp. 244–5: I have modified the translation in a few particulars. Text enclosed within square brackets is not attested by all the witnesses. For details, see Whitelock, *ibid.*.

[3] Abbess of St Mildred's Minster, Thanet. Cf. Brooks, *The Early History*, pp. 35, 204.

[4] Bishop of Rochester.

[5] Abbot of St Augustine's, Canterbury. His disreputable role in the affair raises questions about the fate of his abbey, both during and after the Scandinavian occupation of

111

and men and women – it was impossible for any man to tell how much of that people that was – and they stayed afterwards in that borough as long as they pleased. And when they had then ransacked the whole borough, they went to their ships and took the archbishop with them.

He was then a captive who had been head of the English people and of christendom. There could misery be seen where happiness was often seen before, in that wretched city from which first came [to us] christianity and happiness in divine and secular things. And they kept the archbishop with them till the time when they martyred him.

[1012]   In this year Ealdorman Eadric and all the chief counsellors of England, ecclesiastical and lay, came to London before Easter – Easter Sunday was on 13 April – and they stayed there until the tribute, namely 48,000 pounds, was all paid after Easter. Then on the Saturday the army became greatly incensed against the bishop because he would not promise them any money, but forbade that anything should be paid for him. They were also very drunk, for wine from the south had been brought there. They seized the bishop, and brought him to their assembly on the eve of the Sunday of the octave of Easter, which was 19 April[, and shamefully put him to death there]: they pelted him with bones and with ox-heads, and one of them struck him on the head with the back of an axe, that he sank down with the blow, and his holy blood fell on the ground, and so he sent his holy soul to God's kingdom. And in the morning his body was carried to London, and the bishops Eadnoth[6] and Ælfhun[7] and the citizens received it with all reverence and buried it in St Paul's minster. And God now reveals there the powers of the holy martyr.

When that tribute was paid and the oaths of peace were sworn, the Danish army then dispersed as widely as it had been collected. Then forty-five ships from that army came over to the king, and they promised him to defend this country, and he was to feed and clothe them.

[1013]   In the year after the archbishop was martyred, the king appointed Bishop Lyfing[8] to the archbishopric of Canterbury.

It is hard to estimate the impact of these events on every division of the affairs of the churches and churchpeople of Canterbury. How many ecclesiastics died or were rendered ineffective thereafter, how much material destruction was wrought, and how great was the psychological damage inflicted on the nerve-centre of English christianity, we can only guess. But we may believe that the denizens of Canterbury were better prepared by this experience than were many of their compatriots for the eventual accession, in 1016, of a Danish king to the English throne. One can hardly envy Lyfing his task of attempting not only to restore Church-

---

Canterbury; Ælfmær himself seems to have prospered, however, eventually becoming bishop of Sherborne (1017–?1023).

6 Bishop of Dorchester-on-Thames.

7 Bishop of London.

8 Bishop of Wells.

order in Canterbury as a whole but also to instil a new sense of purpose into the cathedral *familia* after such a blow and amid a continuing succession of momentous events. Lyfing's pontificate lasted but seven years: that he achieved some measure of success in these tasks may be allowed from what follows in this chapter.[9] However, Lyfing seems to represent the end of the second generation of Reform-monasticism.[10] Much was to change, both at Christ Church and in the English Church as a whole, in the years from 1020.[11] Script and book-production constitute one area in which such a transition may be observed.

Lyfing's pontificate (1013–1020) may be measured in a number of different ways. In the archbishop's role as manager and defender of the real property of the cathedral church he is seen to be active;[12] but, from the situation about which Lyfing made memorable complaint to King Cnut,[13] we may suspect that the aftermath of the crises of 1011/12, 1013, and 1016 (to say nothing of the routine mayhem of the whole period from 1011 to 1016) was to be measured locally in terms of the weakening of Christ Church's grip on its endowments. The aggrieved and the opportunistic would both find chances in disturbed conditions to act against the church's interests. Cnut's accession in 1016 may itself have led to further such difficulties as a result of what was in effect, whatever the constitutional niceties, a Scandinavian conquest of England.[14]

Another difficulty attended the archbishop's position: the body of his martyred predecessor lay at London. While times remained troubled and London was a pillar of support for the West Saxon royal dynasty, that was no doubt an eminently suitable location for St Ælfheah. But, as in the case of St Edward a generation before, there are early indications of a developing cult.[15] We must suppose that the Christ Church community

---

[9] Cf. Brooks, *ibid.*, pp. 56 (cf. Gem, 'A recession'), 260, 278–81, 287–90.

[10] Lyfing was a monk and had been an abbot before becoming bishop in 998 or 999. He can be identified with one of the tendencies within the Reform-movement. Cf. Brooks, *The Early History*, p. 256. The next generation of bishops was to be drawn largely from a very different type of cleric.

[11] See Barlow, *The English Church, 1000–1066*, for a fine account of this process.

[12] For example, he obtained a writ from King Cnut (Sawyer, *Anglo-Saxon Charters*, no. 985, of A.D. 1017x1020), confirming the liberties of Canterbury cathedral: this is preserved in a gospel-book – London, British Library, MS. Royal 1.D.ix – on which see below, pp. 116–20. See also Brooks, *The Early History*, p. 287 (and p. 385, n. 91).

[13] In Sawyer, *Anglo-Saxon Charters*, no. 985: Brooks, *The Early History*, p. 288. For a different impression of the impact of unsettled times on Christ Church, see Brooks, *ibid.*, p. 285.

[14] On the tenurial consequences of this conquest, see Fleming, *Kings and Lords*, pp. 1–104.

[15] The Anglo-Saxon Chronicle's annal for 1012 (quoted above) is itself excellent evidence for this; for the Londoners' attachment to St Ælfheah by 1023, see Brooks, *The Early History*, pp. 291–2. The testimony of datable liturgical books – very notably

---

would have wished to gain control of the saint's remains at the earliest opportunity. A great difficulty must have troubled the cathedral community, however. To what extent would the new king, whose father's army had martyred Archbishop Ælfheah, feel slighted or threatened by Canterbury's desire to develop the cult? Eventually, in 1023, the king seems to have played a full part (as he had at *Assandun* in 1020)[16] in the translation of the saint from London to Canterbury. We may sense a general and specific political background to the event – further reconciliation of Dane and English, and further reconciliation of King Cnut and Earl Thorkel.[17] A lengthy account of the translation of St Ælfheah is that given in the D-Chronicle. Again I quote Dorothy Whitelock's version.[18]

[1023]   In this year in St Paul's minster in London, King Cnut gave full permission to Archbishop Æthelnoth and Bishop Brihtwine[19] and to all the servants of God who were with them to take up the archbishop St Ælfheah from the tomb, and they did so on 8 June. And the illustrious king, and the archbishop and the diocesan bishops, and the earls, and very many ecclesiastics and also lay-folk, conveyed his holy body on a ship across the Thames to Southwark, and there entrusted the holy martyr to the archbishop and his companions. And they then bore him with a distinguished company and happy jubilation to Rochester. Then on the third day Queen Emma came with her royal child Hardacnut, and they then all conveyed the holy archbishop with much glory and joy and

London, British Library, MS. Arundel 155, written at Canterbury before 1023 – also points most clearly to the rapid development of cult.

[16] See above, pp. 38–41.

[17] The Anglo-Saxon Chronicle for 1012 records that in the aftermath of Ælfheah's killing, forty-five ships' companies of the Danish army went over to King Æthelred's service. These were led by Thorkel (cf. 1013, on Thorkel's assisting King Æthelred in resisting King Sveinn's attempt on London). When Sveinn eventually triumphed in 1013, Thorkel seems to have rejoined him. In 1017 (or late 1016: Chronicle, *s.a.* 1017), King Cnut made Thorkel earl of East Anglia. In 1021 Cnut banished him. In 1023, according to the C-text alone, reconciliation with Thorkel preceded the translation of St Ælfheah. One wonders whether a specific connexion might be seen here.

[18] *English Historical Documents*, pp. 253–4. In general, the D-text has the character now of a compromise between C and E, now of an amalgamation of their texts. Neil Ker argued that the core of the D-manuscript (London, British Library, MS. Cotton Tiberius B.iv) was written in the mid-1050s, but that fos 68–73, containing annals 1016 (part) to 1043 and 1045 (*rectius* 1044)–1052[1] (*rectius* 1051) (part), are supply-text written in the 1070s or 1080s (Ker, *Catalogue*, pp. 253–5, no. 192). On the other hand, my view is that the whole is datable after 1066 and probably after *ca* 1080 (but before *ca* 1100): Dumville, 'Some aspects of annalistic writing', pp. 24–38 (especially 33–8). On either view, the annal for 1023 here quoted is part of a text datable *ca* 1080 or later. The question must also be put, whether the tone of this annal suggests any direct connexion with Canterbury.

[19] Bishop of Wells.

songs of praise into Canterbury, and thus brought him with due ceremony into Christ Church on 11 June. Afterwards on the eighth day, on 15 June, Archbishop Æthelnoth and Bishop Ælfsige[20] and Bishop Brihtwine and all who were with them placed St Ælfheah's holy body on the north side of Christ's altar, to the praise of God and the honour of the holy archbishop, and to the eternal salvation of all those who daily visit his holy body there with devout hearts and with all humility. May Almighty God have mercy on all Christian men, through the holy merits of St Ælfheah.

What Archbishop Lyfing no doubt desired had been achieved by Æthelnoth, his successor, with the king's goodwill.[21]

There is reason to think that some change occurred in the liturgical practice of Christ Church, Canterbury, during the period marked by the pontificates of Ælfheah and Lyfing, A.D. 1006 x 1020. In the course of his study of the kalendar in the 'Bosworth Psalter', written probably at Christ Church in the period 988 x 1008,[22] Edmund Bishop showed that the evidence of a somewhat later Christ Church kalendar – that in London, British Library, MS. Arundel 155 (written in 1012 x 1023) – indicated a significant impact of the use of Winchester.[23] This liturgical reform might have been undertaken by Ælfheah himself, who had been translated to Canterbury from the see of Winchester, or by Lyfing, formerly bishop of Wells and previously abbot of Chertsey, a house of the Æthelwoldian connexion.[24] At present, there seems to be no evidence which would allow us to consider this reform an aspect specifically of Lyfing's attempt to restore his church's well-being; and it is difficult to judge whether such changes would have been easier for an archbishop to implement in 1006 or in 1013.

That strand in the scriptorial traditions of Christ Church which emanated from the practice of Style-I Anglo-Caroline minuscule[25] must

---

[20] Bishop of Winchester.

[21] MSS. C and E offer much more restrained accounts in the laconic style of annalistic writing. C: 'And afterwards [after his reconciliation with Thorkel] Cnut had St Ælfheah's relics moved from London to Canterbury'. E: 'And in the same year [as a succession to the archbishopric of York] Archbishop Æthelnoth moved the relics of St Ælfheah, the archbishop, from London to Canterbury'. It is just possible (but no more) that a common source lies beneath these two notices of the translation.

[22] On the date, see now Korhammer, 'The origin', p. 175.

[23] Gasquet & Bishop, *The Bosworth Psalter*, pp. 27–34. Because of a severe misdating of MS. Arundel 155, Edmund Bishop thought that this change occurred after the Norman conquest. Cf. Korhammer, 'The origin', p. 179. For a fragmentary Christ Church kalendar (May–August) written before A.D. 1020 and whose text has not yet been published or evaluated, see Paris, Bibliothèque nationale, MS. latin 10062, fos 162–163: Bishop, 'Notes', pp. 415, 420–1.

[24] Knowles *et al.*, *The Heads*, p. 38. Chertsey was one of the houses reformed by Æthelwold in 964.

[25] See chapter III (especially pp. 88, 103–10), above.

have been strengthened by the election of two successive pontiffs schooled in the fashions of the Æthelwoldian houses. It is probably to the time of Archbishop Ælfheah that we should attribute the last known Christ Church essays in Style II.[26] Hybridisation of these styles might seem to have been the natural way forward for the cathedral's scribes.[27]

However, there is some other evidence, albeit of a rather controversial sort, which might testify to determined and successful practice of Style I at Christ Church, Canterbury, in the early eleventh century. According to T.A.M. Bishop, it was three collaborating scribes who produced at that time a superb series of mostly elaborately decorated codices – five gospel-books, one sacramentary, and a copy (unilluminated) of Bede's *Historia ecclesiastica gentis Anglorum* (not to mention two gospel-books of which only small fragments survive).[28] These manuscripts have been assigned origins – individually or as a group – at a number of different scriptoria.[29] They have recently been studied afresh in an important article by T.A. Heslop[30] who has followed T.A.M. Bishop in assigning their scribes to Peterborough Abbey. There is no doubt that these books' minuscule is in the tradition of Style-I Anglo-Caroline; Heslop has made the same point with reference to the majuscule display-scripts found in them.[31] That the group began absolutely no later than the very beginning of the eleventh century is made clear by the Old English script of Rouen, Bibliothèque municipale, MS. Y.6 (274), the 'Missal of Robert of Jumièges', a late form of Anglo-Saxon Square minuscule.[32] Other than this, the evidence for dating these manuscripts hinges on the chronology of an addition to one of its members – London, British Library, MS. Royal 1.D.ix (on fo 44v).[33] This is a copy of an authentic Old English

---

[26] On dating, cf. Bishop, 'Notes', pp. 418–19.

[27] For somewhat earlier attempts, see the discussion in chapter III, above.

[28] 'The Copenhagen gospel-book', pp. 39–41.

[29] See Temple, *Anglo-Saxon Manuscripts*, pp. 69 (no. 47), 83–4 (no. 65), 88–9 (no. 70), 89 (no. 71), 89–91 (no. 72), and 91–2 (no. 73), for summaries of the scholarship on the six illuminated manuscripts in this group. For an earlier treatment of the group, see Homburger, *Die Anfänge*, pp. 65–6. For two suggested additions to the group, see below, p. 117, and also p. 139(–40) and n. 120. For a deletion, see below, n. 116. The New Minster, Winchester, is an origin once suggested for some of these books: for an earlier attribution thither of Copenhagen, Kongelige Biblioteket, G.K.S. 10.2°, see Bishop, 'Notes', p. 333, and of Cambridge, Trinity College, MS. B.10.4 (215), see Ker, *Medieval Libraries*, p. 103 (cf. Heslop, 'The production', p. 153, n. 4, and p. 154[–5], n. 10).

[30] 'The production'.

[31] *Ibid.*, pp. 162–6.

[32] On the closing phases of Anglo-Saxon Square minuscule and their dating, see Dumville, 'Beowulf come lately'. On Rouen MS. Y.6, see Dumville, 'On the dating', p. 52; an origin in the 1020s is too late.

[33] Heslop, 'The production', p. 195; Sawyer, *Anglo-Saxon Charters*, no. 985. For

writ of King Cnut, datable 1017 x 1020: in it the king declared that he had confirmed the liberties of Canterbury Cathedral.[34] The hand of the addition belongs to a known scribe, associable for other reasons too with Christ Church, whom we shall meet shortly. The presence of the writ has usually been taken as evidence that this gospel-book was at Canterbury by 1020. Strictly speaking, neither part of that deduction is conclusive. This version of the writ could in theory have been a royal reference-copy.[35] On chronology we must admit that the writ could have been added at any subsequent date allowed by the script; but in practice, the most likely time for such an act of deliberate preservation would of course be immediately upon issue or receipt of the document. If we allow the double deduction, then London, British Library, MS. Royal 1.D.ix had been written by 1020 and was likewise at Canterbury by that date; its scribal relatives should accordingly be dated in close proximity and consideration should be given to placing their production at Christ Church. One other scribal connexion suggests the same conclusions. Firenze, Biblioteca Laurenziana, MS. Plut. XVII.20 is a gospel-lectionary whose scribe was that of the writ added on BL MS. Royal 1.D.ix, fo 44v; Heslop has identified a series of features – apparently integral to the volume – on fo 1 which connect this gospel-lectionary tightly with the group of Style-I manuscripts under discussion here.[36] The scribe of Firenze MS. Plut. XVII.20 has been identified as a monk of Christ Church, Canterbury.[37]

Before we turn again to Canterbury, it will be well to review briefly another attribution of the aforementioned group of manuscripts – to a scriptorium at Peterborough Abbey,[38] a house reformed or refounded by

---

discussion and a facsimile, see Chaplais, 'The Anglo-Saxon chancery' (1973), p. 59 and plate II (opposite p. 65).

[34] *Anglo-Saxon Writs*, ed. & transl. Harmer, pp. 168–71 and 446–8 (no. 26), issued on a visit of King Cnut to Canterbury Cathedral. Cf. Brooks, *The Early History*, pp. 288–90.

[35] For the other Old English addition (fo 43v) in this manuscript, see the text given by Ker, *Catalogue*, p. 317 (no. 247), a notice of confraternity. Harmer, *Anglo-Saxon Writs*, p. 168, took this to be the admission of Cnut, his brother Harald, and Thorth, Kartoca, and Thuri to confraternity with Christ Church, but that rests on a deduction from the writ on the following folio. On Thorth and Thuri, see *ibid.*, p. 574 (*s.nn.* Thored, Thuri); Ker (*Catalogue*, p. 317) found Thorth and Kartoca together in Sawyer, *Anglo-Saxon Charters*, no. 961 (a genuine charter of Cnut, dated 1024, granting land in Dorset to Orc and preserved in the Abbotsbury archive); the three men were perhaps intimates of the king rather than Dorset nobility.

[36] 'The production', pp. 173–4.

[37] Bishop, *English Caroline Minuscule*, pp. xv–xvi and 22; but cf. below for full discussion of the scribe's career. See also Temple, *Anglo-Saxon Manuscripts*, p. 88 (no. 69).

[38] Bishop, 'The Copenhagen gospel-book'.

Bishop Æthelwold in A.D. 964 x 971.[39] The ascription of these manuscripts to Peterborough rests on deductions from two pieces of evidence. Rouen, Bibliothèque municipale, MS. Y.6 (274), the sacramentary known as the 'Missal of Robert of Jumièges', was written by Bishop's scribe B (one of the scribes of BL MS. Royal 1.D.ix). Its exemplar (or one of its exemplaria) appears to have been a book enjoying some connexion with Peterborough. There is no lack of information tending in that direction, but the precise nature of the relationship remains unclear. Recently, Michael Lapidge has noted the significant Ely and Peterborough elements in its litany.[40] In 1955 Christopher Hohler wrote of one section of this sacramentary that 'it seems obvious that in this part of the book we have an unintelligent fair-copy either of an Ely text with marginal adaptations for Peterborough or of a Peterborough one with adaptations for Ely. . . . The confusion about the dedication makes it tolerably certain that the scribe was not a monk of either house. . . .'[41] Of the kalendar in this manuscript he observed that while it 'implies that the volume which lay before the copyist was a Peterborough book, the fact that it was obsolete and (as reproduced) defective makes it virtually impossible that he was working at or for Peterborough'.[42] These deductions have been rather lost from view in recent writing.[43] The second piece of evidence has been drawn from a manuscript written by Bishop's scribe C, now Oxford, Bodleian Library, MS. Bodley 163 (*S.C.* 2016), fos 2–5 and 8–227, containing Bede's *Historia ecclesiastica* and Æthilwulf's *De abbatibus*. Its twelfth-century provenance was Peterborough Abbey, when some leaves of the Bedan text (fos 1, 6, 7) were supplied in a known Peterborough hand and further texts were added at the end; a final bifolium (fos 250–251) was added (or, at least, written on), which bears a glossary and a book-list considered to be the catalogue of the Peterborough Abbey library.[44] The exemplar of the texts

---

[39] Wulfstan Cantor, *Vita S. Æthelwoldi*, § 24 (edd. & transl. Lapidge & Winterbottom, pp. 40–1), for the event. For discussion see *ibid.* (especially n. 6) and pp. xlviii–xlix, clxi–clxii. Cf. Knowles *et al.*, *The Heads*, p. 59, and Hart, *The Early Charters of Northern England*, pp. 326–8.

[40] *Anglo-Saxon Litanies*, ed. Lapidge, p. 82.

[41] 'Les Saints insulaires', p. 296. The dedication in question is found in the prayer (modified thus in England) to be said at the entrance to the church, one dedicated to the Virgin Mary and SS. Peter, Paul, and Andrew: see Hohler, *ibid.*, pp. 295–6, who has also observed that 'there was no important church with the dedication given in the prayer' but noted that this elaborate dedication represents a conflation of those for Ely and Peterborough. For the text, see *The Missal of Robert of Jumièges*, ed. Wilson, p. 279.

[42] Hohler, 'Les Saints insulaires', p. 301. For earlier studies of this manuscript, see Atkins, 'An investigation', and Tolhurst, 'An examination'.

[43] For connexions of the kalendar in Rouen MS. Y.6 with Christ Church, Canterbury, see Dumville, *Liturgy*, chapter I.

[44] For the hand see Bishop, 'Notes', p. 440; *The Peterborough Chronicle*, facs. edd.

by Bede and Æthilwulf may be preserved as Winchester, Cathedral Library, MS. 1 (although it is possible that the two books are copies of a lost hyparchetype).[45] It has been thought that this transmission could be anchored firmly to the Æthelwoldian houses by reference to Winchester Cathedral MS. 1 which has been declared to have been written there.[46] To accept such an assertion would, however, be to turn on its head our perception of script-history in late Anglo-Saxon England. That that book had arrived at Winchester Cathedral by the fourteenth century is made likely by additional matter concerning St Birinus which it acquired at that time.[47] But the original script is a somewhat crude manifestation of Style-II Anglo-Caroline, replete with Insular features.[48] There is no likelihood that it was written at Winchester; rather, its execution must be placed outside the circle of Æthelwoldian houses. Accordingly, its origin cannot help to locate MS. Bodley 163 within a continuous tradition of that sort.[49] How we assess the argument that BL MS. Royal 1.D.ix and its fellows were written at Peterborough therefore depends on our reaction to these two rather different associations with that house: within this group of nine manuscripts one depends probably on an exemplar from Peterborough and the provenance of another, a century after its writing, was the same abbey. Moreover, that church's buildings had been destroyed by fire in 1116 and it remains uncertain how much of the community's various book-collections (in the library, the refectory, the treasury, and the church itself) survived the conflagration.[50] For my part, I find this juxtaposition of associations little better than coincidental, especially when a variety of other forms of evidence points to connexions with another centre, namely Canterbury Cathedral. This has long been art-historians' preferred attribution for the group, and the additional

---

Whitelock & Clark, p. 14; and *The Historia Brittonum*, ed. Dumville, V, forthcoming; cf. Ker, *Catalogue*, pp. 259-60. For an edition of the glossary, see Lendinara, 'Il glossario'. For the book-list see Lapidge, 'Surviving booklists', pp. 76-82 (no. XIII).

[45] *Bede's Ecclesiastical History*, edd. & transl. Colgrave & Mynors, pp. l-li; *Æthelwulf, De abbatibus*, ed. & transl. Campbell, pp. ix-x, xv-xix. Cf. *Venerabilis Baedae Opera Historica*, ed. Plummer, I.cix-cxiii, cxvi-cxx.

[46] Potter, 'The Winchester Bede', pp. 40-1; *Wulfstan of Winchester*, edd. & transl. Lapidge & Winterbottom, pp. clxxviii-clxxix. An older view, reported in *Venerabilis Baedae Opera Historica*, ed. Plummer, I.cxi, was that it was written at Glastonbury; from the palaeographical point of view this latter would not obviously be impossible, but no direct evidence has been advanced.

[47] On fo 45v: Ker, *Catalogue*, p. 465 (no. 396); *Bede's Ecclesiastical History*, edd. & transl. Colgrave & Mynors, p. li.

[48] As may be seen from the plate printed by Potter, 'The Winchester Bede'.

[49] Indeed, in *The Salisbury Psalter*, edd. Sisam & Sisam, p. 8, n. 2, attention has been drawn to an Insular feature in MS. Bodley 163; this has not yet been fully evaluated.

[50] Anglo-Saxon Chronicle, *s.a.* 1116 E: 'On þisum ylcan geare brænde eall þæt mynstre of Burh 7 eallæ þa husas butan se captelhus 7 se slæpperne; 7 þærto eac brænde eall þa mæste dæl of þa tuna. Eall þis belamp on an frigdæg, þæt wæs .ii. non. august.'

evidence brought forward by Heslop from Firenze MS. Plut. XVII.20 might be thought to strengthen it further.[51]

The point has been made, however, and correctly, that this group of nine manuscripts presents a scribal appearance very different from that of other books from Canterbury.[52] In respect of books produced there in the period up to *ca* 1010, this is undoubtedly so. But, I repeat, art-historians have been quite content to attribute these manuscripts to Canterbury: it is plainly not the case that the art-work is alien to the Canterbury tradition. Further, we must remember that penetration of the Christ Church scriptorium by Style-I Anglo-Caroline can be seen by the beginning of the eleventh century at the very latest. We may, if we wish, take the group represented by BL MS. Royal 1.D.ix to be a further and more complete development of that sort.[53] Concerning chronology, the evidence would seem to suggest that the 'Royal' group preceded the next detectable phase of work in the Canterbury cathedral scriptorium. It would therefore be logical to deduce that Firenze MS. Plut. XVII.20 was the latest member of the 'Royal' group and marginally transitional between it and specimens of the next identifiable scribal phase at Christ Church, Canterbury. However, before any such deductions can be admitted, we must consider what can be attributed with certainty to the Christ Church scriptorium in the generation after the cataclysmic events of A.D. 1011/12.

At the end (fo 183v) of a gospel-book preserved as Hannover, Kestner-Museum, MS. W.M. XXIa, 36, we find the following four-line colophon.[54]

> Pro scriptore precem ne tempnas fundere pater.
> Librum istum monachus scripsit EADUUIUS. cogno-
> mento BASAN. Sit illi longa salus. Uale seruus
> dei .N'. et memor esto mei.

---

[51] 'The production', pp. 173–4.

[52] *Ibid.*, p. 162. This is true, in a different way, of another manuscript (London, British Library, MS Harley 76) showing distinctive scriptorial traditions but having some connexion with developments at Christ Church in this period: see above, p. 33(-4), n. 117.

[53] See Bishop ('Lincoln Cathedral MS 182', p. 74) for a statement of a radically different viewpoint which nonetheless contains within it the germ of what is discussed in the text above: 'When (*c*. 1020) a Gospel Book written in one of Aethelwold's foundations was presented to Christ Church Canterbury, it came into the hands of a Christ Church scribe and artist whose work, extant in a number of important service books and Gospel Books, breaks with a tradition of a centre previously concerned with general literature, copied in a distinct type of Anglo-Caroline' (cf. Bishop, 'Notes', p. 323). But to see the royal writing office as the place of production is yet another option: below, pp. 126–9, 132–5.

[54] For a facsimile, see Bishop, *English Caroline Minuscule*, plate XXII.24. Cf. Heslop, 'The production', pp. 175–6.

The scribe of this book was brought to prominence by the researches of T.A.M. Bishop who referred to him as 'Eadui'.[55] The name is in fact Old English Eadwig, of which Eaduuius and Eaduuinus are conventional latinisations – the latter risking confusion with the name Eadwine, however. The -*g* was dropped in the process of latinisation, no doubt because it had ceased to be sounded as even /g/, much less /g/, in this position in late Old English; latinisation as **Eaduuigus* would perhaps have implied a pronunciation of -*g*- as -/g/-. The same convention may be seen operating with other Old English names in -*wig*, -*sige*, etc..

The form of this colophon presents a difficulty, however. As Michael Lapidge has pointed out to me, it has a metrical character, albeit of a complicated and imperfect sort. It may be laid out in lines of verse.

> Pro scritore precem ne tempnas fundere, pater:
> Librum istum monachus scripsit Eaduuius (cognomento) Basan;
> Sit illi longa salus.
> Uale seruus Dei (N.) et memor esto mei.

Apart from faults involving quantity (*scriptore*, *pater*, *illi*), it is necessary to excise the bracketed words to achieve a scansion. The third line is metrically fragmentary, while the fourth – a pentameter – is in a different metre from the first two, which are hexameters.[56]

It would be possible to suppose that this is merely an incompetent metrical colophon. But two other interpretations also present themselves, both of which would require a preexisting metrical colophon as a source. We could suppose that an 'Eaduuius Basan' had intruded his own name when copying a text which contained a different one or none. Or it could be considered that the whole is a mangled transcript of the colophon which stood in the exemplar (perhaps damaged at this point) of the Hannover manuscript. Of these three options, the first is perhaps the least likely: this is not a satisfactory poem, the text being unmetrical as it stands, for lines 2 and 4 contain hypermetrical elements and line 3 is incomplete, while the manuscript offers no sign that the scribe considered his colophon to be verse. Of the other two possibilities my preference would be for the former. The intrusion of names in lines 2 and 4 and (if we wish to explain faults of quantity thus) the possible rewriting of line 1, both in defiance of metre, would satisfactorily explain the colophon's present shape. The named scribe would therefore have written the extant manuscript. However, until such time as a source may be identified, no certainty is possible. We must allow that

---

[55] *English Caroline Minuscule*, pp. xxiii, 22. Temple, *Anglo-Saxon Manuscripts*, pp. 85 *et passim*, has further de-anglicised the name by referring to the scribe as 'Eadvius'!

[56] I am indebted to Michael Lapidge, Andy Orchard, and Neil Wright for discussion of this colophon.

'Eaduuius cognomento Basan' may not have been the name of the scribe of the Hannover gospel-book. I shall accordingly refer to him in what follows as 'Eadwig'.

The work of 'Eadwig' was recognised by T.A.M. Bishop in ten other specimens.[57] None of these is signed: the identification is purely palaeographical. Four manuscripts offer some dating evidence. We may take first the addition, already mentioned, which 'Eadwig' made on fo 44v of BL MS. Royal 1.D.ix:[58] in as much as the document added belongs to 1017 x 1020, it is likely that 'Eadwig' was writing not later than 1020. Another document of which he was the scribe is BL Stowe Charter 38, a diploma, dated 1018, of King Cnut for Christ Church, Canterbury: it is uncertain what the role of 'Eadwig' as scribe has to say about the genuineness or the circumstances of production of this charter.[59] BL MS. Arundel 155, a psalter mostly in the same hand,[60] was

---

[57] *English Caroline Minuscule*, p. 22. The origin of Bishop's studies of 'Eadwig' may be seen in 1959 ('Notes', p. 94) when he reported C.R. Dodwell's notice of the script of Cambridge, Corpus Christi College, MS. 44 as 'close to' that of London, British Library, MS. Harley 603, fos 28–49 (a section now generally agreed to be by 'Eadwig'). CCCC 44 is a pontifical written (after A.D. 1012, but no specific *terminus ante quem* has been found) in a massive round mid-eleventh-century hand, in the style pioneered by 'Eadwig'. Bishop dissented, however, from a further association made by Dodwell (*The Canterbury School*, p. 1, n. 1): there, Dodwell attributed MSS. CCCC 44 and Harley 603 to St Augustine's Abbey, Canterbury, and described the hybrid (Style I/Style II) Canterbury script of Harley 603, fos 2–27 and 50–73 (the work of a single hand), which he dated *ca* 1000, as 'similar to' that of London, British Library, MS. Cotton Vespasian A.i, fos 155–160; the latter specimen is now generally regarded as being late work by 'Eadwig', coeval rather with fos 28–49 of Harley 603 (cf. nn. 87–88, below). Bishop's resolution of the tangle created by Dodwell has stood the test of time, but has been developed in detail and rendered more sophisticated by Backhouse, 'The making of the Harley Psalter'.

[58] Sawyer, *Anglo-Saxon Charters*, no. 985; cf. above, nn. 33–34. For the problems posed by the other added document (fo 43v), see above, n. 35.

[59] *Ibid.*, no. 950; cf. Bishop, 'Notes', p. 94, and p. 420, n. 2. I am indebted to Susan Kelly for suggesting to me that the non-standard (viz, vertical) format of this single sheet may indicate that it was not a chancery-production (for discussion, see below, pp. 126–7, 130–1). For a recent notice of the charter, with a complete facsimile of the face, see *The Golden Age*, edd. Backhouse *et al.*, pp. 166–7; for other recent discussions see Keynes, *The Diplomas of King Æthelred*, p. 126, n. 136, and Brooks, *The Early History*, p. 288. For the other document in the hand of 'Eadwig', a diploma attributed to King Wihtred and dated 716, see Sawyer, *Anglo-Saxon Charters*, no. 22 (MS. 1), and Brooks, *The Early History*, pp. 289–90.

[60] Bishop, *English Caroline Minuscule*, p. 22; *The Golden Age*, edd. Backhouse *et al.*, pp. 72 and 74 (no. 57), with the speculation (cf. Brooks, *The Early History*, p. 264) that the figure shown abasing himself at St Benedict's feet in the illumination on fo 133r is the scribe (see *The Golden Age*, edd. Backhouse *et al.*, plate XVIII, following p. 176); this speculation has been translated into fantasy by Heslop ('The production', p. 175) who has asserted that BL Arundel 155 'was probably made at Eadwig's own expense and initiative since he is shown presenting it to St Benedict, an act in which the other members of the Christ Church community do not join directly'!

written after 1012, since its kalendar has the feast of St Ælfheah marked
at 19 April; on the other hand, 'Eadwig' did not include the feast of the
translation of St Ælfheah from London to Canterbury (which occurred in
1023, as we have seen) at 8 June, and it has accordingly been supposed
that the book was written before that date. Finally, 'Eadwig' has been
recognised as the contributor of one page of script (fo 23v) to the 'York
Gospels', a manuscript often thought to have been largely written at
Canterbury by *ca* 1000 but which had travelled to York by the time when
local documents were added, before 1023;[61] perhaps 'Eadwig' completed
the gospel-book specifically so that it was ready for despatch northwards.

   Questions arise concerning this scribe's origins, training, employment,
and domicile. One might hope that the 'cognomen', *Basan*, stated in the
colophon would prove helpful in this regard (always remembering,
however, the uncertainty as to whether Eadwig Basan was the name of
our eleventh-century scribe rather than the scribe of the exemplar of one
of the books copied by 'Eadwig'). *Basan* looks as though it might be Old
English, but closer investigation indicates impassable difficulties of
interpretation. A personal name *Bas(s)a* is evidenced in place-names and
Basan could be its genitive. It is unclear, however, why the 'cognomen'
should be the genitive of another personal name. Nor have we any reason
to suppose that *Basan* could stand for a place-name of which it
constituted one element. No other Old English explanation seems to be
available;[62] another approach must be tried.

   In the Old Testament, and particularly in the Psalter, is found a
Hebrew name Basan.[63] In the interpretative literature of late Antiquity we
can discover a number of 'translations' of it. That favoured by St Jerome
was *pinguis*, 'fat'.[64] Embodied in the formula 'Eaduuius cognomento
Basan' we may therefore care to see a couple of monastic jokes, one of
them learned. As a monk, 'Eadwig' – our scribe – would have known the
Psalms well and been instructed in them;[65] indeed, he had occasion to

---

[61] On 'Eadwig' as the scribe of fo 23v see Bishop, 'Notes', p. 186; 'The Copenhagen
gospel-book', p. 37, n. 1 (*ibid.*, Bishop has stated his view of the core-manuscript as
'English Caroline of s. X late'); *English Caroline Minuscule*, p. 22. Cf. Heslop, 'The
production', pp. 166–8; Dumville, 'On the dating', pp. 53–4. On York and Wulfstan
see most recently Keynes, 'The additions in Old English'; the *terminus* (A.D. 1023)
for the additions is provided by Archbishop Wulfstan's death.
[62] I am indebted to Margaret Gelling for discussing with me the limits of possible
interpretation of the 'cognomen' within the framework of Old English philology.
[63] I have noted some fifteen occurrences: Numbers 21:33 (*bis*), IV Kings 10:33, Psalms
21:13, 67:16 (*bis*) and 23, 134:11, 135:20, Isaiah 33:9, Jeremiah 41:9, Ezechiel 27:6,
Micha 7:14, Nahum 1:4, Zachariah 11:2.
[64] Cf. Thiel, *Grundlagen*, pp. 259–60 (Basan); cf. pp. 255 (Baasa), 268 (busa), 365
(Nassa).
[65] That he was a monk is attested by the colophon. If Eadwig Basan was not the scribe of
the Hannover manuscript (and therefore of the other books in the same hand), the
conclusion remains true of Eadwig, whoever he was.

copy them more than once. If his form gave rise to the appellation 'Eadwig the Fat', he was able to use his biblical knowledge to obscure it with learning.

The question of the scribe's name is therefore doubly unhelpful in our search for his career-history. No such Eadwig has been identified in any Anglo-Saxon record.[66] In the colophon to the gospel-book now at Hannover, 'Eadwig' described himself as *monachus*. This designation implies both training and *stabilitas*. We may begin with the hypothesis that 'Eadwig the Fat' had been from the first a monk of Christ Church, Canterbury. At once, difficulties become apparent. Given the quantity of manuscript survival from early eleventh-century Christ Church, it is curious that the highly distinctive scribal style of 'Eadwig' appears suddenly in the record, fully grown. We might have expected to see in slightly earlier Christ Church manuscripts some immature performances or some adumbrations of the wholly developed style.[67] Unless we are to think that one of the Style-I scribes encountered in Christ Church book-production of the years around 1000 is 'Eadwig', writing before the development of his distinctive style, we should do better to suppose that he received his monastic and scribal training elsewhere, coming to Canterbury only in the late 1010s. Otherwise it would be necessary to conclude that he was a prodigy whose first deeds were already those of a master-calligrapher.

Nevertheless, at least one of the unusual elements of his script may be paralleled in Christ Church manuscripts of the preceding period, as we

---

[66] The appeal by Bishop, *English Caroline Minuscule*, p. 22, to a Christ Church obit printed by Boutemy, 'Two obituaries', p. 297, is unimpressive, as Heslop ('The production', p. 154, n. 9) has pointed out. The name was not rare: Searle, *Onomasticon*, p. 191.

[67] On the quantity of survival, see Bishop, 'Notes', pp. 413–23, and *English Caroline Minuscule*, pp. xxv–xxvi; cf. Brooks, *The Early History*, pp. 255–78 (notes on pp. 379–82). On the question of adumbration, some very interesting remarks by Bishop are worth quoting. 'It is [London, British Library, MS. Royal 7.C.iv which] both sums up the calligraphic tendencies of several of the later MSS. in stemma A [of Christ Church scribes] and is evidently the precursor of the script found in Christ Church MSS. of the second and third decades of the eleventh century' ('Notes', p. 415; cf. pp. 422–3 for the 'stemma'); 'the work of some of the later scribes of stemma A seems to mark them as the close precursors of ['Eadwig Basan']. . ., and whose clear, carefully formed, slightly denatured script is . . . outside the limits of this survey' (*ibid.*, p. 420). Finally, Bishop argued (*ibid.*, p. 420, n. 2) that Style II persisted (if briefly) at Christ Church alongside the style of 'Eadwig Basan', on the evidence of additions (made not earlier than 1023) to the Paris kalendar-fragment (n. 23, above). Heslop ('The production', pp. 169–70) has suggested the same for two other manuscripts: London, British Library, MS. Additional 57337 and New York, Pierpont Morgan Library, MS. M.869. On all these manuscripts, see also chapter III, above.

shall see.[68] This would imply either that 'Eadwig' was brought to Canterbury from wherever other Style-I scribes also came or that previous Christ Church books or scribes did have an impact on him as he created his new style of minuscule. What is certain is that the basis of his minuscule is provided by Style-I Anglo-Caroline; but he has absorbed into it Style-II elements. Bishop has written of the style which he traced back to 'Eadwig' that 'this seems to be a developed or degenerate form of Style I, retaining the mass, losing the energy' and has characterised it also as formalistic, deliberate but plain.[69] Likewise, Heslop, in treating of the majuscule display-script used by 'Eadwig', has observed of its constituent elements that 'they partake of several different traditions' and that 'It is almost certainly a simplification to analyse his capitals as though they were the result of an intermingling of elements only from Style I . . . and Style II';[70] that Style I influenced by Style II is the basis of his script seems to be our necessary starting point, however. This mixture has led Heslop to observe that questions are raised thereby about the place of his training.[71]

The evidence provided by the localisable specimens of his script leaves no reasonable doubt that his scriptorium – what Heslop has called 'his main centre of operations' – was Christ Church at Canterbury.[72] Yet there is little in his surviving output to suggest that his career, distinguished as its results were, need be reckoned as extending over a lengthy period. It is striking that those specimens of his writing which permit of dating cluster around and perhaps just before 1020, 1012 x 1023 being the outer limits indicated. In so far as dated or datable items are concerned, therefore, the activities of 'Eadwig' at Christ Church seem best attributed to the later years of Archbishop Lyfing's pontificate. These circumstances suggest another possible interpretation of the twin problems of understanding where 'Eadwig' was trained and what his relationship was with Christ Church, Canterbury. It has been cautiously observed by T.A.M. Bishop that the script practised by 'Eadwig' 'on merely stylistic evidence, might seem to have had a lasting and wide influence'.[73] In fact, 'Eadwig' seems certain to have been the originator of this fourth style of Anglo-Caroline, the practice of which became a scribal mark of Englishness and which outlasted Anglo-Saxon England

---

[68] Below, p. 128 and n. 84.

[69] *English Caroline Minuscule*, pp. xxiii–xxiv.

[70] 'The production', pp. 166–7.

[71] *Ibid.*, p. 167. His training could have been in more than one scriptorium. But it is worth noting that Christ Church, Canterbury, is at present the only scriptorium known to have had practitioners of Style I and Style II working alongside one another (cf. chapter III, above).

[72] *Ibid.*

[73] *English Caroline Minuscule*, p. xxiii.

itself.[74] The question arises as to how his work came to have such extraordinary influence among his fellow-professionals. While one must not underestimate the status and connexions of the cathedral church of Canterbury, it seems to me that some hesitation is in order before we admit that a monk of Christ Church could set such a powerful and enduring trend.

Among the documentary texts in the hand of 'Eadwig' is a diploma of King Cnut for Christ Church, preserved on a single sheet, whose text contains the date 1018.[75] Three deductions are possible from the observation that a Canterbury scribe produced a royal document: the charter is a copy, or a forgery, made at Christ Church; production of diplomas had been delegated by Cnut to the beneficiary; or 'Eadwig' was in 1018 a royal scribe.[76]

The last is an option which has not been seriously pursued, particularly in respect of the diploma. Contemplation of this possibility, however, suggests that its adoption would solve a number of difficulties. We should have reasons why the script of 'Eadwig' was different from that previously practised at Christ Church and why his work is not found in straightforwardly embryonic condition in earlier products of the Christ Church scriptorium. Above all, we should have a very satisfactory explanation of the widespread influence of his style: products of the royal writing office no doubt collectively reached a much wider audience than those of any monk-scribe of Canterbury Cathedral (or any other church). From the reign of Æthelstan, first king of England (and perhaps even from the time of his grandfather, Alfred, king of Wessex), royal scribes had set the pace of fashion in script-development:[77] that the same might be true in Cnut's reign should occasion no surprise. To what extent Cnut (perhaps more, at any rate, than his predecessors) used his own scribes to produce books fit for a king is a nice question: Heslop has attempted to

---

74 For Styles I and II, see above, chapters I–III. For Style III, see chapter II. Henceforth I refer to the script developed by 'Eadwig' as Anglo-Caroline Style IV.

75 Sawyer, *Anglo-Saxon Charters*, no. 950; cf. above, n. 59. See also Chaplais, 'The Anglo-Saxon chancery' (1973), p. 59; Chaplais has there asserted that another (forged) document in the hand of 'Eadwig' is Sawyer, *Anglo-Saxon Charters*, no. 914 (MSS. 3/9), in London, British Library, MS. Cotton Claudius A.iii, fos 2r–6r (Ker, *Catalogue*, p. 239: no. 185, art. a), a suggestion quietly dropped by subsequent scholars except Brooks, *The Early History*, pp. 257–9 (cf. Keynes, *The Diplomas of King Æthelred*, p. 261, on this charter). Brooks has dated the document 1032 x *ca* 1042: if the attribution to 'Eadwig' were to be sustained (but, in my view, it should not be), this would have significant implications for our current perceptions of his career. Cf. also n. 88, below.

76 For discussion of the production of royal diplomas and writs in Cnut's reign, see Chaplais, 'The Anglo-Saxon chancery' (1973), pp. 57–60.

77 Cf. Dumville, 'English Square minuscule script: the background and earliest phases', pp. 174–5, and *Wessex and England*, chapters III–VI.

probe it,[78] but without considering the context in which the Crown might most naturally be an employer of scribal talent.

We still do not know how scribes in the century from A.D. 924 were recruited into royal service. Much less do we know what happened to them after their careers at court.[79] In the last half-century of the Anglo-Saxon state we can see a little more clearly into the world of the royal priest, but still with insufficient clarity for us to answer the question about their source and circumstances of recruitment.[80] In the case of 'Eadwig' it seems fairly clear that by 1020 he was a monk of Christ Church, Canterbury. If he had been a royal scribe in 1018, we should have to suppose that he retired or was attracted into the archbishop's circle, perhaps if Lyfing had admired his calligraphy. Where or whether he had been a monk before entering royal service is not known: we could speculate that (for example) he had already served Lyfing at Wells before 1013.

Such a line of argument throws the spotlight upon the two gospel-books (the Hannover manuscript and BL Add. 34890) and the gospel-lectionary (at Firenze) written by 'Eadwig'. These have not been specifically associated with Christ Church: the attribution rests on what is known of the career of 'Eadwig' at Canterbury. They might have been written there but, alternatively, they might have been executed while their scribe was in the royal service. Heslop has drawn attention to a possible and interesting implication of the colophon in the Hannover manuscript: if it is read without preconceptions, it seems to suggest that the scribe knew the book to have been destined for someone either not yet chosen or chosen by a person other than (s)he who gave 'Eadwig' his orders – at any rate, for someone whom the scribe could not identify.[81] The theory that the commissioning agent was the King (or the Queen), in anticipation of a general need to have such a gift available, has its attractions. It remains speculative. But, in as much as the King undoubtedly had his own scribes, there is no necessary reason to suppose that he commissioned manuscripts by exercising his patronage in ecclesiastical ateliers. That he may have done so is not excluded by this argument, but he was probably able to call upon more immediate professional resources.

'Eadwig the Fat' may, therefore, have been either a native product of Canterbury's Christ Church or a monk-scribe brought thither by Archbishop Lyfing in 1013 or a royal scribe who moved to Christ Church

[78] 'The production', pp. 156–62.
[79] Cf. Dumville, 'English libraries before 1066', pp. 163–4 and 175, n. 41; for a thoroughly revised version of that paper see *Anglo-Saxon Manuscripts*, ed. Richards.
[80] See Barlow, *The English Church, 1000–1066*, pp. 129–37.
[81] 'The production', pp. 175–6. But see also above, pp. 120–2, for a discussion of the colophon and the possible implications of its relationship to its source(s).

in 1018 x 1020. The evidence does not enable us to discriminate with certainty between the possibilities. What does seem reasonably likely, however, is that our scribe's professional floruit, as we see its results displayed in the surviving witnesses, should be placed in the immediate environs of A.D. 1020 and located, after 1018 at least, at Christ Church, Canterbury.

We may turn now to description of our scribe's handwriting. The principal point of reference must of course be the one codex where 'Eadwig Basan' signed his own work – Hannover, Kestner-Museum, MS. W.M. XXIa, 36.[82] Both the majuscule and minuscule scripts employed by 'Eadwig' have a very distinctive appearance; what is more, they stand in very sharp contrast with one another. His serried rows of majuscules seem at first blush to be Rustic Capitals but prove on closer inspection to be mixed majuscules. Among the script's distinguishing features, it may be noted that **S** and **L** are usually tall, **E** occasionally so. A significant characteristic of our scribe's minuscule script is his sporadic employment of small majuscules, particularly **H** and **N**, with the **N** being made very broad.[83] It is noteworthy that this habit of using small majuscules randomly in a minuscule context can be seen in the work of the Style-I scribe at Christ Church who contributed to the writing of, for example, Oxford, Bodleian Library, MS. Bodley 708 (*S.C.* 2609).[84]

The minuscule written by 'Eadwig' is characterised first by its rotundity, an appearance achieved by the bowls of **b**, **d**, **g**, **p**, **q**, by his particular forms of **c** and **e**, and of course by **o** itself. The line of the tops of minim-size letters is straight and regular, but without creating the stiff and regimented aspect which appears in some flat-topped late specimens both of Anglo-Saxon Square minuscule and of Anglo-Caroline.[85] I turn now to specific letter-forms.

a   is usually, though by no means always, of the same height as other ordinary-size letters; but its lower compartment is very small and quite noticeably angled, perhaps in the latter respect suggesting the scribe's awareness of the Uncial form.

---

[82] Bishop, *English Caroline Minuscule*, plate XXII.24.

[83] This is not to say, however, that these features cannot be found outside Style IV. For an example of small, broad, majuscule **N** in London, British Library, MS. Harley 603, fo 54vc15 (not the portion written by 'Eadwig'), see Backhouse, 'The making of the Harley Psalter', p. 103, fig. 4. In fact, the use of this form of **N** has a longer history, reaching back into Continental antecedents.

[84] For discussion of the hand in question, see above, p. 103; for a specimen see Bishop, *English Caroline Minuscule*, plate VIII (*catHedras*, line 7; *adHumilitatis*, sic line 9; for alteration of such a form in line 18, *not* 8, see Bishop, *ibid.*, p. 8).

[85] For some late types of Square minuscule, cf. Dumville, 'Beowulf come lately', and references given there. For late, stiff, flat-topped Anglo-Caroline minuscule of Style IV, see Hinkle, 'The gift', p. 23, fig. 1, on Reims, Bibliothèque municipale, MS. 9.

d   stands upright and with a tall ascender whose top begins in a wedge which tapers gradually downwards. (The same effect may be seen in the ascenders of **b** and **h**, and in **l**.)

e   is round in form, with a very narrow aperture – a squinting eye – which sometimes rises very slightly above the line of minim-strokes. In the Hannover manuscript, **e** does not usually have a horned back. With a following **c** or **i** there is a hint, but no more, in the angling of the eye, of a tall **e** behaving as it might in Insular script.

f   descends well below the ruled line.

g   has a quite distinct short vertical between bowl and hook; the hook is always open.

h   is characterised by a stem whose foot is ticked inwards; the shoulder-stroke turns in, towards the stem, as it approaches the ruled line.

i   has a rather thick approach-stroke, which the other minim-letters share, and either (more usually) a foot or a finishing stroke.

o   often gives the impression of being in continuation with the following letter (as in Style-I Anglo-Caroline), but such continuity seems to be merely apparent, not morphological.

r   sports a somewhat angular top, and its stem descends slightly below the ruled line.

s   has a very distinctive appearance. The stem of Caroline **s** begins with a wedge at the point of join between the two strokes. The top-stroke continues, umbrella-like above much or the whole of the following letter. The stem descends slightly below the ruled line.

t   sometimes has a slightly pierced top.

x   in its lower-left quadrant has a stroke which sweeps back beneath two preceding letters.

Five features require further comment. The principal ascenders – in **b**, **d**, **h**, **l** – are surmounted by a long, tapering wedge which is usually not at all top-heavy. The minim-letters (**i**, **m**, **n**, **u**) all have quite noticeable approach-strokes. The ampersand is used for the word *et* and for final *-et* in longer words. There are three other ligatures: **c+t**, **r+a**, **s+t**. **ct** in ligature is one of the most distinctive features of the hand of 'Eadwig', and very clearly reforms what went before. By the early years of the eleventh century the **ct**-ligature in Anglo-Caroline had gone the way of its counterpart in tenth-century Continental Caroline, becoming absurdly widely spaced, and with a variety of connecting strokes being used. 'Eadwig' introduced an almost rectangular ligature, with the upper and lower elements of nearly equal proportions, the whole looking rather like a reversed **B**. Sometimes that whole is clearly of two-compartment form, but sometimes it is open internally. **ra** in ligature is the form often seen in Style-I Anglo-Caroline and inherited from Continental models, with **a** taking the majuscule **cc**-form. **st** in ligature is tall and relatively narrow, with the cross-stroke of **t** running right across the ligatured form. Finally, 'Eadwig' had a distinctive version of the abbreviated *nomen sacrum*, *Iesus*, writing **IHC** (as if in Greek majuscules, for *IES*) with **i** and **c** indistinguishable from normal minuscule forms but with small-Capital **H** (found also sporadically in miscellaneous words throughout the text).

As has been observed by T.A.M. Bishop and J.M. Backhouse, this scribe's writing does show some development from the style represented in the Hannover manuscript.[86] Two of the specimens attributed to 'Eadwig' have been described as 'late and degenerate',[87] namely, his contributions to the 'Vespasian Psalter' and BL MS. Harley 603. Indeed, Janet Backhouse has gone so far as to see MS. Harley 603, fos 28–49, as work of the scribe's old age.[88] Much study still needs to be undertaken of the internal chronology of his oeuvre. For the moment, it must be sufficient to stress that the contributions by 'Eadwig' to the Harley and Vespasian psalters are by no means of uniform style. In as much as the six folios of additions to the 'Vespasian Psalter' show a few marked variations from the script of the Hannover manuscript, I propose to concentrate on those here. The most noticeable difference is the very frequent use of an **e** with a strongly hooked back, a feature so prominent as to be obtrusive and an impediment to easy recognition of the preceding letter. In general, the approach- and finishing strokes of minim-letters are also more noticeable. A monogram of **o** + reversed **r** is frequently used, both medially and finally in words. The top-stroke of **r** is sometimes more sharply angular. In the abbreviation for *per*, the cross-stroke through the descender of **p** is notably short. More than one form of the ampersand was employed.

In other specimens (Stowe Charter 38, Harley 603) e-caudata, not found in the Vespasian manuscript, is frequently employed.[89] The tall ligature of **r** + **t** occurs in Stowe Ch. 38, where a notably more angular

---

[86] Bishop, *English Caroline Minuscule*, p. 22 (nos 24–5); Backhouse, 'The making of the Harley Psalter', especially p. 107 (fig. 7, showing fo 28r) – on p. 106 she has written that his script here is 'uneven and sometimes almost quavering. It is perhaps not too imaginative to see it as the work of an elderly or infirm man. . . .'

[87] Bishop, *English Caroline Minuscule*, p. 22 (no. 25), on London, British Library, MS. Cotton Vespasian A.i, fos 155–160 (cf. *The Vespasian Psalter*, facs. edd. Wright & Campbell), and hinting at a chronological relationship with the work of 'Eadwig' in Harley 603; on his script in the latter, characterised by Janet Backhouse as 'elderly or infirm', and 'Eadwig' as 'in old age', see *The Golden Age*, edd. Backhouse *et al.*, p. 75. Cf. Gameson, 'The Anglo-Saxon artists', pp. 30–1 and notes, for different emphases.

[88] In 'The making of the Harley Psalter', p. 106, she has written that a 'date in the late [1020s] is a possibility, but this section of the Harley Psalter could equally well have been written out as late as the 1040s'. For another such possibility, cf. n. 75, above.

[89] Bishop, *English Caroline Minuscule*, p. 22 (no. 24), has reported its occurrence in various forms in the Hannover gospel-book written by 'Eadwig'.

r+a ligature is also found, as is an occasional very tall and trailing-headed **a**. These three features recur in Stowe Charter 2, but **e**-caudata is not found. Nonetheless, a consistency in essential, personal character-istics may be seen across the attributed specimens.[90]

Before we pass to consideration of the first generation's diffusion of Style-IV Anglo-Caroline beyond Canterbury, it is important to ask a further question about the sources of influence upon 'Eadwig'. Thus far, I have concentrated on the background at Canterbury and in the royal writing office – in short, upon the internal development of English Caroline minuscule – as well as allowing much to the creative genius of 'Eadwig' himself. However, there is one other and obvious source of inspiration. Anglo-Caroline script began in imitation of some Continental models, and there is no reason why we should deny that that was a continuing process; indeed, there is also good evidence in the eleventh century for the impact of Anglo-Caroline models in some Continental ateliers.

From the abbey of Saint-Bertin at Saint-Omer, a house in constant contact with Canterbury and more generally with England throughout the middle ages, comes evidence which must bear either on the creation or on the diffusion of our Style IV: manuscripts attributed to the abbacy of Odbert (*ca* A.D. 1000), and later, show the characteristic shapes of **a** and **e**, as well as a similar form of **s** and of mixed majuscules, not to mention the (more widely attested) use of small majuscule **N** in minuscule contexts. Continental models need not have been chronologically so proximate, however. An interesting question is posed by Cambridge, Corpus Christi College, MS. 272, the Psalter of Count Achadeus, written at Reims in A.D. 883/4. By the end of the middle ages, this manuscript was in England and perhaps at Christ Church, Canterbury. The extensive marginal commentary in gloss-size script may suggest that the book was already there by the early eleventh century. Either this commentary is written in Style-IV Anglo-Caroline or else (if the usual assumption is correct, that it is coeval with the text) it was one of the sources from which 'Eadwig' drew inspiration.[91]

---

[90] Cambridge, Gonville & Caius College, MS. 732/754 or 734/782, a single-leaf liturgical fragment now mislaid, is a possible exception. A decade ago, Nicholas Webb and I subjected its script to a very close examination and concluded provisionally that it was not by the same scribe as the other specimens attributed to 'Eadwig'. In the absence of the manuscript, I have been unable to review that conclusion while writing this chapter.

[91] On Saint-Bertin and Odbert see Wilmart, 'Les livres de l'abbé Odbert'; Boutemy, 'Odbert de Saint-Bertin et la seconde bible', 'Encore un manuscrit décoré', 'L'enluminure anglaise', 'Un monument capital', and 'Influences carolingiennes'. Cf. also Swarzenski, 'The Anhalt Morgan Gospels'. On other aspects of connexions with England, see Grierson, 'The relations'. I am indebted to Julia Crick for pointing me to Saint-Bertin in this connexion and for suggesting in particular that Saint-Omer,

These two examples alone show that widespread searches in the extensive corpus of Continental Caroline performances from the late eighth to the early eleventh century will be necessary before reasonable certainty can be achieved about the sources which influenced 'Eadwig'. Such a task cannot be undertaken here. But, until it is done, the relative contributions of native and foreign calligraphic inspiration in the creation of Style-IV Anglo-Caroline will not be measurable.

The diffusion of the style – Anglo-Caroline Style IV – seen first in the manuscripts written by 'Eadwig Basan', and therefore presumptively invented by him, seems to have followed rapidly on his datable oeuvre, placed in the immediate environs of A.D. 1020. It is natural to look first at royal diplomas, both as providing a precise chronological sequence and in view of the hypothesis offered above concerning the career of 'Eadwig'. For, in as much as in the tenth century royal scribes seem to have forced the pace of fashion, so we might expect to see the same happening in the eleventh. Save in one possible respect, the results are disappointing.

I begin by listing the relevant diplomas (see p. 133). The divisions between the reigns of the kings of the period – Cnut, Harold I, Harthacnut, Edward II – are marked with horizontal rules. An asterisk indicates a certainly non-contemporaneous single sheet. What is striking, from the palaeographical point of view, about this series is that, after the first document listed – Cnut's diploma, copied by 'Eadwig Basan', in favour of the archbishop of Canterbury –, there is no certain and contemporary surviving specimen of Style-IV Anglo-Caroline until Harthacnut's diploma issued in favour of the Old Minster at Winchester in the last year of his reign. Thereafter, originals of royal diplomas in the name of King Edward are routinely written in Style IV. The documents dated or datable 1019–1040 do not seem to continue what was begun by 'Eadwig Basan'. There is one possible exception. If S.953, dated 1018, is

---

Bibliothèque municipale, MS. 56 should be considered. It is perhaps noteworthy in this context that an Anglo-Caroline manuscript attributed to early eleventh-century Christ Church, Canterbury – Boulogne-sur-mer, Bibliothèque municipale, MS. 189 (for facsimiles see *The Old English Prudentius Glosses*, ed. Meritt, pp. 2, 32, 62, 88, 102) – came into the possession of the abbey of Saint-Bertin (*ibid.*, p. ix; cf. Bishop, 'Notes', p. 415). Wormald, 'Anglo-Saxon initials', suggested that Paris, Bibliothèque nationale, MS. latin 6401A, written in Style-II Anglo-Caroline, represented the sort of English manuscript which Odbert obtained and was influenced by. On CCCC 272, see James, *A Descriptive Catalogue*, II.27–32; its (original) litany has been published by Lapidge, *Anglo-Saxon Litanies*, no. V, who has suspected (p. 65) that it may have served as a model for some long litanies found in late Anglo-Saxon books; but his suggestion that Grimbald might have brought it from Reims to England seems implausible, for it is hard to credit that Count Achadeus, having no doubt paid handsomely for the book's creation, would have been content to see it taken across the sea a year later.

Date	Sawyer[92]	Manuscript	Facsimile[93]	Archive[94]	Beneficiary
1018	950	BL Stowe Ch. 38	OS iii.39	CaCC	Archbishop
*1018	951	Exeter 2524	OS ii.Ex.9	Exeter	Bishop
*1018	953	Exeter 2071	OS ii.Ex.10	Exeter	St Germans
1019	956	Winchester College 7.2.4	OS ii.Wi.Coll.4	WiNM	WiNM
1021x1023	977	BL Cotton Aug. ii.24	BM iv.16	Evesham	Ælfic (monk)
*1021x1023	980	King's Lynn	BA 33	Bury St Edmunds	Bury St Edmunds
*1023	959	Canterbury Ch.Ant. S.261	OS i.20	CaCC	CaCC
1024	961	Dorset R.O., D.124/2	OS ii.Ilch.2	Abbotsbury	Orc
1031	963	BL Cotton Aug. ii.69	BM iv.18	CaCC	Æthelric
1031	971	Exeter 2525	OS ii.Ex.11	Exeter	Hunuwine
1035	974	BL Stowe Ch. 41	OS iii.42	CaCC	Bishop Eadsige
*1016x1035	981	BL Stowe Ch. 40	OS iii.41	CaCC	CaCC
1037x1040	1467	BL Cotton Aug. ii.90	BM iv.20	CaCC	CaCC etc.
*1038x1039	995	King's Lynn	Hervey	Bury St Edmunds	Bury St Edmunds
1042	994	BL Harley Ch. 43.C.8	BM iv.24	WiOM	Bishop
1042x1044	1044	BL Cotton Aug. ii.68	BM iv.25	CaCC	Æthelred
1044	1003	Exeter 2526	OS ii.Ex.12	Exeter	Leofric
1044	1004	Dorset R.O., D.124/3	OS ii.Ilch.3	Abbotsbury	Orc
1044	1005	BL Cotton Aug. ii.59	BM iv.26	CaCC	Ordgar
1045	1008	BL Cotton Ch. viii.9	BM iv.31	WiOM	Bishop

etc.

92 The numbers in this column are those given by Sawyer, *Anglo-Saxon Charters*.

93 References are to the following publications: BM = *Facsimiles*, ed. Bond; OS = *Facsimiles*, ed. Sanders; BA = *Facsimiles*, ed. Keynes; Hervey, *Corolla*.

94 I use the abbreviations employed by Gneuss, 'A preliminary list': CaCC = Christ Church, Canterbury; WiNM = New Minster, Winchester; WiOM = Old Minster, Winchester.

indeed an Exeter forgery of the later eleventh century, it is a remarkably close copy of a document written in his style.[95] On the other hand, S.956 and S.977 are very poor specimens: the scribes were perhaps attempting to incorporate some Style-IV elements into their script, but it cannot be said that they were particularly successful. S.961 is difficult to categorise palaeographically but it is not a representative of Style IV. S.963 and S.971 were both written by one and the same scribe, and both concern land in Devon: their script can be characterised only as regressive. S.981 (MS. 1) seems to me to be post-Conquest in its execution. S.974 is a respectable-enough piece of work, embodying some Style-IV elements: it is certainly the least unsatisfactorily written of Cnut's surviving diplomas post-1018. S.1467 provides no Caroline script for examination: it is a wholly Old-English document. From S.994 (of A.D. 1042), as I have said, the charter-series, in its new attention to bookhand, rejoins the world of book-production and adopts again a respectably calligraphic form of Caroline minuscule. S.994 is written in a large, round hand. S.1044 is a reasonable specimen in Style IV. S.1003 displays what comes to be the classic Exeter interpretation of Style-IV Anglo-Caroline, and may therefore be of somewhat later date than A.D. 1044.[96] S.1004 is an entirely satisfactory essay in Style IV. What this sequence says about the production of royal diplomas under the Anglo-Scandinavian kings remains to be determined.[97] It is possible that charter-production went wholly out of chancery in that period; on the other hand, the 1020s and 1030s may simply represent – like the 970s before them – a poor phase in the history of the royal writing office. Certainly the sequence from 1019 to 1040 is unimpressive both in quantity of survival and in the quality of what remains. During that same period, there were some ecclesiastical scriptoria – Worcester comes at once to mind – which were equally blighted. But, in general, it does not seem to have been an era in which book-production of reasonable quality ceased.

One apparently much earlier document may, however, provide us with some guidance as to the nature and place of professional formation of 'Eadwig Basan'. If it is genuine and contemporary (and commentators

---

[95] Two factors allow that possibility, however. The scriptorium-style of Anglo-Caroline minuscule practised at Exeter during 1050 x 1072 was a strikingly close descendant of the hand of 'Eadwig' himself. And the imitative skill of Exeter forgers in that period was remarkable indeed.

[96] It was ostensibly issued to Leofric when he was chaplain to King Edward (cf. p. 127, above), and therefore before his appointment to the see of Crediton. It is perhaps easier to suppose that the style was developed, in imitation of the script of 'Eadwig', at Exeter in the 1050s; but that it was created in chancery in the preceding decade is by no means yet to be ruled out. See also below, pp. 137–8.

[97] I am grateful to Simon Keynes for discussing with me the diplomatic of the period and the limits of interpretation of the evidence.

have been agreed on this point),[98] S.922 – a diploma of King Æthelred, dated 1009, for land in Derbyshire (Stafford, Salt Library, MS. 84/5/41, from the archive of Burton Abbey)[99] – may be seen to anticipate a number of the features characteristic, a decade later, of the style of 'Eadwig'. There are two possible interpretations: either this is an early specimen of work by 'Eadwig', an identification which I should not care to press, or we see that, already in the last decade of Æthelred's reign, at least one royal-chancery scribe was developing the forms which would issue in the new style, associated with 'Eadwig', by 1018. S.922 is the last of Æthelred's surviving apparent originals; the last but one, S.916 of A.D. 1007 in favour of St Alban's Abbey, is a classic specimen of a late form of Style-I minuscule.[100] Whichever way we interpret the script of S.922 in the context of Æthelred's reign (and we must keep in mind in this process the possibility, however remote, of its being a later copy or forgery), it implies that the royal chancery was in the 1010s still the force for script-development which it had been in the tenth century; it suggests too that 'Eadwig' was at least heir to that development, and perhaps indeed himself an originating force.

A possible implication of the foregoing remarks is that the diffusion of Style-IV Anglo-Caroline might have been achieved in the 1010s by many now lost documentary products of the royal scriptorium. But another possibility exists, that the staff of that writing office was employed also – at least in the first two decades of the eleventh century – in the production of books. Both the 'Royal' group and the earliest manuscripts written by 'Eadwig' would then fall into this category.[101] In so far as such books would have been accompanied by high-status decoration and have enjoyed the prestige of a royal commission, their script might have gained unusual influence. The plainness, relative lightness, and clarity of the Style-IV minuscule no doubt by themselves commended it to many.

The evidence from books is that the diffusion of the style was swift and, by the reign of Edward the Confessor, all but universal. To the half-

---

[98] Sawyer, *Anglo-Saxon Charters*, no. 922; Hart, *The Early Charters of Northern England*, no. 31; *Charters of Burton Abbey*, ed. Sawyer, no. 32; Keynes, *The Diplomas of King Æthelred*, pp. 114, 264; *Facsimiles*, ed. Keynes, p. 6.

[99] *Ibid.*, no. 17.

[100] Bishop, *English Caroline Minuscule*, p. 15 (no. 17); Keynes, *The Diplomas of King Æthelred*, pp. 121–3, 262–3; *Facsimiles*, ed. Keynes, p. 6 (no. 16). However, some advanced features may be seen in an apparently earlier document (London, British Library, MS. Cotton Augustus ii.38: Sawyer, *Anglo-Saxon Charters*, no. 876; *Facsimiles*, ed. Bond, III.36), dated 993; one may wonder whether these add to the textual reasons for uncertainty about the authenticity of this diploma.

[101] Cf. above, pp. 116–20, for discussion of the 'Royal' group, and below, pp. 139–40, for tabulation of the members of both groups. The 'Royal' group could be removed wholly from its connexion with Christ Church, Canterbury, by this means (I discount the attribution to Peterborough).

century between *ca* 1020 and *ca* 1070 we can attribute some two hundred English manuscripts.[102] Although a good many of these contain vernacular texts, for this was Anglo-Saxon England's major period of English-language book-production,[103] there are few manuscripts indeed which contain no Latin. Since, by the time when Style IV was invented, effective discrimination between Caroline script for Latin and Insular script for English had been achieved (although lapses were to occur locally in time and place), this form of Caroline can be seen in almost every book written in England during the half-century just mentioned.[104]

That Style IV spread beyond Canterbury already in the 1020s is made certain by the evidence of datable manuscripts from the New Minster at Winchester. By 1030 at the latest a number of scribes resident there may be seen to have been influenced by the new style: Ælfsige (*Ælsinus*) and his colleagues who wrote Cambridge, Trinity College, MS. R.15.32 (945), in A.D. 1012 x 1035 London, British Library, MSS. Cotton Titus D.xxvi–xxvii, and probably in 1031 London, British Library, MS. Stowe 944.[105]

Before the middle of the century we have evidence from Abingdon, Bath, Crowland, and the Old Minster at Winchester – to mention no others – that the new style had made its impact upon major scriptoria in a variety of locations.[106] As we have seen, royal diplomas of the 1040s were written in Style IV. Innumerable unattributed manuscripts testify to the extent of its diffusion and popularity. Of major centres only Worcester seems to have shown some hesitation in taking up the new fashion, possibly because new styles of Anglo-Caroline had only recently been experimented with there and because in the second quarter of the century – on the evidence of its charters and books – Worcester Cathedral seems to have entered a cultural trough. By the late 1050s,

---

102 I have listed them (according to the numbers given by Gneuss, 'A preliminary list') in 'English libraries before 1066' (1993), n. 88 (a note lost from the original publication in the course of printing).

103 *Ibid.* (1981), pp. 170–1.

104 This may be seen in *Specimina*, ed. Dumville, where illustrations have been chosen to show the interactions of languages and scripts.

105 Bishop, *English Caroline Minuscule*, p. 23 (no. 26), and 'Notes', pp. 189–92. In part at least, MS. Stowe 944 seems to derive from a manuscript written in A.D. 988 x 990. And for a feature of its decoration, see Dumville, 'An episode'.

106 Abingdon: Cambridge, Corpus Christi College, MS. 57 (marginalia – and therefore supply-leaves – perhaps datable 1046/7). Bath: Cambridge, Corpus Christi College, MS. 140 (cf. Dumville, 'Beowulf come lately', p. 61). Crowland: Oxford, Bodleian Library, MS. Douce 296 (*S.C.* 21870); Temple, *Anglo-Saxon Manuscripts*, pp. 96–7 (no. 79). Old Minster, Winchester: London, British Library, MS. Cotton Tiberius C.vi and Oxford, Bodleian Library, MS. Bodley 775 (*S.C.* 2558), on which see Bishop, *English Caroline Minuscule*, p. 23 (no. 27); cf. also Handschin, 'The two Winchester tropers', for Cambridge, Corpus Christi College, MS. 473.

however, Style IV was in full use at Worcester and remained so until the end of the century.[107]

At Worcester, as elsewhere, a rather heavy and monumental grade of Style-IV Anglo-Caroline came into use in the mid-century, particularly for liturgical and paraliturgical books. That development was achieved without giving up the essential peculiarities of the style. This 'liturgical' variety of Style IV is what has long been recognised as the generically English Caroline of the eleventh century, continuing in that respect the monumental proportions of the principal specimens of Style I produced in the approximate period 960–1020.[108]

One centre, at which Style IV was practised with particular care and enthusiasm, should be mentioned in conclusion. At Exeter Cathedral during the episcopate of Leofric, 1050–1072 – and possibly at Crediton from 1046 to 1050, before the transfer of the see –, Style-IV Anglo-Caroline in a form very close to that practised by 'Eadwig Basan' was the fashion of the very active house-scriptorium.[109] Exeter's version has been seen as a particularly distinctive local style, but it is so more in relation to its date than to its format. We know little in detail of Leofric's background, save that he had been a chaplain of Edward the Confessor in the years immediately before the king elevated him to the rank of bishop,[110] but what is certain is that a good many of the books which he

---

[107] For references, see Bishop, *English Caroline Minuscule*, p. xxiv, n. 2, and especially p. 20, n. 1. On the preceding period at Worcester and the writing of Anglo-Caroline Style III, see above, chapter II, especially pp. 68–75.

[108] Cf. Bishop, *English Caroline Minuscule*, p. xi, n. 1: 'To Continental palaeographers what is designated as Style I has seemed typically English, continuing recognizable in the malformed and disproportioned but still round and clear script of . . . English liturgica of s. xi med. and ex.'. Elsewhere (*ibid.*, p. v) Bishop has described this as 'an inbred, distinctively English script'. For the influence of Anglo-Caroline books on the Continent, see for example Boutemy, 'L'enluminure anglaise', and Alexander & Cahn, 'An eleventh century gospel book'. For such influence specifically in Normandy see Alexander, *Norman Illumination*, to which the evidence of Norman charters should be added: Fauroux, *Recueil*, no. 100 (Duke William for Jumièges, A.D. 1035 x 1043) clearly shows the impact of Style-IV Anglo-Caroline (while no. 193, a private document from Rouen, A.D. 1035 x 1040, reminds one of Style II); I am grateful to Simon Keynes for drawing these charters to my attention and supplying me with facsimiles.

[109] Bishop, *English Caroline Minuscule*, pp. 24 (no. 28) and xxiii, and 'Notes', pp. 192–9.

[110] Cf. n. 96, above. For Leofric's career and context see Barlow *et al.*, *Leofric*. Bishop ('Notes', p. 197) has made some very suggestive remarks in this connexion: 'Leofric is said to have been Edward the Confessor's Chancellor [cf. now Keynes, 'Regenbald']; . . . he seems to have been head of the royal secretariat in the early years of the reign. [As I have shown in *Scriptores Regis* on] the twelfth-century royal chancery . . . the *scriptores* of royal charters were sometimes personally dependent on the Chancellor, and they sometimes continued in his service when, in the normal *cursus honorum*, he was preferred to a bishopric. If this tie existed in the eleventh

imported to Exeter were products of the Canterbury scriptoria.[111] We may care to see there the sources of his scriptorial inspiration.

The full history of Style-IV Anglo-Caroline minuscule has yet to be written. When it is, we shall see that from its beginnings at the hand of 'Eadwig Basan' to its apparent demise – as a regional style in East Anglia and the Fenlands – in the mid-twelfth century it enjoyed a long period of national currency. For a half-century in the middle of the eleventh, the Caroline minuscule of 'Eadwig the Fat' was the English style of Latin writing. It was developed and mutated at the hands of many scribes and in many different English scriptoria, but its essential characteristics remained intact. After the Norman conquest it was no less a badge of Englishness, of pre-Conquest training or of education in a house which retained its English traditions.[112] It may be seen sitting awkwardly alongside the writing of scribes trained in the Norman fashion, as Neil Ker so thoroughly demonstrated.[113] It enjoyed considerable success as a regional style in part of Eastern England into a new period of vigorous manuscript production in the mid-twelfth century.[114] And one may argue that it lies behind a twelfth-century 'Romanesque' style seen practised particularly in the western Marches.[115]

---

century, Leofric, at the time of his appointment to the see of the south-west, would not have wanted for the cadre of a writing staff in carrying out his energetic administration of the Cathedral's affairs.' One can see how, by such means, a writing style might spread. One is also bound to wonder where Leofric was trained before he joined the royal service.

[111] For discussion see Conner, *Anglo-Saxon Exeter*. The relationship of Canterbury and Exeter in the third quarter of the eleventh century needs further study.

[112] The point is most eloquently illustrated by Canterbury, Cathedral Library, MS. Cart. Ant. A.2, a memorandum (datable to 1072) on the primacy of the archbishop, and which bears nine autograph *signa*. It is illustrated in *The Palæographical Society Facsimiles*, First series, edd. Bond *et al.*, plate 170. The last signature is that of Wulfstan II, bishop of Worcester, whose distinctively English hand (Anglo-Caroline minuscule in Style IV) stands out in size and rotundity, and therefore clarity, from those of his Norman fellow-signatories. For the text see *The Letters of Lanfranc*, edd. & transl. Clover & Gibson, pp. 38–49 (cf. p. 19 on the manuscript); see also *Regesta Regum Anglo-Normannorum*, edd. Davis *et al.*, I, no. 65. I owe my knowledge of this document to Simon Keynes. See also Bishop, 'Notes', p. 436.

[113] *English Manuscripts*.

[114] Bishop, *English Caroline Minuscule*, pp. xix, xxiii–xxiv; cf. 'Notes', pp. 432–41, 185–92. See also McLachlan, 'The scriptorium of Bury St. Edmunds'.

[115] Cf. Ker, *English Manuscripts*, p. 7 and plate 25.

MANUSCRIPTS ATTRIBUTED TO THE 'ROYAL' AND 'EADWIG' GROUPS

SHELFMARK	SCRIBE(S)	DATE	PROVENANCE
The 'Royal' group			
(1)[116] Cambridge, Pembroke College, 301	C	?	?
(2) London, British Library, Loans 11	C and B	?	Windsor (xiv)
(3)[117] London, British Library, Royal 1.D.ix	B and C	before 1020	Christ Church, Canterbury (1017x1020)
(4) Oxford, Bodleian Library, Bodley 163 (S.C. 2016)	C	?	Peterborough (xii in.)
(5) Copenhagen, Kgl. bibl., G.K.S. 10, 2°	A and B	?	Scandinavia (xvi)
(6)[118] Cambridge, Trinity College, B.10.4 (215)	B	?	?
(7)[119] Oxford, Bodleian Library, lat. bibl. b.1, fos 73-74	B	?	?
(8) Rouen, Bibliothèque municipale, Y.6 (274)	B	before 1051	London, Jumièges (1044x1051)
(9) Winchester, Mr H. Bailey, s.n.	B	?	?
(10)[120] Paris, Bibliothèque nationale, latin 987, fos 85-111	?B	after 1023	?Christ Church, Canterbury
Transitional			
(1) Firenze, Biblioteca Laurenziana, Plut.XVII.20	Eadwig & ?C	?	Continent (xi)
The 'Eadwig' group			
(1) Hannover, Kestner-Museum, W.M. XXIa,36	Eadwig Basan	?	Germany (xi)
(2) Cambridge, Gonville & Caius, 734/782 or 732/754	" (?)	?	?
(3) London, British Library, Additional 34890	"	?	New Minster, Winchester (xi ex.)
(4) London, British Library, Arundel 155, fos 1-191	"	1012x1023	Christ Church, Canterbury
(5) London, British Library, Stowe Charter 2	"	?	Christ Church, Canterbury
(6) London, British Library, Stowe Charter 38	"	1018	Christ Church, Canterbury
(7) London, British Library, Cotton Vespasian A.i, fos 155-160	"	?	?St Augustine's, Canterbury

(8)	London, British Library, Harley 603, fos 28-49	" (& others)	?	?Christ Church, Canterbury
(9)	York, Minster Library, Additional 1, fo 23v	" (& others)	before 1023	York (xi in.)
(10)[121]	Utrecht, Univ. bibl., 32, pentrials	" (?)	?	Christ Church, Canterbury
(11)[122]	Cambridge, Trinity College, B.15.34 (369), fo 1	" & 1 other	?	?
(12)[123]	London, British Library, Cotton Claudius A.iii, fos 2r-6r	"	1032x?1042	Christ Church, Canterbury

116 Elsewhere (Dumville, 'On the dating', pp. 41–2) I have argued that this book is not by Scribe C and should be removed from the group. Its script was first identified with that of MS. Bodley 163 (fos 2–5, 8–227) in 1953 (Bishop, 'Notes', p. 441), but a Peterborough origin was then only very hesitantly accepted for either book. For a lost relative of Pembroke 301, see Alexander & Cahn, 'An eleventh century gospel book', especially pp. 249–54. See also above, p. 33(–4), n. 117.

117 This book has a connexion with the 'Eadwig' group in that it has an Old English document in the hand of 'Eadwig' on fo 44v: see above, pp. 116–17. Backhouse, 'The making of the Harley Psalter', p. 113, n. 23, has mistakenly attributed the other addition (on fo 43v) also to 'Eadwig'.

118 Heslop ('The production', p. 166) has argued that this manuscript was the latest of the surviving series of books to be produced. Bishop (English Caroline Minuscule, p. 22, no. 24) remarked that its 'plan and execution recall, with some points of contrast, those of' London, British Library, MS. Additional 34890, a member of the 'Eadwig' group: but neither Patrick McGurk (who has kindly advised me) nor I have been able to give precision to that observation.

119 This is the fragment noted by Bishop, 'The Copenhagen gospel-book', p. 39 (no. 5); I am grateful to Bruce Barker-Benfield for identifying it for me.

120 This (cf. Temple, Anglo-Saxon Manuscripts, p. 54) was added to the group by D. H. Turner: The Golden Age, edd. Backhouse et al., p. 60 (no. 39). For a very different view, see Heslop, 'The production', p. 170(–1), n. 57: I concur with his (much later) dating.

121 This item has been added to the group by Backhouse, 'The making of the Harley Psalter', p. 112, n. 19.

122 This item has been added by Heslop, 'The production', p. 176; it is not 'fol. 65r' as stated in The Golden Age, edd. Backhouse et al., p. 79. The fundamental importance of the mandorla in this illustration is to be noted, for it is a feature found in five of the manuscripts belonging to the 'Royal' and 'Eadwig' groups; it first appears in London, British Library, MS. Cotton Galba A.xviii, in the English additions (on this book see Dumville, Wessex and England, pp. 73–7), and is to be noted in at least seventeen books illustrated by late Anglo-Saxon artists (Temple, Anglo-Saxon Manuscripts, nos 5, 16, 32, 43, 44, 64, 65, 69, 73, 74, 78, 80, 84, 86, 98, 104, 106; cf. plates 31–2, 84, 94, 144, 150, 210, 212, 232, 233, 241, 244, 253, 263–4, 265, 301, 302, 318); a majority of these books can be associated with Canterbury, but Winchester, Sherborne, Fleury, and Saint-Bertin are also represented. A history of the mandorla in (late) Anglo-Saxon manuscript art would be most welcome.

123 On this item see above, p. 126, n. 75.

V

CONCLUSION

It is possible that one result of the foregoing studies has been to shorten somewhat – by delaying its birth – the life of Anglo-Caroline minuscule. Although there is some modest evidence for knowledge and reception of Caroline manuscripts in England in the ninth century,[1] the earliest direct testimony to the writing of Caroline minuscule in England[2] comes from the late years of King Æthelstan's reign when a foreign scribe, possibly in royal service, copied a poem into a gospel-book which the king gave to Christ Church, Canterbury.[3] In the pontificate of Oda (941–958) foreign

---

[1] Extravagant claims have been made in recent years about Carolingian influence in late eighth- and early ninth-century English cultural life. It remains to be seen whether any of these can be substantiated. Much work is evidently necessary. For a beginning, see Brown, 'Continental symptoms'. The position would be improved if Caroline-minuscule manuscripts could be found which had certainly reached England in the ninth century. According to Pächt et al., Illuminated Manuscripts, III.5 (no. 32), Oxford, Bodleian Library, MS. Bodley 218 (S.C. 2054), written at Tours in the early ninth century and containing Bede on Luke, is one such; this is incorrect, however.

[2] It was a long-held view of Bernhard Bischoff that a group of Caroline manuscripts of late ninth- or early tenth-century date which he could not satisfactorily attribute to a Continental scriptorium or script-province should be accounted for by English scholars; knowing their scepticism on the point, he cautiously described these manuscripts as his Kanalküste group. I am grateful to Professor Bischoff for a number of discussions of this matter: broadly speaking, the opposing positions on the question are as follows. While – given our relative ignorance of so many matters concerning English history in the Alfredian and Edwardian periods – no student of Anglo-Saxon culture could deny absolutely that Caroline writing was adopted in southern England at that date, it would seem strange if a distinctive provincial school of 'Continental' Caroline should have developed there then, leaving no trace in subsequent Anglo-Caroline developments; if there had been Caroline scribes at work in England ca 900, one would have expected them to practise the Caroline script-varieties proper to their origins. It would seem easier to suppose that, somewhere in Continental western Europe, a corner could be found in which the group of manuscripts in question would explain its features satisfactorily. On the other side, the argument was that there was no school or area whose script was close enough to that of the group to justify even a tentative attribution, and that a sufficient number of members of the group had an English provenance to make an attribution of English origin seem a risk worth taking.

[3] See above, pp. 16, 92.

141

scribes and their English imitators are found copying Frithegod's *Breuiloquium uitae sancti Wilfredi* and Oda's preface to it, apparently at Canterbury Cathedral.[4] At about the same time we find evidence of the use of Caroline minuscule of different types in royal diplomas. Indirect testimony to a diploma of the alliterative group, dated 949, suggests that it was written in Caroline script,[5] and an extant apparent original of A.D. 956 certainly was. In the former case we cannot be certain that the scribe was English, while the latter offers features which have allowed the script-model to be characterised as 'possibly Breton'.[6] Perhaps at Worcester, an undated manuscript of penitential texts shows another attempt – with a result not yet seen elsewhere – to come to grips with the Continental hand.[7] Further English testimonies to early attempts to receive Caroline minuscule no doubt await recognition.[8] It is a nice question to what extent the evidence of the datable documents, beginning in the 940s, found in the 'Bodmin Gospels' can be taken in this context of English reception.[9]

What all the examples so far mentioned have in common is that none of them is obviously antecedent to the principal styles of Anglo-Caroline minuscule practised during the heyday of that script, after A.D. 960. Specimens which have seemed to be just that, to show the beginnings of Anglo-Caroline Style II, have been attributed by T.A.M. Bishop to an origin at Glastonbury during the period of Dunstan's abbacy (A.D. 940 x 956).[10] Close examination of that attribution has shown, however, that

---

[4] See above, pp. 92–4.

[5] Sawyer, *Anglo-Saxon Charters*, no. 550; *Facsimiles*, ed. Keynes, no. 43. This survives in an Early Modern script-facsimile. In the middle ages the original document resided in the archives of Evesham Abbey. The group is sometimes associated in its origin with Cenwald, bishop of Worcester (cf. Whitelock, *English Historical Documents*, pp. 372–3; *Charters of Burton Abbey*, ed. Sawyer, pp. xlvii–xlix), on whom see above, pp. 49–52.

[6] Bishop, 'Notes', p. 333; Sawyer, *Anglo-Saxon Charters*, no. 594.

[7] See above, pp. 49–52.

[8] One may compare the evidence from Wales and Cornwall in the first half of the tenth century. From Wales we have one certain example of a hybrid Insular-Caroline performance – Cambridge, Corpus Christi College, MS. 153, fo 17ra; cf. Bishop, 'The Corpus Martianus Capella'. From Cornwall, there is also one certain example, that of the additions to the 'Bodmin Gospels' (see next note). However, there are other Cornish examples, but of less certain date, in the problematic 'Codex Oxoniensis Posterior' – Oxford, Bodleian Library, MS. Bodley 572 (*S.C.* 2026), on which see Lindsay, *Early Welsh Script*, pp. 26–32. In general, see Dumville, *Manuscripts of Wales and Cornwall*.

[9] London, British Library, MS. Additional 9381; cf. Jackson, *Language and History*, pp. 59–60, and Ker, *Catalogue*, p. 159 (no. 126). Olson, *Early Monasteries in Cornwall*, pp. 66–78, has shown that in the tenth century the manuscript was at St Petroc's, Padstow, moving to Bodmin in the eleventh.

[10] *English Caroline Minuscule*, pp. 1–2, and 'An early example of Insular-Caroline'.

evidence to support it is largely wanting. The origins of both the principal early styles of Anglo-Caroline can be sought *ca* A.D. 960, as much as twenty years after the date sometimes suggested.[11] For Style II the effective beginnings would thus be placed at Canterbury in the immediate aftermath of Dunstan's translation thither as archbishop. Style I emerges first in a royal-chancery document of A.D. 961, but one in which Bishop Oswald, newly appointed to the see of Worcester, seems to have had a hand.[12] And its first certain appearance in the circle of Bishop Æthelwold is in the foundation-charter, dated 966, of the New Minster, Winchester; Æthelgar, the abbot, may indeed also have been a former student at Fleury.[13] We may therefore have to allow that the sojourns abroad of three men – Dunstan at Ghent, Osgar and Oswald at Fleury – provided the stimulus to the adoption and rapid development of Caroline writing in England.[14] That the adoption of Caroline script in the 960s was coincident with reception of a revolutionary Benedictine message seems certain.

The evidence of a very remarkable manuscript – which will henceforth be fundamental to the study of the development of Anglo-Caroline minuscule – has also suggested the centrality of the role of Christ Church, Canterbury, in the early history of Style-II Anglo-Caroline. The 'Leofric Missal', as an episcopal book, helps us to identify the cathedral as an early and important player in this process.[15] The manuscripts which have been attributed to Dunstan's Glastonbury might now more satisfactorily be given to his early years at Canterbury. In the received

---

[11] See above, pp. 50–3.

[12] See above, pp. 52–3.

[13] Sawyer, *Anglo-Saxon Charters*, no. 745: London, British Library, MS. Cotton Vespasian A.viii, fos 3–33. On Æthelgar at Fleury, cf. *Wulfstan of Winchester*, edd. & transl. Lapidge & Winterbottom, p. 27, n. 4.

[14] On Osgar at Winchester, see *ibid.*, p. 26(-7), n. 3. For consideration of Fleury's external influence, see Donnat, 'Recherches'. Eric John ('The sources', p. 198; followed by Leclercq, 'The tenth century English Benedictine reform', p. 10) has drawn attention to the significance of a remark in a sermon preached by Odo of Cluny (abbot, 924–942) at Fleury (*Patrologia latina*, ed. Migne, CXXXIII.721-9, at col. 726): 'O quanti sunt etiam in remotissimis trans maria regionibus, qui tantopere gauderent si eis uel semel ad eius sacrum tumulum accredendi possibilitas esset!' It seems certain that this must refer to English devotees of St Benedict who wished to visit the Benedictine 'capital' at Fleury. (For intense Benedictine devotion, see above, p. 77, n. 350, on BL MS. Royal 2.A.xx, whose relevant material perhaps dates from the beginning of Oswald's rule at Worcester, and above, p. 60, n. 265, on BL MS. Harley 2904.) Nor must we forget the importance of Fleury for Archbishop Oda, in whose time at Canterbury we see the practice of Caroline writing at Christ Church; in his case, however, the stimulus might have been provided by Frithegod. On Ghent, cf. the debate between Dauphin ('Le renouveau monastique') and John ('The sources').

[15] See above, pp. 94–6.

history of Style II it has never been evident why a script supposedly developed at Glastonbury made its first Canterbury appearance at St Augustine's Abbey rather than at the cathedral.[16] The distinctive style practised at St Augustine's can now be seen as an offshoot from the Christ Church stem, but one which was nonetheless to influence developments at the cathedral in its turn.[17]

There seems at present to be no evidence which would give priority of origin to Style I or to Style II. Although they emerge contemporaneously into the record, they bespeak different backgrounds and different attitudes. It is by no means obvious that the script of mid-tenth-century Fleury lies behind Anglo-Caroline Style I.[18] Models for Style I seem instead to belong to earlier periods. On the other hand, no Continental model has yet been discovered which is recognisably antecedent to Anglo-Caroline Style II. It is possible that in Flanders or a neighbouring region such an antecedent will in time be recognised, and that Dunstan's exile at Ghent will be seen to have been a specific intermediary in the process of transmission. But it is possible instead, and perhaps at this stage preferable, to view the impetus to develop what we now call Style II as being a local, English reflex of an attitude for which there were Continental models a-plenty. Dunstan, and others, would have been able to see that many specimens of Caroline writing, representing various local traditions, rested on a more or less successful amalgam of Caroline and Insular conventions.[19] Breton manuscripts, of which there must have been a good many in tenth-century England, would have displayed local varieties within such a regional style of Caroline minuscule.[20] Likewise, the core of the 'Leofric Missal', written at Arras not later than the early tenth century, displays a sustained and successful essay in a Caroline style heavily influenced by Insular practices.[21] Examples such as these could have been sufficient to convince English scribes that an eclectically

---

16 See above, pp. 86–103.

17 See above, pp. 90–1, 98–9, 102–3.

18 The script of ninth- and tenth-century Fleury awaits a full palaeographical study: the raw materials have been assembled by Mostert, *The Library of Fleury*.

19 For surveys of the local and regional development of Caroline minuscule on the Continent, see Bischoff, *Latin Palaeography*, pp. 112–27, and *Mittelalterliche Studien*, III.1–38. For Breton gospel-books see *An Early Breton Gospel Book*, facs. edd. Wormald & Alexander.

20 Much work remains to be done on Breton script of the ninth and tenth centuries. For Breton manuscripts' arrival in England in the late ninth and early tenth centuries, see Dumville, *England and the Celtic World*. For a facsimile of one such, see *Saint Dunstan's Classbook*, facs. ed. Hunt, fos 1v–9v. For brief discussion of Breton Caroline minuscule, see Bischoff, *Latin Palaeography*, p. 117, and *Mittelalterliche Studien*, III.15.

21 On the manuscript's history in England, see above, pp. 94–6. For a facsimile from the original portion, see Lega-Weekes, 'Ancient liturgical MS.'.

hybridising approach to the two traditions was an acceptable attitude with adequate precedent in the Carolingian world. In all this we seem to have reason to speak of a number of separate English receptions, or attempted receptions, of Caroline script.[22]

The principal and defining specimens of Style-I Anglo-Caroline are monumental examples, mostly in lavishly decorated liturgical books.[23] This image of Style I is closely associated with manuscripts from the circle of Æthelwold, bishop of Winchester (963–984), thus reflecting his known liturgical interests.[24] Even at Winchester that is not the whole story. The same techniques could be directed to important literary work.[25] Equally, however, the script could be scaled down somewhat and elaborate decoration avoided, whether for hagiography or for Classical poetry.[26] In any event, Style I as practised in Æthelwold's houses seems to have been pure Caroline minuscule based securely on high-grade Continental models. It persisted in use into the first quarter of the eleventh century.[27]

Style I can, however, be seen in two other contexts. In chapter II I have shown how it was the style practised in houses associated with Bishop, then Archbishop, Oswald. Here, too, the monumental grade of Style I was cultivated for important liturgical books.[28] In spite of

22 Cf. Bishop, 'Notes', pp. 331–4.
23 For example: London, British Library, MSS. Additional 49598, Cotton Vespasian A.viii (Sawyer, *Anglo-Saxon Charters*, no. 745), Harley 2904; London, College of Arms, MS. Arundel 22; Besançon, Bibliothèque municipale, MS. 14; Exeter, Cathedral Library, MS. 3548C; Paris, Bibliothèque nationale, MSS. latin 272 and 987; Rouen, Bibliothèque municipale, MS. A.27 (368).
24 Bishop, 'Notes', p. 323, for this characterisation of Æthelwold; on Æthelwold and the liturgy, see *Wulfstan of Winchester*, edd. & transl. Lapidge & Winterbottom, pp. lx–lxxxv.
25 See, for example, the copy of the poetry of Prudentius in London, British Library, MS. Additional 24199: Bishop, *English Caroline Minuscule*, p. xxii; Temple, *Anglo-Saxon Manuscripts*, pp. 71–2 (no. 51) and plates 163, 166; Wieland, 'The Anglo-Saxon manuscripts of Prudentius's *Psychomachia*'. Note that this manuscript has a late mediaeval provenance at Bury St Edmunds: cf. p. 78, n. 360, above.
26 For example, London, British Library, MSS. Royal 13.A.x (fos 63–103) and 15.C.vii (hagiography) and Cambridge, University Library, MS. Kk.5.34 (2076).
27 Rouen, Bibliothèque municipale, MS. A.27 (368) is an example (cf. Dumville, 'On the dating', pp. 51–2). The 'Royal group' (see above, pp. 116–20, 139–40) of mostly liturgical manuscripts, in script transitional between Style I and Style IV, could be included here. Besançon, Bibliothèque municipale, MS. 14, has recently been attributed to *ca* A.D. 1020 (Heslop, 'The production', pp. 153, 174, 182, 188–91), but there are difficulties in detaching it from the comparanda suggested by Bishop (*English Caroline Minuscule*, p. 10); for a facsimile, see Heslop, 'The production', plate I.
28 For example, in London, British Library, MS. Harley 2904, and Cambridge, Sidney Sussex College, MS. 100, part 2, fos 1–13v11. See above, pp. 58–65.

difficulties of identification, it is nevertheless certain that Style-I Anglo-Caroline was being used as a vehicle for staple theological and literary texts.[29] Building on T.A.M. Bishop's work, I have suggested that the origin of some of the relevant manuscripts should be attributed to Oswald's circle. However, there is room for the suspicion that in this context the script had a rather briefer active life, for at least at Worcester other styles seem to have been practised by Archbishop Wulfstan's time (1002–1016x1023).[30]

At Canterbury too, though perhaps not in the time of Archbishop Dunstan (959–988), we find Style I making some impact on the cathedral scriptorium.[31] There is no certain evidence for the production there, in the tenth century, of any pure specimen of Style-I Anglo-Caroline (although one or two doubtful attributions have been made on the basis of later provenance).[32] But it is clear that in the eyes of some members of the Christ Church scriptorium Style I had notable authority, for these scribes can be seen striving to reject Insular characteristics from their evolving calligraphy. Some did indeed achieve the apparent goal of writing a respectable Style-I hand, although it is impossible (I think) not to be conscious of the Insular background of such hands[33] – this is a very different result from that achieved by practitioners in Æthelwold's (and, to a slightly lesser extent, Oswald's) houses. However, in the early eleventh century, whether by a natural progression or under the influence of new archbishops with backgrounds in the Æthelwoldian tradition,[34] we meet an important group of mostly lavishly decorated Style-I liturgical manuscripts which have, if controversially, been assigned an origin at Christ Church.[35] By 1020 Style I seems effectively to have triumphed there, but with such a range of new developments imported that it proves necessary to describe the resulting script with a new label, Anglo-Caroline Style IV.[36]

Questions of definition are raised by this new account of calligraphic practice at Christ Church, Canterbury. The criteria applied by T.A.M. Bishop seem to have ensured that no specimen of Anglo-Caroline showing any sustained Insular features in the morphology of the script could be admitted into the canon of Style-I performances. This seems to

[29] Bishop, *English Caroline Minuscule*, pp. 13, 16, 18–19.
[30] See above, pp. 65–7 (cf. 73–4).
[31] See above, pp. 103–9.
[32] London, British Library, MSS. Royal 1.E.vii–viii and Royal 7.C.iv: see above, pp. 108–10.
[33] See above, pp. 88, 103; for an example, see Bishop, *ibid.*, plate VIII, showing Oxford, Bodleian Library, MS. Bodley 708 (*S.C.* 2609), fo 2r.
[34] See above, pp. 103–4, 115–16.
[35] The 'Royal group': see above, pp. 116–20, 139–40.
[36] See above, chapter IV.

me to be an unrealistically severe criterion. As Bishop himself noted, one can observe Christ Church scribes working to purge their hands of Insular practices.[37] One can also see the deliberate importation of Style-I usages, such as the **r** + **a** ligature, into performances by Christ Church scribes.[38] Late in the tenth century, then, and early in the eleventh, the tendency at Canterbury Cathedral is for some scribes to adopt and imitate Style-I characteristics: some do so more deliberately, some more successfully, than others; some do not try at all. It is important, however, to recognise this mixed history, which has not found a prominent place in the received accounts of Anglo-Caroline writing.

The native Caroline practice of the Canterbury scriptoria was a style deliberately hybridising the Caroline and the Insular to form a mixed Caroline script of Insular aspect. At St Augustine's this ideal was long pursued, for Style-II usages are still apparent in the 1020s and, only slightly less strongly, in the 1040s or 1050s.[39] However, at Christ Church, as we have seen, the last vestiges of Style II cannot be placed later than the early 1020s and a decisive shift to Style-I usage seems to have taken place after a moment most easily identifiable with the vikings' sack of Canterbury in A.D. 1011/12.[40] Style-II Anglo-Caroline may most conveniently be defined as a version of Anglo-Caroline which unashamedly flaunts its Insular connexions. It may be recognised by its use of Insular letter-forms – single-compartment Insular **a** is the one which persists unambiguously throughout the life of the style (although it is employed with absolute consistency by few scribes) – and Insular abbreviations; and frequently it occurs in books with membranes organised in the inherited Insular fashion (HFHF). Style II is not a mere manifestation of an inability (amounting to greater or lesser

---

[37] 'Notes', p. 419.

[38] See above, pp. 88, 103, 108.

[39] For progression in Style II, see the manuscripts of B's Life of St Dunstan: Sankt Gallen, Stadtbibliothek, MS. 337 (written at St Augustine's before 1004); London, British Library, MS. Cotton Cleopatra B.xiii, fos 59–90 (of St Augustine's provenance and probable origin); Arras, Bibliothèque municipale, MS. 1029 (812). I am grateful to Michael Winterbottom for help with the Arras and Sankt Gallen manuscripts. For the early 1020s see Cambridge, University Library, MS. Kk.5.32 (2074), fos 49–60 (cf. Dumville, *Liturgy*, chapter II). Attributed to a mid-century date after 1039 is the famous and massive codex, Cambridge, University Library, MS. Gg.5.35 (1567), of fourteenth-century St Augustine's provenance: on this manuscript cf. Rigg & Wieland, 'A Canterbury classbook' (who, on p. 118, have mistakenly attributed the *ex-libris* inscription – *ibid.*, plate II – to the twelfth century); Gibson *et al.*, 'Neumed Boethian *metra*'; Dronke *et al.*, 'Die unveröffentlichen Gedichte'. The manuscript opens with a splendid illuminated initial **M** in 'Winchester' style (1r; not noticed by Temple, *Anglo-Saxon Manuscripts*). For a specimen of script, see Rigg & Wieland, 'A Canterbury classbook', plate I (showing fo 53r).

[40] See above, pp. 103–20.

incompetence) to cast off inherited local non-Caroline usage. It is the result of a positive willingness to practise an eclectic, even a hybrid, script. It seems to me, therefore, that classification of specimens as belonging to the Style-II tradition which show sporadic traces of Insular morphology in such letters as **c**, **e**, **o**, **q**, **t**, is to risk seeing the trees and not the wood.[41]

In general, Style-II scribes wrote smaller script than their Style-I counterparts. Their manuscripts overwhelmingly contain theological and literary texts: Style-II *liturgica* are relatively scarce, and it may be the case that Anglo-Saxon Square minuscule was used instead for such books.[42] Of the dissemination of Style II it is difficult to speak. No manuscripts securely attributable to an origin at Glastonbury are written in Caroline minuscule. Little work has been done on identifying houses of which Dunstan was spiritual patron. The abbey at Exeter, for example, is thought to have been reformed from Glastonbury in A.D. 968 but, again, no Caroline manuscripts have been securely assigned thither before 1050.[43] For the moment, therefore, localisable Style-II manuscripts are those originating in the two Canterbury minsters.

It is clear that great desiderata in this subject are more precise description of hands and more precise definition of practices within the principal styles. In time, we may hope confidently to attribute Style-I manuscripts to houses associated with either Æthelwold or Oswald on features of their script:[44] but, while some few pointers have been identified, that happy situation has not yet been achieved.[45] Likewise, within Style II we may hope to develop the confidence to say that a given manuscript must, or cannot, have originated at St Augustine's Abbey, Canterbury, purely on the style of its calligraphy. However, it is certain that the necessity to crystallise scribal practice in the form suitable for an introductory palaeographical handbook has led to mistaken perceptions, of the homogeneity of Anglo-Caroline practice at each of the Canterbury

---

[41] Bishop, 'Notes', p. 331, for the list of letters; cf. p. 418. I omit **d** from his list. Persistent use of forms of **f**, **r**, **s**, which trail below the line I should admit as a criterion of definition of Style-II usage, but it is by no means necessarily to be tied to Insular influence.

[42] The principal liturgical books associated with Christ Church in the second half of the tenth century are London, British Library, MS. Additional 37517 and Paris, Bibliothèque nationale, MS. latin 943 (cf. Dumville, 'On the dating', p. 45). At the turn of the century, we meet two in monumental Style-II Anglo-Caroline: see above, pp. 106–7.

[43] For a study of Exeter in that period, see Conner, *Anglo-Saxon Exeter*.

[44] Bishop, *English Caroline Minuscule*, p. xxii, has provided a broad description of the type proper to the houses of the Oswald connexion: 'weighty and rugged'; 'rough energy prevails over the monumental quality'; 'less rounded, slightly compressed'.

[45] See above, pp. 53–6.

houses, gaining a hold on scholarship.[46] Many manuscripts attributed by Mr Bishop to these houses show considerable variety of scribal performance in respect of both specific usage and general aspect. There is a good way to go before a satisfactorily specific history of Canterbury Anglo-Caroline can be written. Many workers are needed in this field.

One may fairly observe that, on present evidence, in the years from *ca* 960 to *ca* 1010 there is an exclusive fit between practice of one Anglo-Caroline style and membership of an identifiable group of houses – except in the case of Canterbury Cathedral (and it is perhaps appropriate that that institution should have been the most catholic in its outlook and practice). If a scribe wrote Style I he or she belonged to one of the houses associated with Æthelwold or Oswald and their immediate heirs (or resided at Christ Church, Canterbury, perhaps in the 990s or later). If a scribe wrote Style II he or she did not belong to houses of those groups and (on the available evidence) is most likely to have been active at Canterbury or at some other house associated with Dunstan.

At Worcester in the years immediately around, and after, 1000 we can see other styles briefly practised. The most distinctive I have named 'Style III' and it appears (on the very limited evidence available) to have been exclusive to that house. My dating of its origin is a generation later than that favoured in 1971 by Mr Bishop.[47] The Worcester cathedral scriptorium seems to have experimented with a number of Caroline forms in these years. One is recognisably derivative of Style I, with proportions changing to the longer, narrower, and more angular; this survived into the time of Wulfstan (1002–1016x1023).[48] Another is a pronouncedly slanting variety derivative of Style I, also with narrower, longer shape, but more elegant in appearance – this is less certainly attributable to Worcester and may in any case be the performance of a single scribe.[49] Finally, a very long and narrow script clearly heavily

---

[46] A case which illustates the genuine difficulties is provided by Salisbury, Cathedral Library, MS. 38 (whose fo 44v has been illustrated by Godfrey, *The Church in Anglo-Saxon England*, plate 12) and MS. 172. Bishop ('Notes', pp. 330 and 333) first associated these books with St Augustine's. In 1963 (*ibid.*, pp. 412–13) he wrote that 'If there is any substance to the concept of a generic style proper to a scriptorium the two Salisbury MSS. were written at St Augustine's'. In 1966 he began to hedge his bets (*Aethici Istrici Cosmographia*, p. xx), writing that they 'have been attributed on the doubtful evidence of mere aspect, and this . . . has some resemblance to that of certain MSS provisionally attributed to Christ Church'. By 1971 (*English Caroline Minuscule*, p. xxvi) he had, albeit hesitantly, assigned them to Christ Church.

[47] See the discussion above, pp. 68–75.

[48] As in London, British Library, MS. Cotton Nero A.i: see above, p. 55.

[49] The group, such as it is, centres on London, British Library, MS. Harley 3376 (for that manuscript see Ker, *Catalogue*, pp. 312–13, no. 240, and 'A supplement', p. 124, no. 240): Bishop, 'The Corpus Martianus Capella', p. 258. It is interesting that the two principal witnesses – the Harley Glossary and the manuscript of excerpts from

influenced by developments in the calligraphy of vernacular usage, was – seemingly briefly – developed as a scriptorium-style in Wulfstan's time: indeed his own hand seems to be approximately of this type.[50]

Developments crucial to the future history – and success – of the script occurred in the 1010s and 1020s. These may first have been pioneered in the royal writing office,[51] but a secure context for them can also be found at Christ Church, Canterbury.[52] We associate the new form with one master-scribe, known from a colophon in one of a number of manuscripts in his very distinctive hand, as 'Eadwig Basan' (although it is not absolutely certain that this was indeed his name).[53] During the middle quarters of the eleventh century the style pioneered by that scribe spread throughout the country. It has been described as a badge of Englishness. I have called it Style-IV Anglo-Caroline. In effect, it represents the triumph of the Style-I tradition, albeit with the adoption of features from Style-II (and other) usage. Its internal history remains to be written: in theory, given its origins, it represents a relatively pure strain of Caroline minuscule, but specimens are not wanting which display abbreviations and other habits characteristic of the Insular scribal tradition – these persist after the Norman conquest,[54] to influence Anglo-Norman (and even, in one or two respects, north-French) usage.[55] What is more, Style IV had had an impact in pre-Conquest Normandy:[56] the relationship of the style with the practice of Caroline minuscule in contemporary Flanders remains to be determined, but there seems to have been some interaction.[57]

As we approach the creation of Style IV, and in the immediately succeeding years, we can see the shading off or the merging of Anglo-Caroline styles into one another. Already at late tenth-century Christ Church we have noted various accommodations of Style I and Style II with one another, from the strivings of some scribes to achieve a purer Caroline style to the deliberate imitation within the Style-II tradition of the monumental Style-I form.[58] As we approach the creation of Style IV

Amalarius's *Liber officialis*, London, British Library, MS. Cotton Vespasian D.xv, fos 102–121 – both very much represent work in progress.

[50] See above, pp. 65–7.
[51] See above, pp. 124–8, 134–5.
[52] See above, pp. 116–32.
[53] See above, pp. 120–4.
[54] Cf. Ker, *Books, Collectors*, p. 148.
[55] For example, the Insular compendium for *enim* survived the Norman conquest and may still be found in English manuscripts after *ca* 1300; it was carried to Normandy and continued to be used there (and in some adjoining parts of northern France) until the early thirteenth century.
[56] Cf. Alexander, *Norman Illumination*.
[57] See above, pp. 131–2.
[58] See above, pp. 88, 103–9.

by 'Eadwig Basan' we find precursory tentatives in the work of some Christ Church scribes: it is fairly certain that a few of that master-scribe's apparently characteristic choices had already come into use in the decade or more before his first datable productions.[59] But he was responsible for assembling the full range of those usages: other scribes who displayed them all were certainly indebted to him. The result is, nonetheless, that we meet not merely Style-I script tending towards Style-IV – such is the condition of the 'Royal group' of hands[60] – but also script-specimens which mix characteristics of Styles I, II, and IV.[61] It seems likely that such hands can be attributed to the 1010s or (at the very latest) the 1020s.

Some of the choices made by 'Eadwig Basan' are perhaps attributable to an awareness of further developments within Continental Caroline usage. From the beginning of the history of Caroline script in England we have to be aware of the possibility of repeated and potentially independent interaction between English developments and aspects of the Continental background. In script, as in text, the Carolingian inheritance carried an air of authority which, during the most fervently Benedictinising years, lost nothing by frequent acts of obeisance at its shrine; but it is difficult for us to pick up the resonances of specific Continental exemplars in late Anglo-Saxon ecclesiastical life. From the late eighth century Caroline manuscripts may have been entering England – in principle, it is very likely that they were.[62] Certainly from the time of the revival engineered by Alfred, king of Wessex (871–899), in the second half of his reign, we can be sure that Carolingian books were being received – from Reims, from Germany, from the Low Countries, from Brittany.[63] Hitherto, art-historians have been more willing to acknowledge and define the influences which these books would have represented.[64] Such work needs to be carried over from their conclusions to see what applications it might have in respect of script.

---

[59] See above, pp. 107–9 (cf. 134–5).

[60] See above, pp. 110, 116–20.

[61] See above, pp. 107–8.

[62] For example, if the *Expositio missae* beginning 'Primum in ordine . . .' is indeed an early Carolingian text (cf. Wilmart, 'Expositio missae', cols 1020–1), the exemplar of Oxford, Bodleian Library, MS. Hatton 93 (*S. C.* 4081) – Lowe, *Codices*, II, no. 241 – may have been written in Caroline minuscule. There is an Anglo-Caroline copy from St Augustine's, Canterbury – London, British Library, MS. Royal 8.C.iii (cf. Bullough, 'Roman books', pp. 49–50) – but its antecedents have not been investigated.

[63] These were the areas with which specific links were forged in Alfred's reign: for the surviving manuscript evidence for the source of imported books of ninth- and early tenth-century date, see my remarks in a review in *Archiv für das Studium der neueren Sprachen und Literaturen* 223 (1986) 388–92, at pp. 389–90; cf. Rella, 'Continental manuscripts'.

[64] Cf. Wormald, 'Continental influence', especially pp. 7–10. Ideological aspects of

It is probable that one such area of impact occurred already in Alfred's reign as the king and his advisers sought a scribal vehicle for their new learning.[65] It is possible that a conscious decision was taken, not to adopt Caroline minuscule. Various decorative aspects of Carolingian books may indeed have been imitated. But, at the level of script, a conscious decision – if taken – was a fateful one, in as much as the literature of the Alfredian renaissance was wholly or largely in the vernacular:[66] Caroline minuscule was never to become the scribal carrier of Old English. Nevertheless, the improved Anglo-Saxon minuscule of Alfred's later years may be seen as a local recognition of the need for reform to be accompanied by a reformed script-style. This perception was carried a stage further in the reign of Edward the Elder (899–924) with the development of English Square-minuscule script:[67] the quest for legibility and formality led to the creation of a new Insular script for a new cultural era. The full flowering of the type, *ca* A.D. 930, coincides with an increased tempo of production of Latin manuscripts in Æthelstan's reign, manuscripts containing also Carolingian texts.[68]

For a generation Square minuscule continued with its own internal development.[69] However, coevally with the emergence of Style-I and Style-II Anglo-Caroline, *ca* A.D. 960, we find the development of Phase-IV Square minuscule, in which square proportions are largely abandoned and some Caroline letter-forms, principally **a**, are adopted. It is difficult to think this coincidental. Phase IV is restricted chronologically to the 960s but in that time was employed in the royal writing office, an institution which in the tenth century seems to have been an engine and arbiter of fashion.[70] Insular traditions reasserted themselves

---

such influence have been pursued by Deshman, '*Benedictus monarcha*' (and, on a somewhat later period, '*Christus rex*').

[65] Cf. Dumville, 'English Square minuscule script: the background and earliest phases', pp. 155–69.

[66] The notable exception is Asser's Life of King Alfred but, while that work is central to our perceptions of the Alfredian renaissance, it seems to have had little impact or circulation. On the other hand, education of an élite-group in Latin was part of the king's programme: but it may be that the results, in terms of a growing need for (in the first instance) foreign manuscripts containing Latin texts, did not become apparent until the next reign (and thus the new century).

[67] Dumville, *Wessex and England*, chapter III, and 'English Square minuscule script: the background and earliest phases', pp. 153–69 (*passim*) and 169–73.

[68] *Ibid.*, pp. 173–8.

[69] Beginning with the charters of the reign of King Edmund I (939–946), a new and more ornate style of Square minuscule is found which characterises the whole of English writing in the period to the reign of Eadwig (955–959): this shows modest internal changes but is the longest-lasting style (Phase III) in the whole history of that script. For discussion, cf. Dumville, *Wessex and England*, pp. 62–6, and 'English Square minuscule script: the mid-century phases'.

[70] For an illustration of Phase IV in a royal diploma (Sawyer, *Anglo-Saxon Charters*, no.

by the end of the 960s,[71] but again at the end of the century we find Caroline forms having an impact on their Insular counterpart. The various monumental types of Square minuscule which have short lives in the years around 1000 sometimes show Caroline attributes – rotundity, for example – and thus appear to be indebted to Style-I Anglo-Caroline.[72] We have seen the same pattern *within* the Anglo-Caroline tradition, with a monumental Style II as a reaction to Style I.[73]

It is worth asking where *both* Anglo-Caroline and Insular (Square) minuscule were written in the second half of the tenth century. At Glastonbury during Dunstan's abbacy a surviving Latin book was written, at that abbot's command, in Square minuscule:[74] there is no certain evidence for the practice there and then of Caroline script.[75] At Canterbury we have evidence of the employment of Square minuscule alongside Anglo-Caroline Style II for Latin writing.[76] The same is true of Square minuscule and Anglo-Caroline Style I at Worcester Cathedral.[77] But from the houses associated with Æthelwold we gain no evidence for the retention of Square minuscule as a vehicle for Latin texts.[78]

---

690), see Bishop, *English Caroline Minuscule*, plate IX (lines 1–11) and p. 9 (no. 11); for a datable example in a vernacular literary context, see *The Parker Chronicle and Laws*, facs. edd. Flower & Smith, fo 28r8–25 (and cf. Dumville, *Wessex and England*, p. 61).

[71] An example is provided by Salisbury, Cathedral Library, MS. 150, perhaps written in or soon after 969: Ker, *Catalogue*, pp. 449–51 (no. 379); for a facsimile, see *The Salisbury Psalter*, edd. Sisam & Sisam, following p. 312 (showing fo 110v). For an Old English document dated 969 (London, British Library, Add. Ch. 19792; Sawyer, *Anglo-Saxon Charters*, no. 1326) and written at Worcester in Square minuscule, see Keller, *Angelsächsische Palaeographie*, II, plate V.

[72] For a discussion of some late types of Square minuscule see Dumville, 'Beowulf come lately'. For a dated example of one such type, see London, British Library, Cotton Charter viii.14 (*Facsimiles*, ed. Bond, III.33; Sawyer, *Anglo-Saxon Charters*, no. 864; *Charters of Rochester*, ed. Campbell, no. 30), the last royal diploma written in Square minuscule to survive.

[73] See above, pp. 106–7.

[74] Oxford, Bodleian Library, MS. Hatton 30 (*S.C.* 4076), a specimen of Phase III: for a facsimile (of part of fo 46r), see Watson, *Catalogue of Dated and Datable Manuscripts c. 435–1600 in Oxford Libraries*, I.84–5 (no. 519), and II, plate 14.

[75] This appears to be true also of Æthelwold's Abingdon (*ca* 954–963): since Æthelwold had been a monk at Dunstan's Glastonbury, one might have expected to find some reflex at Abingdon of Glastonbury practice. The absence of Caroline evidence from both houses may make one wish to stress further the significance of the Continental sojourns of Dunstan and Osgar.

[76] See above, pp. 89–90, 95, 97, 100–1, 148.

[77] See above, pp. 53–4.

[78] Unless one were to argue that Cambridge, Corpus Christi College, MS. 57, of mid-eleventh-century Abingdon provenance, was also written there. It is a substantial specimen of Phase VII (flat-topped) Square minuscule, written *ca* A.D. 1000 (cf. Ker, *Catalogue*, pp. 46–7, no. 34).

This apparently stricter attitude coincides with the exclusivity of usage of the pure Style-I Anglo-Caroline at those same houses. On the other hand, Square minuscule and its eleventh-century replacements were everywhere retained for writing in English. The exclusive association of language and script which was a characteristic of the eleventh-century English scribal tradition began with what must have been a conscious decision on the point in the second half of the tenth century.[79]

Around the millennium and in the first half of the eleventh century we see varying adaptations of the two scripts to one another. The new proportions – long and narrow – developing in vernacular script by the first decade of the eleventh century we have seen in Latin usage in Wulfstan's scriptorium-style at Worcester.[80] Equally, Style-IV Anglo-Caroline seems to have had its own impact on vernacular writing, for in the second quarter of the eleventh century whatever attraction remained for some scribes in the form of Square minuscule was effectively subsumed within the practice of a large, round Anglo-Saxon script prominent but not universal in the middle years of the century.[81] And in specific instances a scribe attempting archaising imitation could successfully create a new hybrid – at mid-eleventh-century Abingdon a Style-IV Anglo-Caroline scribe sought to imitate a large, flat-topped Square minuscule of a half-century earlier when preparing some supply-leaves; the results, though not internally consistent, were an attractive hybrid essay.[82]

These probings of the evidence provided by Anglo-Caroline manuscripts have provided, I think, a number of gains in terms of our ability to attribute individual specimens to particular times and places. Various cautions have, however, been indicated as necessary, not least in approaching the internal development of Caroline writing at Canterbury: a great deal more work must be done on that corpus of material before satisfactory positive conclusions are likely to emerge. In 1971, Mr Bishop argued that the overwhelming body of attributable specimens derives from a mere seven centres: two churches at Canterbury, two at Winchester, Glastonbury, Abingdon, and Worcester.[83] At the end of the Anglo-Saxon period Exeter can be added to the list. The number of

---

[79] On separation of scripts, see *ibid.*, pp. xxv–xxxiii.

[80] See above, pp. 65–7.

[81] For an example, see Keller, *Angelsächsische Palaeographie*, II, plate VIII: London, British Library, Add. Ch. 19797 (*not* 19769, as Keller); Sawyer, *Anglo-Saxon Charters*, no. 1399; written at Worcester, A.D. 1033x1038.

[82] Cambridge, Corpus Christi College, MS. 57 (cf. n. 78, above), fos 8, 19, 22 (and part of 85). For the date of the principal additions to this manuscript (A.D. 1046/7), see Keynes, *The Diplomas of King Æthelred*, p. 239, n. 22, and Gerchow, *Die Gedenküberlieferung*, pp. 245–52, 335–8.

[83] *English Caroline Minuscule*, pp. xiv–xx: I have adapted Mr Bishop's list slightly, to take account both of the material present in his plates and of chronology.

centres of record remains small: for the moment, Abingdon and Glastonbury must be removed from that count, as not providing indubitable offerings.[84] On the other hand, the royal chancery should be added. Mr Bishop also speculated that certain other houses – in particular, Ramsey Abbey – ought to show clearly in the record.[85] In chapter II the possibility of assigning some manuscripts thither (and thus providing the basis for further attributions) began to emerge.[86] And I hope that, in my study of the origins of the Oxford manuscript of the bilingual Benedictine Rule, I have demonstrated how a case might be built for the localisation of a manuscript at a house not previously figuring in the tally of productive centres.[87] Indeed, I hope that in future we shall be able to take Bury St Edmunds more seriously as potentially an active scriptorial and intellectual centre: the pre-Conquest manuscripts having a thirteenth-century Bury provenance deserve study as a group.[88] There remains, nonetheless, a substantial body of unattributed manuscripts requiring close scrutiny.

It has long been argued by art-historians and, to some extent, liturgists that a manuscript might be written in the scriptorium of one house for use in the church of another. We have seen a number of possible eleventh-century instances of this.[89] On the other hand, liturgical or other textual evidence has sometimes been employed to localise or date a manuscript in apparent disregard or defiance of palaeography.[90] The two early eleventh-century Cholsey/Canterbury manuscripts show how such apparently conflicting testimonies can be brought into harmony with one another.[91] However, in the localisation of manuscripts, script must be given primacy over text as an indicator of origin: it constitutes the surface-evidence; script may tell us little or nothing about a work's origin and textual history but, if we have data against which to compare a specimen of Anglo-Caroline script, a positive or negative judgment about the place of origin should be able to be made. In the history of pre-Conquest Anglo-Caroline script there seems to be no evidence for

---

[84] On Glastonbury, see above, pp. 3, 50–1, 86–7, 89–90, 96–8. On Abingdon, cf. Dumville, 'The scriptorium and library of Abingdon Abbey, A.D. 954–1066' (forthcoming).
[85] *English Caroline Minuscule*, p. xvii (cf. p. xv).
[86] See above, pp. 58–65.
[87] See chapter II, above.
[88] See above, p. 78(–9), n. 360.
[89] See above, chapter IV.
[90] For examples, cf. Dumville, 'On the dating'; cf. above, pp. 106–7, 108 n. 127, 118–19. One could add the attribution of Cambridge, Corpus Christi College, MSS. 146 and 411 – both Canterbury cathedral books – to Winchester Cathedral and St Augustine's Abbey, respectively.
[91] Cambridge, University Library, MSS. Ff.1.23 (1156) and Kk.5.32 (2074), fos 49–60: see above, pp. 79–85.

regional styles, whereas after 1066 Style IV, while remaining a badge of Englishness, became eventually, in the last half-century of its life, a regional Fenland script-form. The evidence from before 1066, or even 1100, is specific to particular houses or groups of houses or periods of time, but not to regions (save in as much as Anglo-Caroline does not seem to have penetrated northern England before the eleventh century).[92]

We have seen reason to associate the principal early styles of Anglo-Caroline with families of churches. These party-allegiances seem to have been real enough in the first two generations of the Reform. It remains uncertain how much can be inferred from script about the relative ideological fervour of their principals: but, in so far as what might thus be deduced coheres with inferences drawn from other sources, there is little reason to be over-hesitant about allowing the possibility of an ideological element to such aspects of book-production.[93] One may wonder whether such conclusions could also be drawn from preferences in the selection of texts for copying.[94] A major legacy of the work of David Knowles has been the attribution (but usually without argument or citation of evidence) of numerous Reform-houses to one of the three principal early parties to the movement.[95] These attributions are now beginning to be studied critically:[96] such reconsiderations will need to draw on palaeographical evidence but will also themselves affect palaeographers' perceptions. Only when this task has been wholly carried through shall we be able to measure fully the activity and relative importance of these Benedictine parties in intellectual and monastic history. In particular the churches founded or refounded by Dunstan require especial attention. The complete range of manuscript evidence needs to be examined further for evidence of distinctions too between unreformed churches and those of the revolutionary, monastic movement.[97] At what point such distinctions began to blur and when Caroline

---

[92] On Northumbrian script, cf. Keynes, 'King Athelstan's books', pp. 170-9 and plate VIII; Dumville, 'English Square minuscule script: the background and earliest phases', p. 148(-9), n. 5; Harrsen, 'The Countess Judith'; Hinkle, 'The gift'. On St Margaret's gospel-lectionary – Oxford, Bodleian Library, MS. Lat. liturg. f.5 (*S.C.* 29744) – see Dumville, 'On the dating', pp. 50-1; for its Englishness, see also Frere, *Bibliotheca Musico-liturgica*, I.83 (no. 232).

[93] Cf. pp. 3-4, above.

[94] Cf. Bishop, 'Notes', p. 323.

[95] Knowles, *The Monastic Order*, pp. 31-82 (especially 48-52); cf. Knowles & Hadcock, *Medieval Religious Houses: England and Wales*, *passim*.

[96] See Michael Lapidge's discussion of Æthelwold in this respect: *Wulfstan of Winchester*, edd. & transl. Lapidge & Winterbottom, pp. xliv-l.

[97] It has been argued that the Old English continuous gloss to the Athanasian Creed in Salisbury, Cathedral Library, MS. 150 can be taken as evidence of the approach of an unreformed church: Dorothy Whitelock, in a review in *Review of English Studies*, N.S., 11 (1960) 419-21, followed by Dumville, ' "Beowulf" and the Celtic world', p. 141 and n. 152.

manuscripts began to be written at churches which had never become Benedictine monasteries are issues which have not yet been addressed.

By the end of the second generation of the Reform – that is to say, *ca* 1010–1020 – developments in script seem once again to reflect larger ecclesiastical movements. The creation of Style-IV Anglo-Caroline was itself a process, or an act, which merged elements of Style II into Style I. That this occurred at the principal church of English christianity, and one which had previously pioneered Style II, is perhaps a measure of the penetration of the nation's Church by ecclesiastics representing the ideals of Æthelwold and Oswald. But it is also assuredly an indicator of the blurring of distinctions after a half-century of working against odds in a common cause.[98] After this passage of time the allegiances of the previous two generations, to founding figures now enshrined in an aura of sanctity and passing from the collective living memory of those who knew them, may have come to seem less urgent: at certain specific houses, political or other events caused the supersession of these party-loyalties; elsewhere they were gradually overlain by new realities.[99] There is an argument, though an uncertain one, that after 1016 the nation's Church had a clearer corporate identity. Frank Barlow's superb history of the English Church in the two generations before the Norman conquest may seem to have left little to be said about that era:[100] but the scripts, and especially the Latin books, of the Anglo-Saxon eleventh century have been little investigated; they offer much scope for historical analysis and revision. Such evidence will provide some surprises about the history of major provincial churches in the first half of the century.

[98] *Regularis concordia* (ed. & transl. Symons; cf. *Consuetudinum saeculi X/XI/XII monumenta non-Cluniacensia*, ed. Hallinger, pp. 61–147), a defining text from the heyday of reform in Edgar's reign, is an early example of the cooperation of the various Benedictinising forces. Cf. also Sheerin, 'The dedication', on an important event of A.D. 980.

[99] On the other hand, at Canterbury St Augustine's Abbey seems to have adhered to its traditional practices as much as possible throughout the eleventh century. A full study of its script and book-production in that era is much to be desired.

[100] *The English Church, 1000–1066.*

BIBLIOGRAPHY

ALEXANDER, J.[J.G.] & CAHN, W. 'An eleventh century gospel book from Le Cateau', *Scriptorium* 20 (1966) 248–64 + plates 19–23

ALEXANDER, J.J.G. *Norman Illumination at Mont St Michel, 966–1100* (Oxford 1970)

ÅNGSTRØM, Margareta *Studies in Old English MSS with Special Reference to the Delabialisation of* ў(⟨ū̆ + i) *to* ī̆ (Uppsala 1937)

ARNOLD, Thomas (ed.) *Memorials of St. Edmund's Abbey* (3 vols, London 1890–6)

ARNOLD, Thomas (ed.) *Symeonis Monachi Opera Omnia* (2 vols, London 1882/5)

ATKINS, I. 'An investigation of two Anglo-Saxon kalendars (Missal of Robert of Jumièges and St. Wulfstan's Homiliary)', *Archaeologia* 78 [2nd S., 28] (1928) 219–54

ATKINS, Ivor & KER, N.R. (edd.) *'Catalogus Librorum Manuscriptorum Bibliothecae Wigorniensis' made in 1622–1623 by Patrick Young, Librarian to King James I* (Cambridge 1944)

BACKHOUSE, Janet, *et al.* (edd.) *The Golden Age of Anglo-Saxon Art, 966–1066* (London 1984)

BACKHOUSE, J. 'The making of the Harley Psalter', *British Library Journal* 10 (1984) 97–113

BANTING, H.M.J. (ed.) *Two Anglo-Saxon Pontificals (the Egbert and Sidney Sussex Pontificals* (London 1989)

BARKER, E.E. (ed.) 'Two lost documents of King Athelstan', *Anglo-Saxon England* 6 (1977) 137–43

BARKER, Nicolas (facs. ed.) *The York Gospels* (London 1986)

BARLOW, Frank, *et al. Leofric of Exeter. Essays in Commemoration of the Foundation of Exeter Cathedral Library in A.D. 1072* (Exeter 1972)

BARLOW, Frank *The English Church, 1000–1066. A History of the Later Anglo-Saxon Church* (2nd edn, London 1979)

BATESON, M. 'A Worcester cathedral book of ecclesiastical collections, made c. 1000 A.D.', *English Historical Review* 10 (1895) 712–31

BATESON, M. 'Rules for monks and secular canons after the revival under King Edgar', *English Historical Review* 9 (1894) 690–708

BIRCH, W. de G. 'Historical notes on the manuscripts belonging to Ramsey Abbey', *Journal of the British Archaeological Association*, N.S., 5 (1899) 229–42

BISCHOFF, Bernhard *Latin Palaeography: Antiquity and the Middle Ages* (Cambridge 1990)

BISCHOFF, Bernhard *Mittelalterliche Studien. Ausgewählte Aufsätze zur Schriftkunde und Literaturgeschichte* (3 vols, Stuttgart 1966–81)

BISHOP, T.A.M. (facs. ed.) *Aethici Istrici Cosmographia Vergilio Salis-burgensi rectius adscripta. Codex Leidensis Scaligeranus 69* (Amsterdam 1966)

BISHOP, T.A.M. 'An early example of Insular-Caroline', *Transactions of the Cambridge Bibliographical Society* 4 (1964–8) 396–400 + plate XXIX

BISHOP, T.A.M. 'An early example of the Square minuscule', *Transactions of the Cambridge Bibliographical Society* 4 (1964–8) 246–52 + plates XVIII–XIX

BISHOP, T.A.M. *English Caroline Minuscule* (Oxford 1971)

BISHOP, T.A.M. 'Lincoln Cathedral MS 182', *Lincolnshire History and Archaeology* 2 (1967) 73–6 + plates I–II

BISHOP, T.A.M. 'Notes on Cambridge manuscripts', *Transactions of the Cambridge Bibliographical Society* 1 (1949–53) 432–41; 2 (1954–8) 185–99 (+ plates X–XI), 323–36 (+ plates XIII–XIV); 3 (1959–63) 93–5, 412–23 (+ plates XIII–XV)

BISHOP, T.A.M. *Scriptores Regis. Facsimiles to Identify and Illustrate the Hands of Royal Scribes in Original Charters of Henry I, Stephen, and Henry II* (Oxford 1961)

BISHOP, T.A.M. 'The Copenhagen gospel-book', *Nordisk Tidskrift för Bok-och Biblioteksväsen* 54 (1967) 33–41

BISHOP, T.A.M. 'The Corpus Martianus Capella', *Transactions of the Cambridge Bibliographical Society* 4 (1964–8) 257–75 + plates XX–XXII

BLAKE, E.O. (ed.) *Liber Eliensis* (London 1962)

BOND, Edward A[ugustus] (ed.) *Facsimiles of Ancient Charters in the British Museum* (4 vols, London 1873–8)

BOND, Edward Augustus, *et al.* (edd.) *The Palæographical Society Facsimiles of Manuscripts and Inscriptions* (2 series, London 1873–94)

BOUTEMY, A. 'Encore un manuscrit decoré par Odbert de Saint-Bertin (Leyde B.P.L. 190)', *Scriptorium* 4 (1950) 245–6 + plate 27(*b*)

BOUTEMY, A. 'Influences carolingiennes dans l'oeuvre de l'abbé Odbert de Saint-Bertin (circ. ann. 1000)', *Forschungen zur Kunstgeschichte und christlichen Archäologie* 3 (1957) 427–33

BOUTEMY, A. 'L'enluminure anglaise de l'époque saxonne (Xe–XIe siècles) et la Flandre française', *Bulletin de la Société nationale des antiquaires de France* (1956) 42–50

BOUTEMY, A. 'Les feuillets de Damme', *Scriptorium* 20 (1966) 60–5 + plates 7(*b*)–10

BOUTEMY, A. 'Odbert de Saint-Bertin et la seconde bible de Charles le Chauve', *Scriptorium* 4 (1950) 101–2

BOUTEMY, A. (ed.) 'Two obituaries of Christ Church, Canterbury', *English Historical Review* 50 (1935) 292–9

BOUTEMY, A. 'Un monument capital de l'enluminure anglo-saxonne: le manuscrit 11 de Boulogne-sur-mer', *Cahiers de civilisation médiévale, Xe–XIIe siècles* 1 (1958) 179–82 + figg. 1–2

BRESSIE, R. (ed.) 'MS Sloane 3548, folio 158', *Modern Language Notes* 54 (1939) 246–56

BRETT, C. (ed. & transl.) 'A Breton pilgrim in England in the reign of King Æthelstan', in *France and the British Isles in the Middle Ages and*

Renaissance, edd. G. Jondorf & D.N. Dumville (Woodbridge 1991), pp. 43–70

BRETT, M. 'John of Worcester and his contemporaries', in *The Writing of History in the Middle Ages*, edd. R.H.C. Davis *et al.* (Oxford 1981), pp. 101–26

BROOKS, Nicholas *The Early History of the Church of Canterbury. Christ Church from 597 to 1066* (Leicester 1984)

BROWN, Michelle P. *Anglo-Saxon Manuscripts* (London 1991)

BROWN, M.P. 'Continental symptoms in Insular codicology: historical perspectives', in *Pergament*, ed. P. Rück (Sigmaringen 1991), pp. 57–62

BULLOUGH, D.A. 'Roman books and Carolingian *renovatio*', *Studies in Church History* 14 (1977) 23–50

BULLOUGH, D.A. 'The Continental background of the Reform', in *Tenth-century Studies*, ed. D. Parsons (Chichester 1975), pp. 20–36 *and* 210–14

BULLOUGH, D.A. 'The educational tradition in England from Alfred to Aelfric: teaching *utriusque linguae*', *Settimane di studio del Centro italiano di studi sull'alto medioevo* 19 (1971) 453–94 *and* 547–54

CABROL, Fernand & LECLERCQ, H. (edd.) *Dictionnaire d'archéologie chrétienne et de liturgie* (15 vols in 30, Paris 1903–53)

CAMPBELL, A[listair] (ed. & transl.) *Æthelwulf, De abbatibus* (Oxford 1967)

CAMPBELL, A[listair] (ed.) *Charters of Rochester* (London 1973)

CAMPBELL, Alistair (ed.) *Frithegodi Monachi Breuiloquium Vitæ Beati Wilfredi et Wulfstani Cantoris Narratio Metrica de Sancto Swithuno* (Zürich 1950)

CARAMAN, P.G. 'The character of the late Saxon clergy', *Downside Review* 63 [N.S., 44] (1945) 171–89

CARLEY, J.P. 'Two pre-Conquest manuscripts from Glastonbury Abbey', *Anglo-Saxon England* 16 (1987) 197–212

CHADWICK, Nora K. (ed.) *Celt and Saxon. Studies in the Early British Border* (Cambridge 1963; rev. imp., 1964)

CHAMBERLIN, John (ed.) *The Rule of St. Benedict: the Abingdon Copy edited from Cambridge, Corpus Christi College MS. 57* (Toronto 1982)

CHAPLAIS, P. 'The Anglo-Saxon chancery: from the diploma to the writ', in *Prisca Munimenta*, ed. F. Ranger (London 1973), pp. 43–62

CLARK, C. 'Notes on a *Life* of three Thorney saints, Thancred, Torhtred and Tova', *Proceedings of the Cambridge Antiquarian Society* 69 (1979) 45–52

CLASSEN, E. & HARMER, F.E. (edd.) *An Anglo-Saxon Chronicle from British Museum, Cotton MS., Tiberius B.IV* (Manchester 1926)

CLEMOES, P. 'Ælfric', in *Continuations and Beginnings*, ed. E.G. Stanley (London 1966), pp. 176–209

CLEMOES, Peter *Manuscripts from Anglo-Saxon England* (Cambridge 1985)

CLEMOES, P. 'The Old English Benedictine Office, Corpus Christi College, Cambridge, MS 190, and the relations between Ælfric and Wulfstan: a reconsideration', *Anglia* 78 (1960) 265–83

CLOVER, Helen & GIBSON, M. (edd. & transl.) *The Letters of Lanfranc, Archbishop of Canterbury* (Oxford 1979)

COLGRAVE, Bertram & MYNORS, R.A.B. (edd. & transl.) *Bede's Ecclesiastical History of the English People* (Oxford 1969)

COLGRAVE, Bertram (ed. & transl.) *Felix's Life of Saint Guthlac* (Cambridge 1956)

CONNER, Patrick W. *Anglo-Saxon Exeter. A Tenth-century Cultural History* (Woodbridge 1992)

COXE, Henry O. *Catalogus Codicum MSS. qui in Collegiis Aulisque Oxoniensibus hodie adservantur* (18 vols in 2, Oxford 1852)

CRAWFORD, S.J. 'Byrhtferth of Ramsey and the anonymous Life of St. Oswald', in *Speculum Religionis, being Essays and Studies in Religion and Literature from Plato to Von Hügel, presented by Members of the Staff of University College, Southampton, to their President, Claude G. Montefiore* (Oxford 1929), pp. 99–111

CRAWFORD, S.J. (ed. & transl.) *Byrhtferth's Manual (A.D. 1011), now edited for the first time from MS. Ashmole 328 in the Bodleian Library* London 1929)

DARLINGTON, R.R. 'Ecclesiastical reform in the late Old English period', *English Historical Review* 51 (1936) 385–428

DARLINGTON, R.R. (ed.) *The Cartulary of Worcester Cathedral Priory (Register I)* (London 1968)

DAUPHIN, H. 'Le renouveau monastique en Angleterre au Xe siècle et ses rapports avec la réforme de Saint Gérard de Brogne', *Revue bénédictine* 70 (1960) 177–96

DAVEY, W. 'The commentary of the Regius Psalter: its main source and influence on the Old English gloss', *Mediaeval Studies* 49 (1987) 335–51

DAVIS, G.R.C. *Medieval Cartularies of Great Britain. A Short Catalogue* (London 1958)

DAVIS, H.W.C., et al. (edd.) *Regesta Regum Anglo-Normannorum, 1066–1154* (4 vols, Oxford 1913–69)

DAVIS, H.W.C. (ed.) 'The liberties of Bury St. Edmunds', *English Historical Review* 24 (1909) 417–31

DAVIS, R.H.C., et al. (edd.) *The Writing of History in the Middle Ages. Essays presented to Richard William Southern* (Oxford 1981)

DAVRIL, Anselme (ed.) *The Monastic Ritual of Fleury (Orléans, Bibliothèque Municipale, MS 123 [101])* (London 1990)

DEANESLY, Margaret *Sidelights on the Anglo-Saxon Church* (London 1962)

DEANESLY, Margaret *The Pre-Conquest Church in England* (2nd edn, London 1963)

DE BRÚN, Pádraig & HERBERT, M. *Catalogue of Irish Manuscripts in Cambridge Libraries* (Cambridge 1986)

DE LA MARE, A.C. & BARKER-BENFIELD, B.C. (edd.) *Manuscripts at Oxford: an Exhibition in Memory of Richard William Hunt (1908–1979), Keeper of Western Manuscripts at the Bodleian Library, Oxford, 1945–1975, on Themes selected and described by Some of his Friends* (Oxford 1980)

DELISLE, L. 'Vers et écriture d'Orderic Vital', *Journal des Savants*, N.S., 1 (1903) 429–40

DENHOLM-YOUNG, N. *Handwriting in England and Wales* (2nd edn, Cardiff 1964)

DESHMAN, R. '*Benedictus monarcha et monachus*. Early medieval ruler theology and the Anglo-Saxon reform', *Frühmittelalterliche Studien* 22 (1988) 204–40 + plates XVIII–XXVIII

DESHMAN, R. '*Christus rex et magi reges*: kingship and christology in Ottonian and Anglo-Saxon art', *Frühmittelalterliche Studien* 10 (1976) 367–405 + plates XII–XXIII

DESHUSSES, J. & HOURLIER, J. 'Saint Benoît dans les livres liturgiques', *Studia Monastica* 21 (1979) 143–204

DODWELL, C.R. *Anglo-Saxon Art. A New Perspective* (Manchester 1982)

DODWELL, C.R. *The Canterbury School of Illumination, 1066–1200* (Cambridge 1954)

DONNAT, L. 'Recherches sur l'influence de Fleury au Xe siècle', in *Études ligériennes d'histoire et d'archéologie médiévales*, ed. R. Louis (Auxerre 1975), pp. 165–74

DOUGLAS, D.C. (ed.) *Feudal Documents from the Abbey of Bury St. Edmunds* (London 1932)

DOUGLAS, D.[C.] (ed.) 'Fragments of an Anglo-Saxon survey from Bury St. Edmunds', *English Historical Review* 43 (1928) 376–83

DRAGE, Elaine M. 'Bishop Leofric and the Exeter Cathedral Chapter, 1050–1072: a Reassessment of the Manuscript Evidence' (unpublished D. Phil. dissertation, University of Oxford 1978)

DRONKE, P., *et al.* 'Die unveröffentlichen Gedichte der Cambridger Liederhandschrift (CUL Gg.5.35)', *Mittellateinisches Jahrbuch* 17 (1982) 54–95

DUMVILLE, D.N. 'An early text of Geoffrey of Monmouth's *Historia Regum Britanniae* and the circulation of some Latin histories in twelfth-century Normandy', *Arthurian Literature* 4 (1985) 1–36

DUMVILLE, D.N. 'An episode in Edmund Campion's "Historie of Ireland" ', *Éigse. A Journal of Irish Studies* 16 (1975/6) 131–2

DUMVILLE, D.N. ' "Beowulf" and the Celtic world: the uses of evidence', *Traditio* 37 (1981) 109–60

DUMVILLE, D.N. 'Beowulf come lately. Some notes on the palaeography of the Nowell Codex', *Archiv für das Studium der neueren Sprachen und Literaturen* 225 (1988) 49–63

DUMVILLE, D.N. 'Biblical apocrypha and the early Irish: a preliminary investigation', *Proceedings of the Royal Irish Academy* 73 C (1973) 299–338

DUMVILLE, David N. *Britons and Anglo-Saxons in the Early Middle Ages* (Aldershot 1992)

DUMVILLE, D.N. 'Copying an exemplar written in Insular script and correcting the results', *Filologia Mediolatina* 1 (1993)

DUMVILLE, David N. *England and the Celtic World in the Ninth and Tenth Centuries* (Woodbridge, forthcoming)

DUMVILLE, D.N. 'English libraries before 1066: use and abuse of the manuscript evidence', in *Insular Latin Studies*, ed. M.W. Herren (Toronto 1981), pp. 153–78; 2nd edn in *Anglo-Saxon Manuscripts*, ed. M.P. Richards (New York 1993)

DUMVILLE, D.N. 'English Square minuscule script: the background and earliest phases', *Anglo-Saxon England* 16 (1987) 147–79 + plates I–VII

DUMVILLE, D.N. 'English Square minuscule script: the mid-century phases', *Anglo-Saxon England* (forthcoming)

DUMVILLE, David N. *Histories and Pseudo-histories of the Insular Middle Ages* (Aldershot 1990)

DUMVILLE, David N. *Liturgy and the Ecclesiastical History of Late Anglo-Saxon England: Four Studies* (Woodbridge 1992)

DUMVILLE, David N. *Manuscripts of Wales and Cornwall, A.D. 800–1150* (Woodbridge, forthcoming)

DUMVILLE, D.N. 'On the dating of some late Anglo-Saxon liturgical manuscripts', *Transactions of the Cambridge Bibliographical Society* 10 (1991–) 40–57

DUMVILLE, D.N. [review of H. Sauer (ed.), *Theodulfi Capitula in England* (1978)], *Archiv für das Studium der neueren Sprachen und Literaturen* 223 (1986) 388–92

DUMVILLE, D.N. 'Some aspects of annalistic writing at Canterbury in the eleventh and early twelfth centuries', *Peritia: Journal of the Medieval Academy of Ireland* 2 (1983) 23–57

DUMVILLE, David N. (ed.) *Specimina Codicum Palaeoanglicorum* (Copenhagen, forthcoming)

DUMVILLE, David [N.] & KEYNES, S. (gen. edd.) *The Anglo-Saxon Chronicle. A Collaborative Edition* (23 vols, Cambridge 1983–)

DUMVILLE, David N. (ed.) *The Historia Brittonum* (10 vols, Cambridge 1985–)

DUMVILLE, David N. *Wessex and England from Alfred to Edgar. Six Essays on Political, Cultural, and Ecclesiastical Revival* (Woodbridge 1992)

DUMVILLE, D.N. 'Wulfric cild', *Notes and Queries* 238 [N.S., 40] (1993) 5–9

FARIS, M.J. (ed.) *The Bishops' Synod ("The First Synod of St. Patrick"). A Symposium with Text, Translation, and Commentary* (Liverpool 1976)

FAUROUX, Marie (ed.) *Recueil des actes des ducs de Normandie de 911 à 1066* (Caen 1961)

FAUSBØLL, Else (facs. ed.) *Fifty-six Ælfric Fragments. The Newly-found Copenhagen Fragments of Ælfric's* Catholic Homilies (Copenhagen 1986)

FELL, C.E. 'Edward, king and martyr, and the Anglo-Saxon hagiographic tradition', in *Ethelred the Unready*, ed. D. Hill (Oxford 1978), pp. 1–13

FERRABINO, Aldo (ed.) *Atti del X Congresso internazionale di scienze storiche, Roma, 4–11 Settembre 1955* (Roma 1957)

FINBERG, H.P.R. *The Early Charters of the West Midlands* (2nd edn, Leicester 1972)

FISHER, D.J.V. 'The anti-monastic reaction in the reign of Edward the Martyr', *Cambridge Historical Journal* 10 (1950–2) 254–70

FLEMING, Robin *Kings and Lords in Conquest England* (Cambridge 1991)

FLOWER, Robin & SMITH, H. (facs. edd.) *The Parker Chronicle and Laws (Corpus Christi College, Cambridge, MS. 173). A Facsimile* (London 1941)

FOWLER, Roger (ed.) *Wulfstan's Canons of Edgar* (London 1972)

FRANZEN, Christine *The Tremulous Hand of Worcester. A Study of Old English in the Thirteenth Century* (Oxford 1991)

FRERE, Walter Howard *Bibliotheca Musico-liturgica. A Descriptive Handlist of the Musical and Latin-liturgical MSS. of the Middle Ages preserved in Great Britain and Ireland* (2 vols, London 1894–1932)

164

FRY, Timothy (ed.) *The Rule of St. Benedict* (Collegeville, Minn. 1981)

FRYDE, E.B., *et al.* (edd.) *Handbook of British Chronology* (3rd edn, London 1986)

GALBRAITH, V.H. (ed.) The East Anglian see and the abbey of Bury St. Edmunds', *English Historical Review* 40 (1925) 222-8

GALLOWAY, A. 'On the medieval and post-medieval collation of St. Dunstan's "Aethicus" (Leiden, Rijksuniv. Bibl. Scaliger 69)', *Scriptorium* 43 (1989) 106-11

GAMESON, R. 'The Anglo-Saxon artists of the Harley 603 Psalter', *Journal of the British Archaeological Association* 143 (1990) 29-48 + plates III-VI

GANSHOF, F.L. 'L'église et le pouvoir royal dans la monarchie franque sous Pépin III et Charlemagne', *Settimane di studio del Centro italiano di studi sull'alto medioevo* 7 (1959) 95-141 *and* 314-18

GANZ, Peter (ed.) *The Role of the Book in Medieval Culture. Proceedings of the Oxford International Symposium, 26 September-1 October, 1982* (2 vols, Turnhout 1986)

GASQUET, F.A. & BISHOP, E. *The Bosworth Psalter* (London 1908)

GELLING, Margaret *The Early Charters of the Thames Valley* (Leicester 1979)

GEM, R. 'A recession in English architecture during the early eleventh century, and its effect on the development of the Romanesque style', *Journal of the British Archaeological Association*, 3rd S., 38 (1975) 28-49

GEM, R. 'Church architecture in the reign of King Æthelred', in *Ethelred the Unready*, ed. D. Hill (Oxford 1978), pp. 105-14

GERCHOW, Jan (ed.) *Die Gedenküberlieferung der Angelsachsen, mit einem Katalog der* libri vitae *und Necrologien* (Berlin 1988)

GIBSON, Margaret [T.] (ed.) *Boethius, his Life, Thought and Influence* (Oxford 1981)

GIBSON, M.T., *et al.* 'Neumed Boethian *metra* from Canterbury: a newly recovered leaf of Cambridge, University Library, Gg.5.35 (the "Cambridge Songs" manuscript)', *Anglo-Saxon England* 12 (1983) 141-52 + plates IV-VI

GJERLØW, Lilli *Adoratio Crucis: the Regularis Concordia and the Decreta Lanfranci. Manuscript Studies in the Early Medieval Church of Norway* (Oslo 1961)

GJERLØW, L. 'Fragments of a lectionary in Anglo-Saxon script found in Oslo', *Nordisk Tidskrift för Bok- och Biblioteksväsen* 44 (1957) 109-22

GNEUSS, H. 'Anglo-Saxon libraries from the Conversion to the Benedictine reform', *Settimane di studio del Centro italiano di studi sull'alto medioevo* 32 (1984) 643-99

GNEUSS, H. 'A preliminary list of manuscripts written or owned in England up to 1100', *Anglo-Saxon England* 9 (1981) 1-60

GNEUSS, H. 'Englands Bibliotheken im Mittelalter und ihr Untergang', in *Festschrift für Walter Hübner*, edd. D. Riesner & H. Gneuss (Berlin 1964), pp. 91-121

GNEUSS, Helmut *Hymnar und Hymnen im englischen Mittelalter. Studien zur Überlieferung, Glossierung und Übersetzung lateinischer Hymnen in England mit einer Textausgabe der lateinisch-altenglischen Expositio Hymnorum* (Tübingen 1968)

Bibliography

GNEUSS, H. 'Liturgical books in Anglo-Saxon England and their Old English terminology', in *Learning and Literature in Anglo-Saxon England*, edd. M. Lapidge & H. Gneuss (Cambridge 1985), pp. 91–141

GNEUSS, H. 'The origin of Standard Old English and Æthelwold's school at Winchester', *Anglo-Saxon England* 1 (1972) 63–83

GODFREY, John *The Church in Anglo-Saxon England* (Cambridge 1962)

GOODWIN, A. *The Abbey of St. Edmundsbury* (Oxford 1931)

GRANSDEN, A. 'Baldwin, abbot of Bury St Edmunds, 1065–1097', *Proceedings of the Battle Conference on Anglo-Norman Studies* 4 (1981) 65–76 *and* 187–95

GRANSDEN, Antonia *Historical Writing in England* (2 vols, London 1974/82)

GRANSDEN, A. 'The legends and traditions concerning the origins of the abbey of Bury St Edmunds', *English Historical Review* 100 (1985) 1–24

GRANSDEN, A. 'The question of the consecration of St Edmund's church', in *Church and Chronicle in the Middle Ages*, edd. I. Wood & G.A. Loud (London 1991), pp. 59–86

GRANSDEN, A. 'Traditionalism and continuity during the last century of Anglo-Saxon monasticism', *Journal of Ecclesiastical History* 40 (1989) 159–207

GRANT, Raymond J.S. (ed.) *Cambridge, Corpus Christi College 41: the Loricas and the Missal* (Amsterdam 1978)

GRANT, Raymond J.S. *The B Text of the Old English Bede. A Linguistic Commentary* (Amsterdam 1989)

GREMONT, D. & DONNAT, L. 'Fleury, Le Mont Saint-Michel et l'Angleterre à la fin du Xe et au début du XIe siècle à propos du manuscrit d'Orléans No. 127 (105)', in *Millénaire monastique du Mont Saint-Michel*, edd. J. Laporte *et al.* (4 vols, Paris 1967), I.751–93

GRETSCH, M. 'Æthelwold's translation of the *Regula Sancti Benedicti* and its Latin exemplar', *Anglo-Saxon England* 3 (1974) 125–51

GRETSCH, Mechthild *Die Regula Sancti Benedicti in England und ihre altenglische Übersetzung* (München 1973)

GRETSCH, M. 'Die Winteney-Version der *Regula Sancti Benedicti*: eine frühmittelenglische Bearbeitung der altenglischen Prosaübersetzung der Benediktinerregel', *Anglia* 96 (1978) 310–48

GRIERSON, P. 'The relations between England and Flanders before the Norman conquest', *Transactions of the Royal Historical Society*, 4th S., 23 (1941) 71–112

GRODECKI, L., *et al.* *Le Siècle de l'an mil* (Paris 1973)

HAFNER, Wolfgang (ed.) *Der Basiliuskommentar zur Regula S. Benedicti. Ein Beitrag zur Autorenfrage karolingischer Regelkommentare* (Münster i.W. 1959)

HALLINGER, Kassius (ed.) *Consuetudinum saeculi X/XI/XII monumenta non-Cluniacensia* (Siegburg 1984)

HAMILTON, B. 'The monastic revival in tenth century Rome', *Studia Monastica* 4 (1962) 35–68

HAMILTON, N.E.S.A. (ed.) *Willelmi Malmesbiriensis monachi De Gestis Pontificum Anglorum libri quinque* (London 1870)

HANDSCHIN, J. 'The two Winchester tropers', *Journal of Theological Studies* 37 (1936) 34–49 *and* 156–72

HARMER, F.E. (ed. & transl.) *Anglo-Saxon Writs* (Manchester 1952)

HARRIS, R.M. 'An illustration in an Anglo-Saxon psalter in Paris', *Journal of the Warburg and Courtauld Institutes* 26 (1963) 255–63

HARRSEN, M. 'The Countess Judith of Flanders and the library of Weingarten Abbey', *Papers of the Bibliographical Society of America* 24 (1930) 1–13 + plates I–VIII

HART, C. [R.] 'Athelstan "Half King" and his family', *Anglo-Saxon England* 2 (1973) 115–44

HART, C. [R.] 'Eadnoth, first abbot of Ramsey, and the foundation of Chatteris and St Ives', *Proceedings of the Cambridge Antiquarian Society* 56/57 (1964) 61–7

HART, C. [R.] 'The B text of the *Anglo-Saxon Chronicle*', *Journal of Medieval History* 8 (1982) 241–99

HART, C. [R.] 'The church of St Mary of Huntingdon', *Proceedings of the Cambridge Antiquarian Society* 59 (1966) 105–111

HART, C. [R.] & SYME, A. 'The earliest Suffolk charter', *Proceedings of the Suffolk Institute of Archaeology and History* 36 (1985–8) 165–81 + plate X

HART, C[yril] R. *The Early Charters of Eastern England* (Leicester 1966)

HART, C[yril] R. *The Early Charters of Northern England and the North Midlands* (Leicester 1975)

HART, C. [R.] 'The East Anglian chronicle', *Journal of Medieval History* 7 (1981) 249–82

HART, C. [R.] 'The hidation of Huntingdonshire', *Proceedings of the Cambridge Antiquarian Society* 61 (1968) 55–66

HART, C. [R.] 'The Mersea charter of Edward the Confessor', *Essex Archaeology and History* 12 (1980) 94–102

HART, C. [R.] 'The site of *Assandun*', *History Studies* 1 (1968) 1–12

HART, C. [R.] 'Two queens of England', *The Ampleforth Journal* 82 (1977), pt 2, pp. 10–15 & 54

HEIMANN, A. 'Three illustrations from the Bury St. Edmunds Psalter and their prototypes. Notes on the iconography of some Anglo-Saxon drawings', *Journal of the Warburg and Courtauld Institutes* 29 (1966) 39–59 + plates 7–13

HENEL, Heinrich (ed.) *Aelfric's De temporibus anni* (London 1942)

HERREN, Michael W. (ed.) *Insular Latin Studies. Papers on Latin Texts and Manuscripts of the British Isles: 550–1066* (Toronto 1981)

HERVEY, Francis (ed. & transl.) *Corolla Sancti Eadmundi. The Garland of Saint Edmund, King and Martyr* (London 1907)

HERVEY, Francis (ed.) *Corpus Christi College, Oxford, MS. 197. The History of King Eadmund the Martyr and of the Early Years of his Abbey* (London 1929)

HESLOP, T.A. 'The production of *de luxe* manuscripts and the patronage of King Cnut and Queen Emma', *Anglo-Saxon England* 19 (1990) 151–95 + plates I–IV

HESSEL, A. 'Studien zur Ausbreitung der karolingischen Minuskel', *Archiv für Urkundenforschung* 7 (1918–21) 197–202 *and* 8 (1922/3) 16–25

HESSEL, A. 'Zur Entstehung der karolingischen Minuskel', *Archiv für Urkundenforschung* 8 (1922/3) 201–14

HILL, David (ed.) *Ethelred the Unready: Papers from the Millenary Conference* (Oxford 1978)

HINKLE, W.M. 'The gift of an Anglo-Saxon gospel book to the abbey of Saint-Remi, Reims', *Journal of the British Archaeological Association*, 3rd S., 33 (1970) 21–35 + plates VII–IX

HOBSON, A.R.A. (ed.) *Fourth International Congress of Bibliophiles, London, 27 September–2 October, 1965: Transactions* (London 1967)

HOFFMANN, Erich *Die heiligen Könige bei den Angelsachsen und den skandinavischen Völkern: Königsheiliger und Königshaus* (Neumünster 1975)

HOFSTETTER, W. 'Winchester and the standardization of Old English vocabulary', *Anglo-Saxon England* 17 (1988) 139–61

HOFSTETTER, Walter *Winchester und der spätaltenglische Sprachgebrauch. Untersuchungen zur geographischen und zeitlichen Verbreitung altenglischer Synonyme* (München 1987)

HOHLER, C.[E.] 'Les Saints insulaires dans le missel de l'archevêque Robert', in *Jumièges. Congrès scientifique du XIIIe centenaire, Rouen, 10–12 juin 1954* (2 vols, Rouen 1955), I.293–303

HOHLER, C.E. 'Some service-books of the later Saxon Church', in *Tenth-century Studies*, ed. D. Parsons (Chichester 1975), pp. 60–83 *and* 217–27

HOMBURGER, Otto *Die Anfänge der Malschule von Winchester im X. Jahrhundert* (Leipzig 1912)

HOMBURGER, O. 'Eine spätkarolingische Schule von Corbie', *Forschungen zur Kunstgeschichte und christlichen Archäologie* 3 (1957) 412–26

HOMBURGER, O. [review of E.G. Millar, *English Illuminated Manuscripts from the Xth to the XIIIth Century* (1926)], *Art Bulletin* 10 (1927/8) 399–402

HORSTMAN, Carl (ed.) *Nova Legenda Anglie: as collected by John of Tynemouth, John Capgrave, and Others, and first printed, with New Lives, by Wynkyn de Worde a.d. mdxui* (2 vols, Oxford 1901)

HOUGHTON, Bryan *Saint Edmund – King and Martyr* (Lavenham 1970)

HUNT, R.W., *et al. A Summary Catalogue of Western Manuscripts in the Bodleian Library at Oxford* (7 vols in 8, Oxford 1922–53; rev. imp., München 1980)

HUNT, R.W. (facs. ed.) *Saint Dunstan's Classbook from Glastonbury. Codex Biblioth. Bodleianae Oxon. Auct. F.4.32* (Amsterdam 1961)

HUNTER BLAIR, Peter *Anglo-Saxon Northumbria* (London 1984)

HUNTER BLAIR, P. 'Some observations on the *Historia Regum* attributed to Symeon of Durham', in *Celt and Saxon*, ed. N.K. Chadwick (Cambridge 1963; rev. imp., 1964), pp. 63–118

JACKSON, Kenneth *Language and History in Early Britain. A Chronological Survey of the Brittonic Languages, 1st to 12th c. A.D.* (Edinburgh 1953)

JAMES, Montague Rhodes *A Descriptive Catalogue of the Manuscripts in the Library of Corpus Christi College, Cambridge* (2 vols, Cambridge 1909–12)

JAMES, Montague Rhodes *On the Abbey of S. Edmund at Bury* (Cambridge 1895)

JOHN, Eric *Land Tenure in Early England. A Discussion of Some Problems* (Leicester 1960; rev. imp., 1964)

JOHN, Eric *Orbis Britanniae and Other Studies* (Leicester 1966)

JOHN, E. ' "Saecularium prioratus" and the Rule of St. Benedict', *Revue bénédictine* 75 (1965) 212–39

JOHN, E. 'St Oswald and the tenth-century Reformation', *Journal of Ecclesiastical History* 9 (1958) 159–72

JOHN, E. 'The church of Winchester and the tenth-century Reformation', *Bulletin of the John Rylands Library* 47 (1964/5) 404–29

JOHN, E. 'The King and the monks in the tenth-century Reformation', *Bulletin of the John Rylands Library* 42 (1959/60) 61–87

JOHN, E. 'The sources of the English monastic reformation. A comment', *Revue bénédictine* 70 (1960) 197–203

JONDORF, Gillian & DUMVILLE, D.N. (edd.) *France and the British Isles in the Middle Ages and Renaissance. Essays by Members of Girton College, Cambridge, in Memory of Ruth Morgan* (Woodbridge 1991)

KAUFFMANN, C.M. *Romanesque Manuscripts, 1066–1190* (London 1975)

KEIM, H.W. 'Aeþelwold und die Mönchreform in England', *Anglia* 41 [N.F., 29] (1917) 405–43

KELLER, Wolfgang *Angelsächsische Palaeographie. Die Schrift der Angelsachsen mit besonderer Rücksicht auf die Denkmäler in der Volkssprache* (2 vols, Berlin 1906)

KELLER, Wolfgang *Die litterarischen Bestrebungen von Worcester in angelsächsischer Zeit* (Strassburg 1900)

KELLER, Wolfgang *Zur Litteratur und Sprache von Worcester im X. und XI. Jahrhundert. Erster Teil: litterarische Bestrebungen in Worcester bis zum Tode des Erzbischofs Oswald (992)* (Strassburg 1897)

KELLY, S. 'Anglo-Saxon lay society and the written word', in *The Uses of Literacy in Early Mediaeval Europe*, ed. R. McKitterick (Cambridge 1990), pp. 36–62

KEMP, B.R. 'The monastic dean of Leominster', *English Historical Review* 83 (1968) 505–15

KER, N.R. 'A supplement to *Catalogue of Manuscripts containing Anglo-Saxon*', *Anglo-Saxon England* 5 (1976) 121–31

KER, N.R. *Books, Collectors and Libraries. Studies in the Medieval Heritage* (London 1985)

KER, N.R. *Catalogue of Manuscripts containing Anglo-Saxon* (Oxford 1957; rev. imp., 1990)

KER, N.R. *English Manuscripts in the Century after the Norman Conquest* (Oxford 1960)

KER. N.R. *Medieval Libraries of Great Britain. A List of Surviving Books* (2nd edn, London 1964)

KER, N.R. (facs. ed.) *The Pastoral Care. King Alfred's Translation of St. Gregory's Regula Pastoralis: MS. Hatton 20 in the Bodleian Library at Oxford; MS. Cotton Tiberius B.XI in the British Museum; MS. Anhang 19 in the Landesbibliothek at Kassel* (Copenhagen 1956)

KEYNES, Simon & KENNEDY, A. (edd. & transl.) *Anglo-Saxon Ely* (Woodbridge, forthcoming)

KEYNES, Simon *Anglo-Saxon Manuscripts and Other Items of Related Interest in the Library of Trinity College, Cambridge* (3rd edn, Binghamton, N.Y. 1992)

KEYNES, Simon (ed.) *Facsimiles of Anglo-Saxon Charters* (London 1991)

KEYNES, S. 'King Athelstan's books', in *Learning and Literature in Anglo-Saxon England*, edd. M. Lapidge & H. Gneuss (Cambridge 1985), pp. 143–201 + plates I–XVI

KEYNES, S. 'Regenbald the Chancellor (*sic*)', *Anglo-Norman Studies* 10 (1987) 185–222

KEYNES, S. 'Royal government and the written word in late Anglo-Saxon England', in *The Uses of Literacy in Early Mediaeval Europe*, ed. R. McKitterick (Cambridge 1990), pp. 226–57

KEYNES, S. 'The additions in Old English', in *The York Gospels*, facs. ed. N. Barker (London 1986), pp. 81–99

KEYNES, S. 'The declining reputation of King Æthelred the Unready', in *Ethelred the Unready*, ed. D. Hill (Oxford 1978), pp. 227–53

KEYNES, Simon *The Diplomas of King Æthelred 'the Unready', 978–1016. A Study in their Use as Historical Evidence* (Cambridge 1980)

KNOWLES, [M.] David & HADCOCK, R.N. *Medieval Religious Houses: England and Wales* (2nd edn, London 1971)

KNOWLES, M.D. 'The early community at Christ Church, Canterbury', *Journal of Theological Studies* 39 (1938) 126–31

KNOWLES, [M.] David, *et al. The Heads of Religious Houses: England and Wales, 940–1216* (Cambridge 1972)

KNOWLES, [M.] David *The Monastic Order in England. A History of its Development from the Times of St Dunstan to the Fourth Lateran Council, 940–1216* (2nd edn, Cambridge 1963)

KOEHLER, Wilhelm R.W. (ed.) *Medieval Studies in Memory of A. Kingsley Porter* (2 vols, Cambridge, Mass. 1939)

KORHAMMER, [P.] Michael (ed.) *Die monastischen Cantica im Mittelalter und ihre altenglischen Interlinearversion. Studien und Textausgabe* (München 1976)

KORHAMMER, P.M. 'The origin of the Bosworth Psalter', *Anglo-Saxon England* 2 (1973) 173–87 + plate IV

KORHAMMER, [P.] Michael, *et al.* (edd.) *Words, Texts and Manuscripts. Studies in Anglo-Saxon Culture presented to Helmut Gneuss on the Occasion of his Sixty-fifth Birthday* (Cambridge 1992)

KOTTJE, Raymund & MAURER, H. (edd.) *Monastische Reformen im 9. und 10. Jahrhundert* (Sigmaringen 1989)

LAPIDGE, M. 'Abbot Germanus, Winchcombe, Ramsey and the "Cambridge Psalter" ', in *Words, Texts and Manuscripts*, edd. [P.] M. Korhammer *et al.* (Woodbridge 1992), pp. 99–129

LAPIDGE, M. 'Æthelwold as scholar and teacher', in *Bishop Æthelwold, his Career and Influence*, ed. B. Yorke (Woodbridge 1988), pp. 89–117

LAPIDGE, M. 'A Frankish scholar in tenth-century England: Frithegod of Canterbury/Fredegaud of Brioude', *Anglo-Saxon England* 17 (1988) 45–65 + plates I–V

LAPIDGE, Michael (ed.) *Anglo-Saxon Litanies of the Saints* (London 1991)

Bibliography

Bibliography

LAPIDGE, M. 'Byrhtferth and the *Vita S. Ecgwini*', *Mediaeval Studies* 41 (1979) 331–53

LAPIDGE, M. 'Byrhtferth of Ramsey and the early sections of the *Historia Regum* attributed to Symeon of Durham', *Anglo-Saxon England* 10 (1982) 97–122

LAPIDGE, Michael & DUMVILLE, D. (edd.) *Gildas: New Approaches* (Woodbridge 1984)

LAPIDGE, Michael & GNEUSS, H. (edd.) *Learning and Literature in Anglo-Saxon England. Studies presented to Peter Clemoes on the Occasion of his Sixty-fifth Birthday* (Cambridge 1985)

LAPIDGE, M. 'St Dunstan's Latin poetry', *Anglia* 98 (1980) 101–6

LAPIDGE, M. (ed. & transl.) 'Some Latin poems as evidence for the reign of Athelstan', *Anglo-Saxon England* 9 (1981) 61–98

LAPIDGE, M. (ed.) 'Surviving booklists from Anglo-Saxon England', in *Learning and Literature in Anglo-Saxon England*, edd. M. Lapidge & H. Gneuss (Cambridge 1985), pp. 33–89

LAPIDGE, M. 'The hermeneutic style in tenth-century Anglo-Latin literature', *Anglo-Saxon England* 4 (1975) 67–111

LAPIDGE, M. 'The revival of Latin learning in late Anglo-Saxon England', in *Manuscripts at Oxford*, edd. A.C. de la Mare & B.C. Barker-Benfield (Oxford 1980), pp. 18–22

LAPIDGE, Michael & WINTERBOTTOM, M. (edd. & transl.) *Wulfstan of Winchester, The Life of St Æthelwold* (Oxford 1991)

LAPORTE, J., *et al.* (edd.) *Millénaire monastique du Mont Saint-Michel* (4 vols, Paris 1967)

LECLERCQ, J. 'The tenth century English Benedictine reform as seen from the Continent', *The Ampleforth Review* [sic] (1980) 8–23

LEGA-WEEKES, E. 'Ancient liturgical MS. discovered in Exeter cathedral library', *Devon and Cornwall Notes and Queries* 9 (1916/17) 32–5

LENDINARA, P. (ed.) 'Il glossario del ms. Oxford, Bodleian Library, Bodley 163', *Romanobarbarica* 10 (1988/9) 485–516

LEROQUAIS, V. *Les Sacramentaires et les missels manuscrits des bibliothèques publiques de France* (4 vols, Paris 1924)

LINDSAY, W.M. *Early Welsh Script* (Oxford 1912)

LIUZZI, F. 'Notazione musicale del sec. XI in un manoscritto dell'Eneide', *Studi medievali*, N.S., 5 (1932) 67–77

LOBEL, M.D. *The Borough of Bury St. Edmund's. A Study in the Government and Development of a Monastic Town* (Oxford 1935)

LOGEMAN, H. (ed.) *The Rule of S. Benet. Latin and Anglo-Saxon Interlinear Version* (London 1888)

LOUIS, René (ed.) *Études ligériennes d'histoire et d'archéologie médiévales. Mémoires et exposés présentés à la Semaine d'études médiévales de Saint-Benoît-sur-Loire du 3 au 10 juillet 1969* (Auxerre 1975)

LOURDAUX, W. & VERHELST, D. (edd.) *Benedictine Culture, 750–1050* (Leuven 1983)

LOWE, E.A. (ed.) *Codices Latini Antiquiores. A Palaeographcial Guide to Latin Manuscripts prior to the Ninth Century* (11 vols & supplement, Oxford 1934–71)

171

Bibliography

LOYN, Henry R. (facs. ed.) *A Wulfstan Manuscript containing Institutes, Laws and Homilies: British Museum Cotton Nero A.I* (Copenhagen 1971)

LUCAS, P.J. 'MS. Hatton 42: another manuscript containing Old English', *Notes and Queries* 224 [N.S., 26] (1979) 8

MACKINLAY, J.B. *Saint Edmund, King and Martyr. A History of his Life and Times with an Account of the Translations of his Incorrupt Body, etc., from Original MSS.* (London 1893)

McKITTERICK, Rosamond (ed.) *The Uses of Literacy in Early Mediaeval Europe* (Cambridge 1990)

McLACHLAN, E.P. 'The scriptorium of Bury St. Edmunds in the third and fourth decades of the twelfth century: books in three related hands and their decoration', *Mediaeval Studies* 40 (1978) 328–48 + plates I–IV

MACRAY, W. Dunn (ed.) *Chronicon Abbatiæ Rameseiensis, a Sæc. X. usque ad an. circiter 1200: in quatuor partibus* (London 1886)

MASON, Emma *St Wulfstan of Worcester, c. 1008–1095* (Oxford 1990)

MAWER, A., *et al. The Place-names of Worcestershire* (Cambridge 1927)

MERITT, Herbert Dean (ed.) *The Old English Prudentius Glosses at Boulogne-sur-Mer* (Stanford, Cal. 1959)

MEYVAERT, P. 'Towards a history of the textual transmission of the *Regula S. Benedicti*', *Scriptorium* 17 (1963) 83–110

MIGNE, J.-P. (ed.) *Patrologiæ [latinæ] cursus completus. . .* (221 vols, Paris 1844–64)

MILLAR, Eric G. *English Illuminated Manuscripts from the Xth to the XIIIth Century* (Paris 1926)

MILLER, Thomas *Place Names in the English Bede and the Localisation of the MSS.* (Strassburg 1896)

MOSTERT, M. 'Le séjour d'Abbon de Fleury à Ramsey', *Bibliothèque de l'École des Chartes* 144 (1986) 199–208

MOSTERT, Marco *The Library of Fleury. A Provisional List of Manuscripts* (Hilversum 1989)

MOSTERT, Marco *The Political Theology of Abbo of Fleury. A Study of the Ideas about Society and Law of the Tenth-century Monastic Reform Movement* (Hilversum 1987)

NAPIER, A[rthur] S. & STEVENSON, W.H. (edd.) *The Crawford Collection of Early Charters and Documents now in the Bodleian Library* (Oxford 1895)

NAPIER, Arthur S. (ed.) *The Old English Version of the Enlarged Rule of Chrodegang together with the Latin Original. An Old English Version of the Capitula of Theodulf together with the Latin Original. An Interlinear Old English Rendering of the Epitome of Benedict of Aniane* (London 1916)

NELSON, Janet L. *Politics and Ritual in Early Medieval Europe* (London 1986)

NIVER, C. 'The psalter in the British Museum, Harley 2904', in *Medieval Studies in Memory of A. Kingsley Porter*, ed. W.R.W. Koehler (Cambridge, Mass. 1939), II.667–87

O'DONOVAN, M.A. (ed.) *Charters of Sherborne* (London 1988)

OETGEN, J. 'The Old English *Rule* of St. Benedict', *American Benedictine Review* 26 (1975) 38–53

O'KEEFFE, K.O'B. 'The text of Aldhelm's *Enigma* no. c in Oxford, Bodleian Library, Rawlinson C.697 and Exeter Riddle 40', *Anglo-Saxon England* 14 (1985) 61–73

OLSON, Lynette *Early Monasteries in Cornwall* (Woodbridge 1989)

ORTENBERG, V. (ed.) 'Archbishop Sigeric's journey to Rome in 990', *Anglo-Saxon England* 19 (1990) 197–246

PÄCHT, Otto, *et al*. *Illuminated Manuscripts in the Bodleian Library, Oxford* (4 vols, Oxford 1966–74)

PANTIN, W.A. 'The pre-Conquest saints of Canterbury', in *For Hilaire Belloc*, ed. D. Woodruff (London 1942), pp. 146–72

PARKES, M.B. 'A note on MS Vatican, Bibl. Apost., lat. 3363', in *Boethius, his Life, Thought and Influence*, ed. M. Gibson (Oxford 1981), pp. 425–7

PARSONS, David (ed.) *Tenth-century Studies. Essays in Commemoration of the Millennium of the Council of Winchester and Regularis Concordia* (Chichester 1975)

PELLEGRIN, Elisabeth *Bibliothèques retrouvées. Manuscrits, bibliothèques et bibliophiles du moyen âge et de la renaissance* (Paris 1988)

PLUMMER, Charles (ed.) *Venerabilis Baedae Opera Historica* (2 vols, Oxford 1896)

POLLARD, G. 'Some Anglo-Saxon bookbindings', *The Book Collector* 24 (1975) 130–59

PONTIFEX, D. 'St Dunstan in his first biography', *Downside Review* 51 [N.S., 32] (1933) 20–40 *and* 309–25

POTTER, S. 'The Winchester Bede', *Wessex* 3 (1934–6), no. 2, pp. 39–45

PRESCOTT, A. 'The structure of English pre-Conquest benedictionals', *British Library Journal* 13 (1987) 118–58

RÄDLE, Fidel *Studien zu Smaragd von Saint-Mihiel* (München 1974)

RAINE, James (ed.) *The Historians of the Church of York and its Archbishops* (3 vols, London 1879–94)

RAND, Edward Kennard *Studies in the Script of Tours, I, A Survey of the Manuscripts of Tours* (2 vols, Cambridge, Mass. 1929)

RANGER, Felicity (ed.) *Prisca Munimenta. Studies in Archival & Administrative History presented to Dr A.E.J. Hollaender* (London 1973)

RELLA, F.A. 'Continental manuscripts acquired for English centers in the tenth and early eleventh centuries: a preliminary checklist', *Anglia* 98 (1980) 107–16

RICHARDS, Mary P. (ed.) *Anglo-Saxon Manuscripts: Basic Readings* (New York 1993)

RIDYARD, Susan J. *The Royal Saints of Anglo-Saxon England. A Study of West Saxon and East Anglian Cults* (Cambridge 1988)

RIESNER, Dieter & GNEUSS, H. (edd.) *Festschrift für Walter Hübner* (Berlin 1964)

RIGG, A.G. & WIELAND, G.R. 'A Canterbury classbook of the mid-eleventh century (the "Cambridge Songs" manuscript)', *Anglo-Saxon England* 4 (1975) 113–30 + plates I–II

ROBERTSON, A.J. (ed. & transl.) *Anglo-Saxon Charters* (2nd edn, Cambridge 1956)

ROBINSON, J.A. 'Byrhtferth and the Life of St Oswald', *Journal of Theological Studies* 31 (1929/30) 35–42

ROBINSON, J. Armitage *St Oswald and the Church of Worcester* (London [1919])

ROBINSON, J. Armitage *Somerset Historical Essays* (London 1921)

ROBINSON, J.A. 'The early community at Christ Church, Canterbury', *Journal of Theological Studies* 27 (1925/6) 225–40

ROBINSON, J. Armitage *The Saxon Bishops of Wells. A Historical Study in the Tenth Century* (London [1918])

ROBINSON, J. Armitage *The Times of Saint Dunstan* (Oxford 1923)

ROLLASON, David [W.] *Saints and Relics in Anglo-Saxon England* (Oxford 1989)

ROLLASON, D.W. 'The cults of murdered royal saints in Anglo-Saxon England', *Anglo-Saxon England* 11 (1983) 1–22

ROLLASON, D[avid] W. *The Mildrith Legend. A Study in Early Medieval Hagiography in England* (Leicester 1982)

ROSENWEIN, Barbara H. *Rhinoceros Bound: Cluny in the Tenth Century* (Philadelphia, Pa 1982)

ROSIER, James L. (ed.) *Philological Essays. Studies in Old and Middle English Language and Literature in Honour of Herbert Dean Meritt, Professor of English Philology, Stanford University* (The Hague 1970)

ROUSE, R.H. 'Bostonus Buriensis and the author of the *Catalogus scriptorum ecclesiae*', *Speculum* 41 (1966) 471–99

RUBIN, Ida E. (ed.) *Studies in Western Art. Acts of the Twentieth International Congress of the History of Art, Volume One, Romanesque and Gothic Art* (Princeton, N.J. 1963)

RÜCK, Peter (ed.) *Pergament: Geschichte, Struktur, Restaurierung, Herstellung* (Sigmaringen 1991)

SAMARAN, Charles & MARICHAL, R. (edd.) *Catalogue des manuscrits en écriture latine portant des indications de date, de lieu ou de copiste* (Paris 1959–)

SANDERS, W. Basevi (ed.) *Facsimiles of Anglo-Saxon Manuscripts* (3 vols, Southampton 1878–84)

SANDGREN, Folke (ed.) *Otium et Negotium. Studies in Onomatology and Library Science presented to Olof von Feilitzen* (Stockholm 1973)

SAUER, Hans (ed.) *Theodulfi Capitula in England. Die altenglischen Übersetzungen zusammen mit dem lateinischen Text* (München 1978)

SAUER, H. 'Zur Überlieferung und Anlage von Erzbischof Wulfstans "Handbuch" ', *Deutsches Archiv für Erforschung des Mittelalters* 36 (1980) 341–84

SAWYER, P.H. *Anglo-Saxon Charters. An Annotated List and Bibliography* (London 1968)

SAWYER, P.H. (ed.) *Charters of Burton Abbey* (London 1979)

SAWYER, P.H. 'Charters of the Reform movement: the Worcester archive', in *Tenth-century Studies*, ed. D. Parsons (Chichester 1975), pp. 84–93 *and* 228–30

SAWYER, P. [H.] 'The royal *tun* in pre-Conquest England', in *Ideal and Reality in Frankish and Anglo-Saxon Society*, edd. P. Wormald *et al.* (Oxford 1983), pp. 273–99

SCHMITZ, Philibert *Histoire de l'ordre de Saint Benoît* (7 vols, Maredsous 1942–56)

SCHRÖER, [M.M.] Arnold (ed.) *Die angelsächsischen Prosabearbeitungen der Benediktinerregel* (Kassel 1885–8; 2nd edn, by H. Gneuss, Darmstadt 1964)

SCHRÖER, M.M. Arnold (ed.) *Die Winteney-Version der Regula S. Benedicti, lateinisch und englisch* (Halle a.S. 1888; rev. imp., by M. Gretsch, Tübingen 1978)

SCHROLL, Mary Alfred *Benedictine Monasticism as reflected in the Warnefrid-Hildemar Commentaries on the Rule* (New York 1941)

SCOTT, John (ed. & transl.) *The Early History of Glastonbury. An Edition, Translation and Study of William of Malmesbury's* De Antiquitate Glastonie Ecclesie (Woodbridge 1981)

SEARLE, William George *Onomasticon Anglo-Saxonicum. A List of Anglo-Saxon Proper Names from the Time of Beda to that of King John* (Cambridge 1897)

SEMMLER, J. 'Benedictus II: una regula – una consuetudo', in *Benedictine Culture, 750–1050*, edd. W. Lourdaux & D. Verhelst (Leuven 1983), pp. 1–49

SEMMLER, J. 'Das Erbe der karolingischen Klosterreform im 10. Jahrhundert', in *Monastische Reformen im 9. und 10. Jahrhundert*, edd. R. Kottje & H. Maurer (Sigmaringen 1989), pp. 29–77

SGARBI, R. 'Sulla tradizione manoscritto della versione in inglese antico della *Regola* di S. Benedetto', *Aevum* 58 (1984) 149–57

SHARPE, R. 'Gildas as a Father of the Church', in *Gildas: New Approaches*, edd. M. Lapidge & D. Dumville (Woodbridge 1984), pp. 193–205

SHARPE, R. 'The date of St. Mildreth's translation from Minster-in-Thanet to Canterbury', *Mediaeval Studies* 53 (1991) 349–54

SHEERIN, D.J. 'The dedication of the Old Minster, Winchester, in 980', *Revue bénédictine* 88 (1978) 261–73

SIMS-WILLIAMS, Patrick *Religion and Literature in Western England, 600–800* (Cambridge 1990)

SISAM, Celia & SISAM, K. (edd.) *The Salisbury Psalter edited from Salisbury Cathedral MS. 150* (London 1959)

SISAM, Kenneth *Studies in the History of Old English Literature* (Oxford 1953; rev. imp., 1962)

SOUTER, A. 'Contributions to the criticism of Zmaragdus's *Expositio libri comitis*', *Journal of Theological Studies* 9 (1907/8) 584–97

SOUTER, A. 'Further contributions to the criticism of Zmaragdus's *Expositio libri comitis*', *Journal of Theological Studies* 23 (1921/2) 73–6

SOUTER, A. 'Prolegomena to the commentary of Pelagius on the Epistles of St Paul', *Journal of Theological Studies* 7 (1905/6) 568–75

SPANNAGEL, Alfred & ENGELBERT, P. (edd.) *Smaragdi Abbatis Expositio in Regulam S. Benedicti* (Siegburg 1974)

STANLEY, Eric Gerald (ed.) *Continuations and Beginnings. Studies in Old English Literature* (London 1966)

STENTON, F.M. *Anglo-Saxon England* (3rd edn, Oxford 1971)

STEVENSON, William Henry (ed.) *Asser's Life of King Alfred* (Oxford 1904; rev. imp., by D. Whitelock, 1959)

STORK, Nancy Porter (ed.) *Through a Gloss darkly. Aldhelm's Riddles in the British Library MS Royal 12. C.xxiii* (Toronto 1990)

STUBBS, William (ed.) *Memorials of Saint Dunstan, Archbishop of Canterbury* (London 1874)

SWARZENSKI, H. 'The Anhalt Morgan Gospels', *Art Bulletin* 31 (1949) 77–83

SYMONS, T. 'Notes on the life and work of St Dunstan', *Downside Review* 80 (1962) 250–61 *and* 355–66

SYMONS, Thomas (ed. & transl.) *Regularis Concordia Anglicae Nationis Monachorum Sanctimonialiumque. The Monastic Agreement of the Monks and Nuns of the English Nation* (Edinburgh 1953)

SYMONS, T. 'St Dunstan in the "Oswald" tradition', *Downside Review* 90 (1972) 119–24

SYMONS, T. 'Some notes on English monastic origins', *Downside Review* 80 (1962) 55–69

SYMONS, T. 'The English monastic reform of the tenth century', *Downside Review* 60 [N.S., 41] (1942) 1–22, 196–222, 268–79

SYMONS, T. 'The introduction of monks at Christ Church, Canterbury', *Journal of Theological Studies* 27 (1925/6) 409–11

SYMONS, T. 'The monastic reforms of King Edgar', *Downside Review* 39 [N.S., 20] (1921) 38–51

SYMONS, T. 'The Regularis Concordia and the Council of Winchester', *Downside Review* 80 (1962) 140–56

TEMPLE, Elzbieta *Anglo-Saxon Manuscripts, 900–1066* (London 1976)

THIEL, Matthias *Grundlagen und Gestalt der Hebräischkenntnisse des frühen Mittelalters* (Spoleto 1973)

THOMPSON, Edward Maunde *An Introduction to Greek and Latin Palaeography* (Oxford 1912)

THOMPSON, E[dward] Maunde *Catalogue of Ancient Manuscripts in the British Museum, Part II, Latin* (London 1884)

THOMPSON, Edward Maunde, *et al.* (edd.) *The New Palaeographical Society Facsimiles of Ancient Manuscripts* (2 series, London 1903–30)

THOMSON, Rodney M. *The Archives of the Abbey of Bury St Edmunds* (Woodbridge 1980)

THOMSON, R.M. 'The library of Bury St Edmunds Abbey in the eleventh and twelfth centuries', *Speculum* 47 (1972) 617–45

THOMSON, R.M. 'The Norman conquest and English libraries', in *The Role of the Book in Medieval Culture*, ed. P. Ganz (2 vols, Turnhout 1986), II.27–40

THOMSON, Rodney [M.] *William of Malmesbury* (Woodbridge 1987)

THORPE, Benjamin (ed. & transl.) *The Anglo-Saxon Chronicle according to the Several Original Authorities* (2 vols, London 1861)

TOLHURST, J.B.L. 'An examination of two Anglo-Saxon manuscripts of the Winchester school: the Missal of Robert of Jumièges, and the Benedictional of St. Æthelwold', *Archaeologia* 83 (1933) 27–44

TRONCARELLI, Fabio *Tradizioni perdute. La "Consolatio Philosophiae" nell'alto medioevo* (Padova 1981)

TUPPER, F., jr 'History and texts of the Benedictine reform of the tenth century', *Modern Language Notes* 8 (1893) 172–84 (cols 344–67)

TURNER, C.H. 'The churches at Winchester in the early eleventh century', *Journal of Theological Studies* 17 (1915/16) 65–8

TURNER, Cuthbert Hamilton (facs. ed.) *Early Worcester MSS: Fragments of Four Books and a Charter of the Eighth Century belonging to Worcester Cathedral* (Oxford 1916)

TURNER, D.H., et al. *The Benedictines in Britain* (London 1980)

TURNER, D.H. (ed.) *The Claudius Pontificals (from Cotton MS. Claudius A.iii in the British Museum)* (London 1971)

URE, James M. (ed.) *The Benedictine Office. An Old English Text* (Edinburgh 1957)

VAUGHAN, Richard (ed.) *The Chronicle attributed to John of Wallingford* (London 1958) [Camden Miscellany, vol. 21, item 1]

VEZIN, J. 'Leofnoth. Un scribe anglais à Saint-Benoît-sur-Loire', *Codices Manuscripti* 3 (1977) 109–20

VEZIN, J. 'Manuscrits des dixième et onzième siècles copiés en Angleterre en minuscule caroline et conservés à la Bibliothèque nationale de Paris', in *Humanisme actif. Mélanges d'art et de littérature offerts à Julien Cain* (2 vols, Paris 1968), II.283–96

VEZIN, J. [review of *Aethici Istrici Cosmographia*, ed. T.A.M. Bishop (1966)], *Bibliothèque de l'École des Chartes* 124 (1966) 532–5

VOLLRATH, Hanna *Die Synoden Englands bis 1066* (Paderborn 1985)

VOLLRATH, H. 'König Edgar und die Klosterreform in England: die "Ostersynode" der "Vita S. Oswaldi auctore anonymo" ', *Annuarium historiae conciliorum* 10 (1978) 67–81

WALLACE-HADRILL, J.M. *The Frankish Church* (Oxford 1983)

WARNER, George F[rederic] & GILSON, J.P. *British Museum Catalogue of Western Manuscripts in the Old Royal & King's Collections* (4 vols, London 1921)

WARNER, George Frederic & WILSON, H.A. (facs. edd.) *The Benedictional of Saint Æthelwold, Bishop of Winchester 963–984* (Oxford 1910)

WARREN, F.E. 'An Anglo-Saxon missal at Worcester', *The Academy* 28 (1885) 394–5

WARREN, F.E. (ed.) *The Leofric Missal as used in the Cathedral of Exeter during the Episcopate of its First Bishop, A.D. 1050–1072, together with Some Account of the Red Book of Derby, the Missal of Robert of Jumièges, and a Few Other Early Manuscript Service Books of the English Church* (Oxford 1883)

WATSON, Andrew G. *Catalogue of Dated and Datable Manuscripts c. 435–1600 in Oxford Libraries* (2 vols, Oxford 1984)

WHITELOCK, Dorothy (ed. & transl.) *Anglo-Saxon Wills* (Cambridge 1930)

WHITELOCK, D. 'A note on the career of Wulfstan the homilist', *English Historical Review* 52 (1937) 460–5

WHITELOCK, D[orothy], et al. (edd.) *Councils & Synods with Other Documents relating to the English Church, I, A.D. 871–1204* (2 parts, Oxford 1981)

WHITELOCK, Dorothy (transl.) *English Historical Documents c. 500–1042* (2nd edn, London 1979)

WHITELOCK, Dorothy *From Bede to Alfred. Studies in Early Anglo-Saxon Literature and History* (London 1980)
WHITELOCK, Dorothy *History, Law and Literature in 10th–11th Century England* (London 1981)
WHITELOCK, D. [review of C. Sisam & K. Sisam (edd.), *The Salisbury Psalter* (1959)], *Review of English Studies*, N.S., 11 (1960) 419–21
WHITELOCK, Dorothy (ed.) *Sermo Lupi ad Anglos* (3rd edn, London 1963)
WHITELOCK, Dorothy *Some Anglo-Saxon Bishops of London* (London 1975)
WHITELOCK, D. 'The appointment of Dunstan as archbishop of Canterbury', in *Otium et Negotium*, ed. F. Sandgren (Stockholm 1973), pp. 232–47
WHITELOCK, D. 'The authorship of the account of King Edgar's establishment of monasteries', in *Philological Essays*, ed. J.L. Rosier (The Hague 1970), pp. 125–36
WHITELOCK, D. 'The conversion of the Eastern Danelaw', *Saga-book of the Viking Society* 12 (1937–45) 159–76
WHITELOCK, Dorothy & CLARK, C. (facs. edd.) *The Peterborough Chronicle (the Bodleian Manuscript Laud Misc. 636)* (Copenhagen 1954)
WHITELOCK, D. 'The pre-Viking Age Church in East Anglia', *Anglo-Saxon England* 1 (1972) 1–22
WIELAND, G.R. 'The Anglo-Saxon manuscripts of Prudentius's *Psychomachia*', *Anglo-Saxon England* 16 (1987) 213–31
WIELAND, Gernot R. (ed.) *The Canterbury Hymnal edited from British Library MS. Additional 37517* (Toronto 1982)
WILLIAMS, A. '*Princeps Merciorum gentis*: the family, career and connections of Ælfhere, ealdorman of Mercia, 956–83', *Anglo-Saxon England* 10 (1982) 143–72
WILLIAMS, R.D. 'The Worcester fragments of Statius' *Thebaid*', *Classical Review* 61 (1947) 88–90
WILLIAMS, R.D. 'Two manuscripts of Statius' *Thebaid*', *Classical Quarterly* 42 (1948) 105–12
WILMART, André (ed.) *Analecta Reginensia. Extraits des manuscrits latins de la reine Christine conservés au Vatican* (Roma 1933)
WILMART, André *Codices Reginenses Latini* (2 vols, Roma 1937/45)
WILMART, A. 'Expositio missae', in *Dictionnaire d'archéologie chrétienne et de liturgie*, edd. F. Cabrol & H. Leclercq (15 vols in 30, Paris 1903–53), V, cols 1014–27
WILMART, A. 'Les livres de l'abbé Odbert', *Bulletin historique trimestriel de la Société des antiquaires de la Morinie* 14 (1922–9) 169–88
WILMART, A. (ed.) 'The prayers of the Bury Psalter', *Downside Review* 48 [N.S., 29] (1930) 198–216
WILSON, David M. *Anglo-Saxon Art from the Seventh Century to the Norman Conquest* (London 1984)
WILSON, H.A. (ed.) *The Missal of Robert of Jumièges* (London 1896)
WINTERBOTTOM, Michael (ed.) *Three Lives of English Saints* (Toronto 1972)
WITTERS, W. 'Smaragde au moyen âge. La diffusion de ses écrits d'après la tradition manuscrite', in *Études ligériennes d'histoire et d'archéologie médiévales*, ed. R. Louis (Auxerre 1975), pp. 361–76

WOOD, Ian & LOUD, G.A. (edd.) *Church and Chronicle in the Middle Ages. Essays presented to John Taylor* (London 1991)

WOODRUFF, Douglas (ed.) *For Hilaire Belloc. Essays in Honour of his 72nd Birthday* (London 1942)

WORMALD, Francis & ALEXANDER, J. (facs. edd.) *An Early Breton Gospel Book. A Ninth-century Manuscript from the Collection of H.L. Bradfer-Lawrence 1887–1965* (Cambridge 1977)

WORMALD, F. 'Anglo-Saxon initials in a Paris Boethius manuscript', *Gazette des Beaux-arts*, 6th S., 62 (1963) 63–70

WORMALD, F. 'Continental influence on English medieval illumination', in *Fourth International Congress of Bibliophiles*, ed. A.R.A. Hobson (London 1967), pp. 4–16 + plates I–III

WORMALD, F. 'Decorated initials in English MSS. from A.D. 900 to 1100', *Archaeologia* 91 (1945) 107–35

WORMALD, Francis (ed.) *English Benedictine Kalendars after A.D. 1100* (2 vols, London 1939/46)

WORMALD, Francis *English Drawings of the Tenth and Eleventh Centuries* (London 1952)

WORMALD, Francis (ed.) *English Kalendars before A.D. 1100* (London 1934)

WORMALD, F. 'L'Angleterre', *apud* L. Grodecki *et al.*, *Le Siècle de l'an mil* (Paris 1973), pp. 226–55

WORMALD, F. 'Late Anglo-Saxon art: some questions and suggestions', in *Studies in Western Art*, I, ed. I.E. Rubin (Princeton, N.J. 1963), pp. 19–26 + plate VIII

WORMALD, F. 'The Insular script in late tenth century English Latin MSS', *Atti del X Congresso internazionale di scienze storiche, Roma, 4–11 Settembre 1955*, ed. A. Ferrabino (Roma 1957), pp. 160–5

WORMALD, P. 'Æthelwold and his Continental counterparts: contact, comparison, contrast', in *Bishop Æthelwold, his Career and Influence*, ed. B. Yorke (Woodbridge 1988), pp. 13–42

WORMALD, Patrick, *et al.* (edd.) *Ideal and Reality in Frankish and Anglo-Saxon Society. Studies presented to J.M. Wallace-Hadrill* (Oxford 1983)

WRIGHT, C.E. *English Vernacular Hands from the Twelfth to the Fifteenth Centuries* (Oxford 1960)

WRIGHT, David H. & CAMPBELL, A. (facs. edd.) *The Vespasian Psalter: British Museum Cotton Vespasian A.I* (Copenhagen 1967)

YORKE, Barbara (ed.) *Bishop Æthelwold, his Career and Influence* (Woodbridge 1988)

ZELZER, K. 'Untersuchungen zu einer Gesamtedition des frühnachkaroling-ischen Kommentars zur Regula S. Benedicti aus der Tradition des Hildemar von Corbie', *Revue bénédictine* 91 (1981) 373–82

INDEX OF ANGLO-SAXON CHARTERS

Documents are cited according to the reference-number given by Sawyer, *Anglo-Saxon Charters*.

INDEX OF MANUSCRIPTS

Index of Manuscripts

HANNOVER

Kestner Museum

W.M. XXIa, 36 18, 120–2, 123–4, 127, 128–30, 139–40, plate XIII

HEREFORD

Cathedral Library

O.6.xi 8–9

KING'S LYNN

Borough Archives

KL/C2/61 (*olim* Ae. 34) 40, 133
KL/C2/62 (*olim* Ae. 35) 133

KØBENHAVN

Kongelige Biblioteket

G.K.S. 10.2° 75, 116, 139–40
G.K.S. 1595.4° 66

Rigsarkivet

Aftagne pergamentfragmenter 637–664, 669–671, 674–698 68

LAWRENCE

University of Kansas Library

Pryce P2A:1 55

LEIDEN

Bibliotheek der Rijksuniversiteit

Scaliger 69 89, 96

LINCOLN

Cathedral Library

182 33–4, 58, 102

LONDON

British Library

Additional 9381 142
24199 78, 145
28188 59, 60–1, 62–3
34652 12
34890 127, 139–40
37517 60–1, 100, 108, 115, 148
40074 8–9, 98
46204 56
49598 2, 18, 21, 25, 53, 107, 145
57337 60–1, 106–7, 124

Additional Charter 19788 48
19792 153
19793 70–3
19794 20, 22, 29, 54–5, 56–7, 75–6
19795 66
19797 67, 154
19798 67
19799 67
19800 67–8
19801 68
Arundel 60 59, 60–1, 62–3, 64
155 60–1, 107, 113–14, 115, 122–3, 139–40
237 13
Cotton Augustus ii.6 29–30
12 29–30
24 133, 134
38 135
39 2, 16, 18, 19, 25–6, 52–3, 98, 152–3
41 16, 52, 142
59 133
67 29–30
68 133, 134
69 133, 134
90 133, 134
96 83–4
Caligula A.xv 140
Charter viii.6 142
viii.9 133
viii.14 153
viii.18 29–30
viii.38 29–30
Claudius A.i 16, 93, 142
A.iii 55, 60–1, 65, 126, 139–40
B.iv 140
D.iii 11, 12
Cleopatra B.xiii 90, 147
Domitian A.i 102
A.viii 12
Faustina A.x 11, 12–13, 15
Galba A.xiv 19, 59–61
A.xviii 140
Iulius A.ii 19
D.vii 81–3
E.vii 78–9

185

OSLO

Riksarkivet
Lat. fragm. 201   64
        204   64
        207   64
        208   64
        210   64
        223   64
        226   64
        228   64

OXFORD

Bodleian Library
Ashmole 328 (*S.C.* 6882/7420) 19
Auct. D.2.14 (*S.C.* 2698) 78
    D.inf.2.9 (*S.C.* 2638) 102
    F.1.15 (*S.C.* 2455) 91, 102
    F.4.32 (*S.C.* 2176) 3, 50–1, 52, 97, 144
Barlow 4 (*S.C.* 6416) 8, 49
Bodley 130 (*S.C.* 27609) 78–9
    163 (*S.C.* 2016) 118–19, 139–40
    218 (*S.C.* 2054) 141
    240 (*S.C.* 2469) 42
    297 (*S.C.* 2468) 32–3, 36, 40, 41, 42
    311 (*S.C.* 2122) 55
    451 (*S.C.* 2401) 8
    543 (*S.C.* 2588) 8, 67
    572 (*S.C.* 2026) 97, 142
    579 (*S.C.* 2675) 94–6, 99, 102–3, 143, 144
    708 (*S.C.* 2609) 18, 88, 99, 103, 107, 128, 146
    718 (*S.C.* 2632) 60–1, 100
    775 (*S.C.* 2558) 136
    865 (*S.C.* 2737) 12
Douce 296 (*S.C.* 21870) 60–1, 62, 64, 136
Eng. hist. a.2 (*S.C.* 31346), no. VII 19, 135
Hatton 30 (*S.C.* 4076) 3, 50–1, 153
    38 (*S.C.* 4090) 19
    40 (*S.C.* 4104) 8
    42 (*S.C.* 4117) 3, 49, 97
    48 (*S.C.* 4118) 8
    76 (*S.C.* 4125) 68
    93 (*S.C.* 4081) 151
Junius 11 (*S.C.* 5123) 105, 106

Lat. bibl. b.1   139–40
  liturg. f.5 (*S.C.* 29744) 156
  misc. a.3   55
  theol. c.3 (*S.C.* 31382) 97
  theol. c.4 (*S.C.* 1926*) 54, 76
Laud lat. 81 (*S.C.* 768)   60–1
  misc. 482 (*S.C.* 1054) 52, 60–1, 68
  misc. 636 (*S.C.* 1003) 31, 118–19
Marshall 19 (*S.C.* 5265) 106
Rawlinson C.697 (*S.C.* 12541) 78, 97
Tanner 3 (*S.C.* 9823) 55

Corpus Christi College
197   11, 13, 15, 19–35, 37, 54–5, 56–7, 69, 75–8, 155

St John's College
194   92

PARIS

Bibliothèque nationale
latin 272   145
  943   100, 148
  987   53, 139–40, 145, plate XIV
  4210   8
  6401   57–8, 93, 140
  6401A   93, 131–2, plate XI
  7299   59
  7585   102
  8431   16, 93, 142
  8824   12, 60–1, 64
  10062   108, 115, 124
  12050   18
  12638   8
  14380   33
  n.a.l. 1627 54–5

PRINCETON (New Jersey)

Scheide Library
M.140   29–30

REIMS

Bibliothèque municipale
9   6, 128

ROMA

Biblioteca Apostolica Vaticana
lat. 3363   3, 51, 97
Reg. lat. 12   33–4, 37, 41–3, 47–8, 60–2, 64, 78, 140
  489   8–9, 98, 99
  1671   69–75, plates VI–VII

GENERAL INDEX

Aachen (synod of, 816) 8
Abbo (abbot of Fleury) 59, 84
  commissioned metrical Life of St Dun-
    stan 84, 90
  Passio sancti Eadmundi 35-8, 44, 47, 84
  preface (to Dunstan) 84
Abbotsbury (Dorset) 117, 133
Abingdon (Berkshire) 14, 16, 18, 26, 46,
  52, 57-8, 60, 76, 82, 84, 89, 102,
  104, 136, 153-5
Achadeus (count) 131-2
Æfic (monk) 133
Ælfflæd (wife of Byrhtnoth, ealdorman) 36
Ælfgar (ealdorman of East Anglia) 35-6
Ælfgifu: *see* Emma.
Ælfheah (bishop of Winchester; arch-
  bishop of Canterbury) 51, 103-4,
  111-12, 114-16
Ælfhere (ealdorman) 79
Ælfhun (bishop of London) 112
Ælfmær (abbot of St Augustine's, Canter-
  bury; bishop of Sherborne) 111-12
Ælfric (abbot of St Albans; bishop of
  Ramsbury; archbishop of Canter-
  bury) 47, 82-3, 100, 103-4
Ælfric I (bishop of East Anglia) 42
Ælfric II (bishop of East Anglia) 42
Ælfric III, 'the Good' (bishop of East
  Anglia) 42
Ælfric of Bath (scribe) 28
Ælfric (abbot of Eynsham) 27
  De temporibus anni 71
  Grammar 12, 20
  Lives of Saints 78
  Sermones catholici 68
Ælfsige I (bishop of Winchester; arch-
  bishop of Canterbury) 103
Ælfsige II (bishop of Winchester) 115
Ælfsige/*Ælsinus* (scribe at Winchester)
  136
Ælfstan: *see* Lyfing.
Ælfthryth (queen to Edgar) 13-14, 81
Ælfweard (abbot of Evesham; bishop of
  London) 67

Ælfweard (king's reeve) 111
Ælfwine (abbot of Ramsey; bishop of East
  Anglia) 32, 34, 38, 43
Ælfwold III (bishop of Crediton) 51
Ælfwold (Ealdorman Æthelwine's brother),
  thane 45, 48, 72-3
Ætheldryth, St (of Ely) 9
Æthelflæd of Damerham (queen to Edmund
  I) 36
Æthelgar (abbot of New Minster, Winches-
  ter; bishop of Selsey; archbishop of
  Canterbury) 51, 104, 143
Æthelnoth (archbishop of Canterbury)
  32-4, 37, 39, 51, 114-15
Æthelred 'the Unready' (king of England)
  80-4, 96, 114, 135
Æthelred (*optimas* of King Edward 'the
  Confessor') 133
Æthelric (thane) 133
Æthelstan (king of England) 16, 45, 50,
  87, 92, 126, 141, 152
Æthelstan 'Half-king' (ealdorman of East
  Anglia) 37-8, 40, 45-7
Æthelweard (Ealdorman Æthelwine's son)
  45
Æthelwine (ealdorman of East Anglia)
  44-5, 67, 72-3, 77, 79-80, 82
Æthelwold (bishop of Winchester) 2-4,
  8-10, 15-18, 21, 25-8, 45-6, 52-3,
  57-8, 63, 65, 67, 75, 78, 104, 118,
  143, 145, 157; *and see* saints, cult
  of.
'Æthelwoldian script' 5, 110
Libellus Æthelwoldi 9-10, 13
Old English translation of the Benedictine Rule 10-28, 30, 33, 56, 69,
  75-8, 155
  preface to 12-13, 17, 46
  Wintney version (early Middle English
    recension) of 11-13, 15
Reform-houses 18, 115-20, 145-6,
  148-9, 153, 156
school at Winchester 14
vocabulary of 10

189

Maldon (Essex) 45
Malmesbury (Wiltshire) 105–6
mandorla 140
Marches (western) 138
Margaret, St (of Scotland) 156
marginalia 65, 76–7, 97, 131, 136
Mercia 50–1, 61, 63
metrical colophon 121–4, 127, 150
missals 4, 34, 77, 94–9, 103, 106, 110, 116, 118, 143–4

neums 65, 70
Normandy 150
Northumbria 59, 61, 63, 65, 156
Norway 64
Noua legenda Anglie 42
nuns/nunneries 11, 81, 84

Oda (bishop of Ramsbury; archbishop of Canterbury) 50, 52, 57, 92–7, 103, 141
his preface to Frithegod's *Breuiloquium* 142
Odbert (abbot of Saint-Bertin) 131–2
Odo (abbot of Cluny) 143
Offa (king of Mercia) 65
Old English: *see* vernacular.
Orc (thane) 117, 133
Ordgar (ealdorman) 13
Ordgar (thane) 133
ordines
for the consecration of an archbishop 107
for the dedication of a church 118
Ording (abbot of Bury St Edmunds) 31
Oscytel (bishop of Dorchester-on-Thames; archbishop of York) 52
Osgar (abbot of Abingdon) 57, 86, 143, 153
Osulf (kinsman to Archbishop Oswald) 48
Oswald (bishop of Worcester; archbishop of York) 4, 26, 44–5, 47–8, 50–3, 56–9, 63–5, 67, 73–6, 79, 86, 94, 109, 143, 145–6, 157; *and see* saints, cult of.
Reform-houses of 146, 148–9
Oswald II (monk of Ramsey; nephew of Archbishop Oswald) 67

palaeography
Caroline minuscule 1, 3, 16–17, 19–28, 48, 50, 52, 54–5, 57
Continental Caroline 1–3, 93, 106, 129, 131–2, 144–5, 151

abbreviations (used at Fleury) 33
Anglo-Caroline 1, 3–4, 7–78, 86, 93, 128–9, 132, 134, 136, 141–2
Style I 2–5, 18, 24–8, 33, 52–4, 56–9, 64–5, 68–71, 74–6, 86, 88, 95, 101–10, 115–17, 120, 124–5, 128–9, 135, 137, 143–50, 152–3, 157; *and see* 'Æthelwoldian script'.
Style II 2–4, 17–18, 24, 26–8, 50–3, 58, 75, 86–7, 89–91, 95, 97–8, 101–3, 106, 116, 119, 124–5, 132, 137, 142–4, 147–50, 152–3, 157
Style III 5, 68–75, 126, 137, 149
Style IV 5–6, 18, 28, 33, 64, 67, 74–5, 95, 101, 108, 111–40, 146, 150–1, 154–5, 157
hybrid of Styles I and II 116, 122, 145, 157
hybrid of Styles I and IV 145, 151
hybrid of Styles I, II, and IV 108–9, 151
Gothic script 70
Insular minuscule 2, 19–30, 51–2, 62, 71, 89, 97, 99, 101–3, 119, 136, 144, 146–7, 150, 152–3
Anglo-Saxon Square minuscule 3, 5, 17–21, 25–9, 51, 53–4, 68, 74–8, 87–9, 91, 93, 95, 97–9, 100–1, 116, 128, 148, 152–4
Phase I 78, 89
Phase II 88–9, 95
Phase III 14, 51, 71, 88, 92, 95, 152–3
Phase IV 14, 52, 98, 152
Phase VII 154
hybrid Insular-Caroline 2, 5, 17, 24–5, 51, 54, 87, 89, 93, 95–7, 102, 105, 107, 142, 145, 147–8, 154
Rustic Capital script 128
official correction 23, 27, 30
script-differentiation between Latin and Old English 15, 19–22, 24–7, 52, 66, 69, 71, 74, 76–7, 116, 136, 152–4
Uncial script 128
paschal tables 34; *and see computistica.*
passional 68
patronage 16, 40, 46–7, 67, 83, 94, 127, 148
Pershore (Worcestershire) 45, 57, 77
Peterborough (Northamptonshire) 31, 45, 67, 110, 116–19, 135, 139–40

General Index

Tavistock (Devon) 96, 104
Thames (River) 114
Theodred (bishop of London) 35, 38, 46
Theodulf (of Orléans) 20
Thetford (Norfolk) 87
Thorkel/Thurkill 'the Tall' (earl of East Anglia) 32, 34, 38–9, 114–15
Thorney (Cambridgeshire) 45
Thorth (courtier of King Cnut) 117
Thuri (courtier of King Cnut) 117
Tours 2, 48, 55, 141
tropers 136

Upwood (Huntingdonshire) 44
Uuius (abbot of Bury St Edmunds) 32, 47

Vergil 69–71, 73–5
vernacular texts 9, 12, 20, 27, 30–1, 56, 64, 68, 87, 105, 117, 121, 123, 134, 136, 139–40, 152–3, 155–6; *and see* glosses; palaeography, script-differentiation between Latin and Old English.
vikings 8, 87, 96, 110, 147; *and see* Danish army; Scandinavia.

Wales/Welsh 97, 142
Wallingford (Berkshire) 84
Wells (Somerset) 51, 103–4, 112, 114–15, 127
Westbury-on-Trym   (Gloucestershire) 44–5, 77
Westminster (Middlesex) 100
Wiccia: see Hwicce.
Wihtred (king of Kent) 122
wills 35, 42, 46, 104
William 'the Conqueror' (duke of Normandy, king of England) 30, 137
William (of Malmesbury)
  Gesta pontificum Anglorum 80
  Uita sancti Dunstani 12–13
Winchcombe (Gloucestershire) 45, 48, 57–9, 77, 79–80, 82–3

Winchester (Hampshire) 4–5, 14–15, 18, 25–6, 28, 52–3, 56–7, 59, 61–4, 69, 76–7, 86, 89, 103–4, 107, 109, 115, 139–40, 143, 145
  New Minster 2, 14, 53, 65, 104, 110, 116, 133, 136, 139, 143, 154
  Nunnaminster 8, 14
  Old Minster 2, 56, 59, 66, 73, 98, 105, 107, 118, 132–3, 136, 154
Windsor (Berkshire) 139
Wintney (Hampshire) 11; *and see* Æthelwold, Old English translation of the Benedictine Rule, Wintney version.
women aristocrats 46
Worcester 3–5, 8, 14, 17, 20, 22, 44–5, 48–9, 51–8, 61–2, 65–9, 70–7, 84, 94, 104, 134, 136–7, 142–3, 146, 149, 153–4; *and see Liber Wigorniensis.*
writs 37, 113, 116–17, 122, 126
Wulfhelm (bishop of Wells; archbishop of Canterbury) 95, 103
Wulfhere (king of Mercia) 48
Wulfred (archbishop of Canterbury) 100
Wulfric (abbot of St Augustine's, Canterbury) 84
Wulfsige (abbot of Ramsey) 45
Wulfsige (abbot of Westminster; bishop of Sherborne) 100
Wulfstan (bishop of London; bishop of Worcester; archbishop of York) 39, 49, 55, 65–8, 74, 82, 146, 149–50, 154
  Benedictine Office 55
  Canons of Edgar 55
  Sermo Lupi ad Anglos 67
Wulfstan II (bishop of Worcester) 68, 138
Wulfstan (*cantor*/precentor) 105
  Uita sancti Æthelwoldi 28, 57, 118

York 44, 48–9, 65, 67, 82, 107, 115, 123, 139–40

196

DATE DUE

HIGHSMITH 45-220